OLDIES BUT GOODIES

OLDIES BUT GOODIES

THE ROCK 'N' ROLL YEARS

BY
STEWART GOLDSTEIN
AND ALAN JACOBSON

MASON / CHARTER

NEW YORK 1977

Library of Congress Cataloging in Publication Data
Goldstein, Stewart.
    Oldies but goodies.
    1. Rock music—Discography. I. Jacobson, Alan,
joint author. II. Title.
ML156.4.P6G63   016.784   76-28242
ISBN 0-88405-365-2
ISBN 0-88405-431-4 (paperback)

CONTENTS

With Thanks To

Pepi
Rosalind
Jan
Vi

. . . without whose tolerance, patience and
hard work this book would not have been.

To

Jeanne
Lee

. . . for their knowledge and cooperation.

To the artists who made it all happen.

To "oldie freaks" everywhere; we hope you get
as much out of this book as we put into it. . . .

FOREWORD

When I entered junior high school in 1954, I didn't realize how perfect the timing was. I was thirteen years old and rock 'n' roll was being born. Being a teen-ager, my interests began to develop in clothing, cars, girls and, of course, music.

A neighbor taught me to do the bop, the dance first associated with rock 'n' roll. I remember practicing with the record "Hearts of Stone" by the Charms.

Rock 'n' roll and I grew up together. Through my junior high school years I was on hand for the emergence of such groups as the Drifters, Crew Cuts, Bill Haley & the Comets; while I was learning to dance, an unknown singer named Presley was beginning a career that would lead to immortality.

In 1954 songs like "Earth Angel" and "Shake, Rattle and Roll" were transforming rhythm & blues to pop. By 1955, pop was rock 'n' roll, and Bill Haley & the Comets helped us all "Rock Around the Clock."

My own interests centered around music and drama, and rock 'n' roll became an ally. I listened to and loved it all.

Alan was a couple of years younger, but shared my great love of rock 'n' roll. We grew up in the same city, but never met until 1968, after the rock 'n' roll era had ended.

Memories lingered . . . both of us spoke of the oldies . . . and then it happened . . . almost by accident.

We decided to tape record the oldies for our own pleasure. It became necessary to compile a list before we began collecting. After listing and taping over 2700 songs, our interests and memories grew even stronger. A trivia debate took place between the two of us. We made up a Top 100, those songs we thought to be the best of the oldies. With this much work already done (over two years), why not go all the way? Why not write a book so that everyone could share the oldies?

So, after more than three years of collecting, organizing, cataloging and verifying, we invite you to take off your shoes, sit back and relax; you are about to embark upon a journey through a lost (but not forgotten) era. It is lost to all but those who lived it.

Here are the best of the best—the top oldies from 1953 to 1965.

Music had a very special meaning during the fifties and sixties. The freedom of expression enjoyed by the youth of the seventies was not present then; sexual freedom, drug use, long hair and the like—the age of "doing your own thing"—had not yet evolved. Music was one of the few forms of identification that young people could call their own.

By merely glancing through the song titles, one can see this identification; the majority of the oldies dealt with such subjects as cars, clothes, going steady, school and music, a reflection of what the young people were all about.

The impact made by rock 'n' roll is evidenced by the great interest in nostalgia today. Those of us who grew up with the oldies still hold them vividly within our memory; something still "clicks" in us when we see or hear something from our teen years.

While movies, T.V., books and other forms of nostalgia are all around us, none is more prevalent than music. Most pop radio stations today still play some of the oldies and many stations throughout the country are devoted strictly to the oldie sounds.

Recording artists from the fifties and sixties may be found performing in almost every major city in the country. On a recent visit to Las Vegas, I found more than half a dozen oldie artists appearing. In Miami Beach, several clubs feature oldie artists almost exclusively, and, of course, many of today's recording artists are recording songs that were hits in the fifties and sixties.

The impact felt over twenty years ago has caused this book to be written. It is intended to represent those songs which typified the sound of the fifties and sixties; a period when pop music was the best ever; the time when rock 'n' roll ruled; the years of Elvis, the Platters, Bill Haley & the Comets—songs of which it's said today: "They don't write them like that anymore."

1953 is the earliest year covered in the book. The songs listed in '53 and '54 are intended to represent a sound that had emerged from standards to rhythm & blues to rock 'n' roll. While 1965 is the most recent year covered, the Beatles' arrival on the music scene in 1964 signaled the end of the oldies. The few post-Beatles songs in this book are here because they were the last to have the old sound, and extended even into the new, revolutionary Rock Era.

Certain artists and songs popular in the fifties and sixties have been omitted or limited. While a number of these were popular, we feel they do not typify the sound of the times. For the most part, the "sound" was pure rock 'n' roll, with the "Doo-Wah" and "Dip Dip Dip." These were the true oldies. We have, however, also included songs that may not be called oldies by strict definition, but enjoyed great popularity and were accepted by the teen-age record-buying public. For this reason we will consider such songs as "Melody of Love," "Jamaica Farewell," "Secret Love,". "The Ballad of Davy Crockett" and "High Hopes" to be oldies. The separation of oldies and non-oldies is based on our own opinion.

The book contains, but is not limited to, every oldie that made the Top 40 between 1955 and 1963, the major years of rock 'n' roll. You will also find songs from the formative years of 1953 and 1954 as well as those songs from 1964 and 1965 that survived the arrival of the "British sound."

Those songs reaching the Top 40 between 1955 and 1963, but not considered oldies by the authors, may be found in a special section which lists the non-oldies year by year. Some artists (Perry Como, Tony Bennett, Frank Sinatra, The Kingston Trio, etc.) may be found in both the oldie and non-oldie lists. Names like the Supremes and Sonny and Cher are absent, because theirs is not considered the oldie sound by our definition. And, of course, no Beatles, Rolling Stones, etc. This is, primarily, a collection of those songs whose sound, impact or popularity has earned them our label, "Oldies but Goodies."

In addition, you will find the authors' Top 100, the statistical Top 100, the Top 100 oldie instrumentals, all the #1 songs of the oldie era, most productive artists and many other items of interest to "oldie freaks." There is even a trivia quiz to test your knowledge.

So, now turn back the hands of time as you experience history, as we present the List of Gold; the Best of the Best; those "OLDIES BUT GOODIES."

Stewart Goldstein

Note: This book has been written in part from statistics, but with great consideration given to impact, popularity and classic oldie sounds of the songs. In some cases, the authors' opinions are in evidence. In some of the trivia catagories, not all songs are listed, but rather the most popular ones. Date shown next to songs represents the date the song first hit the charts.

Paul Anka *(United Artists)*

INTRODUCTION

All of us who love rock 'n' roll, performers and fans alike, have a favorite year. Mine is 1957. "Diana" was a hit, and my career was under way. I was fortunate enough to become involved early. I witnessed the growth of rock 'n' roll throughout the 50s and 60s. I saw rock 'n' roll grow into one of the major forces in musical history.

We've come a long way since those days, but many of us remember as if it was only yesterday. We remember a more carefree time; a time of first dates, first cars, problems with parents and staying after school; a time when music meant more to us, perhaps, than any other time in history; a time when songs reflected the way we lived and the things we loved. Each of us remembers a certain artist or a particular song that stirs a memory and brings a smile to our face today, more than twenty years after the birth of rock 'n' roll.

While the rock 'n' roll era may be gone, it is certainly not forgotten. I doubt that it will ever be . . . It has been immortalized by the likes of Elvis Presley, Chuck Berry and Bill Haley and the Comets. Songs like "Heartbreak Hotel," "The Great Pretender," "Rock Around the Clock" (maybe a few Anka hits, too) and others seem to stay around forever. Movies, television, Broadway and the record industry continue to bring back the "good old days." And now, the whole story has been brought to us in print.

In their book, Stewart and Alan pay rock 'n' roll its due reward. It's a detailed and thoroughly fascinating tribute to the "Oldies But Goodies," whether you want to analyze, compare, research or just remember and enjoy. It contains the significant songs of the rock 'n' roll era: from 1953, when rock 'n' roll was an embryo, to the 1964 arrival of the Beatles and beyond.

Thank you, fellas, for giving us all a chance to look back. We now have a permanent record of a most outstanding part of our past. From the casual fan to the most involved "Oldie Freak," I'm sure your readers will find your book a continuing source of pleasure.

Paul Anka

Author's Note: At age 15, Paul Anka wrote and recorded his first hit, "Diana." In the 19 years that have followed, he has remained a consistent star (see 1959 introduction). While other performers come and go, Anka's talent has stood the test of time. Nothing says more for an artist's talent than the rare ability to remain "on top" year after year.

1
OLDIE LIST 1953-1965

(Songs with * next to them were #1 songs)

Nat "King" Cole *(Capitol)*

1953

There were 160 million people in America in 1953. The Korean War had ended; Eisenhower was president and hemlines on ladies' skirts were up to just below the knee. Fur collars and hoop earrings were "in." Bermuda shorts became popular for men.

On Broadway, *The Seven Year Itch* was a smash, and William Inge won the Pulitzer Prize for *Picnic.* At the movies, *From Here to Eternity* was the big Oscar winner. "I Love Lucy" and "Dragnet" were T.V. favorites.

Music was beginning to experience a change. The "standard" sound was still popular ("I Believe," "Doggie in the Window"); pop artists included Dean Martin and Teresa Brewer, with such songs as "That's Amore" and "Ricochet." But another type of music, rhythm & blues, was rapidly growing in popularity. Rhythm & blues had been primarily associated with black people. It featured drums, saxophone and a definite "beat" that was the backbone of the song.

The rhythm & blues sound began working its way into the pop field, and was to serve as a transition from standards to rock 'n' roll.

1953 saw the beginning of two groups that were to become all-time superstars. The Drifters, with lead singer Clyde McPhatter, had "Money Honey," the first of a string of hits that kept them on top even beyond the "official" end of the oldie era.

Bill Haley & the Comets began their rise in 1953 with "Crazy Man Crazy." A later recording, "Rock Around the Clock," went on to become the largest selling oldie of all time, and the "theme song" of rock 'n' roll.

Haley's music was built almost entirely around the rhythm & blues concept.

JANUARY

FEBRUARY

MARCH
*Song from Moulin Rouge. . . . . Percy Faith (with Felicia Sanders)

APRIL

MAY
Crazy Man Crazy. . . . . Bill Haley & the Comets

3

JUNE

Song from Moulin Rouge . . . . Mantovani

JULY

Crying in the Chapel. . . . . Sonny Til & the
Orioles
Crying in the Chapel. . . . . June Valli

AUGUST

Shake a Hand . . . . Faye Adams
Dragnet. . . . . Ray Anthony

SEPTEMBER

OCTOBER

Ricochet . . . . Teresa Brewer
Money Honey . . . . Drifters[1]
A Sunday Kind of Love . . . . Harptones

NOVEMBER

That's Amore . . . . Dean Martin

DECEMBER

[1]Lead singer Clyde McPhatter later established a very successful solo career.

4

1954

The top movie of 1954 was *On the Waterfront,* starring Marlon Brando. Dr. Jonas Salk discovered a polio vaccine, and Roger Bannister broke the four-minute mile.

Two "launchings" took place in '54; the atomic-powered submarine "Nautilus," and a music form to be labeled rock 'n' roll.

Along with the now-fading standards such as "Mr. Sandman," "Secret Love" and "Little Things Mean a Lot," rhythm & blues tunes such as "Hearts of Stone" by the Charms hit the pop charts; the rise of Bill Haley & the Comets continued and in '54, "Shake, Rattle and Roll" was their biggest hit.

1954 could be called a tug-of-war year. Three different forms of music were in a battle. The old standards were trying to maintain the popularity they had enjoyed through the forties and early fifties.

Rhythm & blues was extremely popular, producing such songs in '54 as "Honey Love" (Drifters) and "Sh-Boom" (Chords).

But the third form, rock 'n' roll, was on the move. Through cover versions (a pop artist's recording of an R & B hit) songs that were already popular on the R & B charts were brought to the pop charts. "Sh-Boom" was recorded by the Crew Cuts; "Hearts of Stone" was a hit by the Fontane Sisters.

A young man from Tupelo, Mississippi, began his recording career in '54 with "That's All Right." Two years later, his career would begin in earnest, and he would become perhaps the most amazing success story in the history of music. His name, of course, Elvis Presley.

With Presley, Bill Haley, the Drifters and others on its side, rock 'n' roll would win the war and, within a year, would rule the music world.

JANUARY
* Secret Love . . . . Doris Day
From the Vine Came the Grape. . . . . Gaylords
* Let Me Go Lover. . . . . Joan Weber

FEBRUARY
From the Vine Came the Grape. . . . . Hilltoppers

MARCH
Lovey-Dovey. Clovers
Life Is But a Dream . . . . Harptones

5

APRIL

Gee . . . . Crows
The Wind. . . . . Diablos
* Little Things Mean a Lot . . . . Kitty Kallen
Cherry Pie . . . . Marvin & Johnny
Work with Me Annie. . . . . Midnighters
Goodnite, Sweetheart, Goodnite . . . . Spaniels
Shake Rattle and Roll . . . . Joe Turner

MAY

Honey Love . . . . Drifters
The Letter . . . . Medallions

JUNE

Sh-Boom . . . . Chords
* Sh-Boom . . . . Crew Cuts
Goodnight Sweetheart . . . . McGuire Sisters
Sexy Ways . . . . Midnighters

JULY

Chapel in the Moonlight. . . . . Kitty Kallen
Cara Mia . . . . David Whitfield

AUGUST

Shake, Rattle and Roll . . . . Bill Haley & the
Comets
Hearts of Stone . . . . Jewels
Tick Tock. . . . . Marvin & Johnny
Annie Had a Baby . . . . Midnighters
Blue Moon of Kentucky . . . . Elvis Presley[1]
Good Rockin' Tonight . . . . Elvis Presley
I Forgot to Remember to Forget . . . . Elvis Presley
Mystery Train . . . . Elvis Presley
That's All Right . . . . Elvis Presley

SEPTEMBER

Papa Loves Mambo. . . . . Perry Como
Moments to Remember . . . . Four Lads

---

[1]The five songs shown here were recorded by Presley on Sun Records before he began his rise to stardom with R.C.A.

6

OCTOBER

* Mr. Sandman . . . . Chordettes

NOVEMBER

Hearts of Stone . . . . Charms
Dim Dim the Lights . . . . Bill Haley & the
                                              Comets
* Sincerely . . . . Harvey & the
                                              Moonglows
That's All I Want From You . . . . Jaye P. Morgan

DECEMBER

Let Me Go Lover . . . . Teresa Brewer
Melody of Love . . . . David Carrol
No More . . . . DeJohn Sisters
Ling Ting Tong . . . . Five Keys
* Hearts of Stone . . . . Fontane Sisters
Sincerely . . . . McGuire Sisters
Earth Angel . . . . Penguins
Melody of Love . . . . Billy Vaughn

1955

This was a year of "firsts." For the first time, the Dodgers beat the Yankees in the World Series. One of the greatest groups ever, the Platters, had their first hits, "Only You" and "The Great Pretender." A legend was born in '55: the man some people credit with being the largest single influence on rock 'n' roll was first heard from. "Maybelline" launched the recording career of Chuck Berry—a career that led to stardom in '55 and that is still going strong today.

Another legend took the country by storm in '55. Fess Parker came to us as Davy Crockett, King of the Wild Frontier. Coonskin caps were everywhere. And, of course, "The Ballad of Davy Crockett" became a #1 record.

In '55, rock 'n' roll was here to stay. Bill Haley & the Comets recorded "Rock Around the Clock," which was to become the theme song of rock 'n' roll, and the largest selling oldie of all time. It was the group's biggest year. Rock 'n' roll had arrived and would dominate the musical scene until the Beatles' "arrival" in 1964.

Rhythm & blues did not fade away, but did take a back seat to rock 'n' roll. Many R & B artists enjoyed great success in the pop field, and became known as pop artists. Names like Bo Diddley, the Five Keys and Fats Domino flooded the pop scene. Fats had his first big hit, "Ain't It a Shame" in 1955, and went on to become a superstar.

In the fashion world, pink and black became the rage for men, and women wore spiked heels and pop-beads.

As rock 'n' roll grew, so grew the record industry. Recording companies enjoyed phenomenal success.

JANUARY

Tweedle Dee	Lavern Baker
Ling Ting Tong	Charms
Ko Ko Mo	Perry Como
Earth Angel	Crew Cuts
Ko Ko Mo	Crew Cuts
* Melody of Love	Four Aces
Tweedle Dee	Georgia Gibbs
Crazy Otto	Johnny Maddox
No More	McGuire Sisters

FEBRUARY

Pledging My Love	Johnny Ace
Rock Love	Fontane Sisters
Mambo Rock	Bill Haley & the Comets
* Ballad of Davy Crockett	Bill Hayes
Dance with Me Henry	Etta James
How Important Can It Be	Joni James
Ballad of Davy Crockett	Fess Parker
* Cherry Pink & Apple Blossom White	Prez Prado

MARCH

Close Your Eyes	Five Keys
Dance with Me Henry	Georgia Gibbs
Birth of the Boogie	Bill Haley & the Comets
Lonely Nights	Hearts
Unchained Melody	Al Hibbler

APRIL

Don't Be Angry	Nappy Brown
Unchained Melody	Roy Hamilton

MAY

Bo Diddley	Bo Diddley
This Is My Story	Gene & Eunice
*Rock Around the Clock	Bill Haley & the Comets[1]
Thirteen Women	Bill Haley & the Comets
The House of Blue Lights	Chuck Miller
Story Untold	Nutmegs

JUNE

Ain't That a Shame	Pat Boone
Story Untold	Crew Cuts
W-P-L-J	Four Deuces
Heaven and Paradise	Don Julian & the Meadowlarks
Mary Lee	Rainbows

[1]Largest selling "oldie" of all time. Considered by many to be the theme song of rock 'n' roll.

Chuck Berry *(Universal Attractions)*

Fats Domino *(Dona Kay)*

Kay Starr *(R.C.A.)*

JULY

Ain't It a Shame. . . . . Fats Domino
Ko Ko Mo . . . . Gene & Eunice
Razzle Dazzle . . . . Bill Haley & the
                                                    Comets
Two Hound Dogs. . . . . Bill Haley & the
                                                    Comets
Come Home. Bubber Johnson
It's Almost Tomorrow . . . . Snooky Lanson[1]
If You Don't Want My Love . . . . Jaye P. Morgan
Pepper-Hot Baby . . . . Jaye P. Morgan
Hummingbird . . . . Les Paul & Mary
                                                    Ford
Only You . . . . Platters
Feel So Good . . . . Shirley & Lee

AUGUST

Wake the Town and Tell the People . . . . . . Les Baxter
Seventeen . . . . Boyd Bennett &
                                                    the Rockets
Maybelline. . . . . Chuck Berry
Wake the Town and Tell the People . . . . . . Mindy Carson
Hummingbird . . . . Chordettes
Love Is a Many Splendored Thing. . . . . . . Don Cornell
Tina Marie . . . . Perry Como
Gum Drop . . . . Crew Cuts
The Yellow Rose of Texas . . . . Johnny Desmond
Seventeen . . . . Fontane Sisters
* Love Is a Many Splendored Thing . . . . . . Four Aces
No Arms Can Ever Hold You. . . . . Gaylords
I Hear You Knockin'. . . . . Smiley Lewis
Daddy-O . . . . Bonnie Lou
The Longest Walk . . . . Jaye P. Morgan

SEPTEMBER

My Bonnie Lassie . . . . Ames Brothers
No Other Arms . . . . Pat Boone
At My Front Door . . . . El Dorados
* The Yellow Rose of Texas. . . . . Mitch Miller
Dog Face Soldier . . . . Russ Morgan
Croce Di Oro . . . . Patti Page

[1]Lanson starred in the T.V. Show, "Your Hit Parade."

12

OCTOBER

Autumn Leaves . . . . Steve Allen
Black Denim Trousers . . . . Cheers
Shifting Whispering Sands. . . . . Rusty Draper
Daddy-O . . . . Fontane Sisters
The Yellow Rose of Texas . . . . Stan Freberg
He . . . . Al Hibbler
You Are My Love. . . . . Joni James
He . . . . McGuire Sisters
Black Denin Trousers . . . . Vaughn Monroe
No Arms Can Ever Hold You. . . . . Georgie Shaw
I Hear You Knockin'. . . . . Gale Storm[1]
Shifting Whispering Sands. . . . . Billy Vaughn
* Autumn Leaves. . . . . Roger Williams
Autumn Leaves . . . . Victor Young

NOVEMBER

My Boy Flat Top . . . . Boyd Bennett &
                       the Rockets
Lullaby of Birdland. . . . . Blue Stars
At My Front Door . . . . Pat Boone
Gee Whittakers . . . . Pat Boone
Speedo . . . . Cadillacs
It's Almost Tomorrow . . . . David Carroll
Band of Gold . . . . Kit Carson
Band of Gold . . . . Don Cherry
All At Once You Love Her . . . . Perry Como
Angels in the Sky . . . . Crew Cuts
It's Almost Tomorrow . . . . Dream Weavers
Are You Satisfied . . . . Rusty Draper
Dungaree Doll. . . . . Eddie Fisher
Nuttin' For Christmas . . . . Fontane Sisters
* Sixteen Tons. . . . . Ernie Ford
Memories of You . . . . Four Coins
Nuttin' For Christmas . . . . Barry Gordon
ABC Boogie . . . . Bill Haley & the
                       Comets
Burn That Candle. . . . . Bill Haley & the
                       Comets
Rock-A-Beatin' Boogie . . . . Bill Haley & the
                       Comets
Only You . . . . Hilltoppers

[1]Gale Storm was best known as T.V.'s "My Little Margie" when she started singing.

13

Teenage Prayer . . . . Gloria Mann
* Memories Are Made of This . . . . Dean Martin
* The Great Pretender. . . . . Platters
Lisbon Antigua . . . . Nelson Riddle
It's Almost Tomorrow . . . . Jo Stafford
When You Dance. . . . . Turbans
Nuttin' For Christmas . . . . Joe Ward
Wanting You. . . . . Roger Williams
Nuttin' For Christmas . . . . Ricky Zahnd

DECEMBER
My Boy Flat Top . . . . Dorothy Collins[1]
Mostly Martha. Crew Cuts
Nuttin' for Christmas. . . . . Stan Freberg
See You Later, Alligator . . . . Bill Haley & the
Comets[2]
My Treasure . . . . Hilltoppers
Go On With the Wedding. . . . . Kitty Kallen
Tutti Fruitti . . . . Little Richard
Convicted . . . . Oscar McLollie
Go On With the Wedding. . . . . Patti Page
Chain Gang . . . . Bobby Scott
* Rock and Roll Waltz . . . . Kay Starr
Memories Are Made of This . . . . Gale Storm
Teenage Prayer . . . . Gale Storm

[1]Dorothy Collins was another star of "Your Hit Parade."
[2]This title became an "in" expression with the kids of the mid-fifties.

14

1956

1956 saw the re-election of Eisenhower and Nixon and the increased availability of color television.

In boxing, Floyd Patterson, at age twenty-one, became the youngest man ever to win the heavyweight championship of the world.

Movie star Grace Kelly (she recorded "True Love" with Bing Crosby) married Prince Ranier of Monaco. The big movies of '56 were *The King and I, Around the World in 80 Days* (a hit by Mantovani and Victor Young in '57) and *The Ten Commandments.* Broadway hits included *My Fair Lady* and *Auntie Mame.*

The year 1956 was one of the most important years of the rock 'n' roll era. This was due primarily to two recording artists.

Pat Boone began his rise to stardom in '56 with songs like "Don't Forbid Me" and "I Almost Lost My Mind" (both #1 songs). He would go on to become the second most productive oldie artist of all time; second to the man who was to be known as The King—Elvis Presley.

Elvis actually began his career in 1954, with five barely known records on the Sun label. It was 1956, however, when he was to become a star. Under the management of Colonel Tom Parker, and signed to a recording contract with R.C.A., Elvis was brought before the nation on the Ed Sullivan show and sang his first and perhaps greatest hit, "Heartbreak Hotel." This was followed quickly by the two-sided smash, "Don't Be Cruel" and "Hound Dog." He made the first of many movies, and its title song, "Love Me Tender," was an almost instant million seller. In '56, he produced an incredible nineteen hits, three of them reaching #1 in the country. From 1956 until now, Elvis was, and is, The King.

Though Elvis dominated 1956, there were other smash hits, such as Gogi Grant's "The Wayward Wind," Guy Mitchell's "Singing the Blues," and Jim Lowe's "The Green Door." 1956 also produced three "classics" of the oldie era: Fats Domino's "Blueberry Hill," the Platters' "My Prayer," and a song by the Five Satins that many consider the greatest oldie ballad of all, "In the Still of the Nite."

The year 1956 also marked the establishment of a new star, Andy Williams.

Frankie Lymon & the Teenagers contributed the classic, "Why Do Fools Fall in Love."

After "Tutti Fruitti" in 1955, Little Richard had his biggest years in '56, '57 and '58; 1956 featured "Long Tall Sally," "Slippin' and Slidin'," "Rip It Up" and "Ready Teddy."

15

Little Richard *(courtesy Specialty Records, Inc.)*

Gene Vincent and the Blue Caps *(Capitol)*

Johnny Cash *(Columbia)*

Four Lads *(Columbia)*

JANUARY

I'll Be Home	Pat Boone
Tutti Fruitti	Pat Boone
Devil or Angel	Clovers
Seven Days	Dorothy Collins
Seven Days	Crew Cuts
I'll Be Home	Flamingos
No, Not Much	Four Lads
Theme From the Threepenny Opera (Moritat)	Richard Hayman[1]
11th Hour Melody	Al Hibbler
Theme From the Threepenny Opera (Moritat)	Dick Hyman Trio
Seven Days	Clyde McPhatter
Lisbon Antigua	Mitch Miller
Ninety-Nine Years	Guy Mitchell
Don't Go To Strangers	Vaughn Monroe
Theme from the Threepenny Opera (Moritat)	Billy Vaughn
That's Your Mistake	Otis Williams & the Charms

FEBRUARY

Forever Darling	Ames Brothers
*Theme From the Threepenny Opera (Moritat)	Louis Armstrong
Poor People of Paris	Les Baxter
Cry Baby	Bonnie Sisters
A Tear Fell	Teresa Brewer
Bo Weevil	Teresa Brewer
11th Hour Melody	Lou Busch
Our Love Affair	Tommy Charles
Eddie My Love	Chordettes
Hot Diggity	Perry Como
Why Do Fools Fall in Love	Diamonds
Bo Weevil	Fats Domino
Eddie My Love	Fontane Sisters
Lovely One	Four Voices
Lipstick & Candy & Rubber Sole Shoes	Julius La Rosa
Mr. Wonderful	Teddi King
Mr. Wonderful	Peggy Lee

[1]Later became the vocal, "Mack the Knife," by Bobby Darin.

18

Why Do Fools Fall in Love . . . . Frankie Lymon &
the Teenagers
Lovely Lies. Manhattan
Brothers
Innamorata. Dean Martin
Poor People of Paris . . . . Russ Morgan
To You My Love . . . . Nick Noble
Theme from the
Threepenny Opera (Moritat). . . . . Les Paul & Mary
Ford
Blue Suede Shoes. . . . . Carl Perkins
I'm Just a Dancing Partner . . . . Platters
* Heartbreak Hotel. . . . . Elvis Presley[1]
I Was the One. . . . . Elvis Presley
Why Do Fools Fall in Love . . . . Gale Storm
Eddie My Love . . . . Teen Queens
Eloise . . . . Kay Thompson
Innamorata. Jerry Vale
Mr. Wonderful. . . . . Sarah Vaughn
Theme from the
Threepenny Opera (Moritat). . . . . Lawrence Welk
Beyond the Sea . . . . Roger Williams

MARCH
Main Title from the
Man With the Golden Arm. . . . . Elmer Bernstein
Ivory Tower . . . . Cathy Carr
Wild Cherry . . . . Don Cherry
Too Young To Go Steady . . . . Nat "King" Cole
Rock Island Line . . . . Lonnie Donegan
Rock Right. Georgia Gibbs
R-O-C-K . . . . Bill Haley & the
Comets
The Saints Rock 'n Roll . . . . Bill Haley & the
Comets
Main Title & Molly-O . . . . Dick Jacobs
Long Tall Sally . . . . Little Richard
Theme From the
Man With the Golden Arm. . . . . Richard Maltby
Theme From the
Man With the Golden Arm. . . . . Billy May
The Magic Touch . . . . Platters

[1]This is the song that "started it all" for Elvis.

19

Blue Suede Shoes . . . . Elvis Presley
Port Au Prince . . . . Nelson Riddle
Ivory Tower . . . . Otis Williams &
                                          the Charms
Church Bells May Ring . . . . Willows

APRIL
It Only Hurts For a Little While. . . . . Ames Brothers
Long Tall Sally . . . . Pat Boone
Moonglow & Theme From Picnic . . . . George Cates
Little Girl of Mine . . . . Cleftones
On the Street Where You Live. . . . . Vic Damone
Church Bells May Ring . . . . Diamonds
I'm In Love Again . . . . Fats Domino
My Blue Heaven . . . . Fats Domino
A Little Love Can Go a Long, Long Way . . . Dream Weavers
My Little Angel. . . . . Four Lads
Standing on the Corner . . . . Four Lads
*The Wayward Wind. . . . . Gogi Grant
Slippin' and Slidin' . . . . Little Richard
I Want You To Be My Girl . . . . Frankie Lymon &
                                          the Teenagers
Walk Hand in Hand . . . . Tony Martin
Delilah Jones. . . . . McGuire Sisters
Picnic . . . . McGuire Sisters
The Happy Whistler . . . . Don Robertson
Moonglow & Theme From Picnic . . . . Morris Stoloff
Ivory Tower . . . . Gale Storm

MAY
* I Almost Lost My Mind . . . . Pat Boone
I'm In Love With You . . . . Pat Boone
A Sweet Old Fashioned Girl . . . . Teresa Brewer
Portuguese Washerwomen . . . . Joe "Fingers" Carr
Born To Be With You . . . . Chordettes
The Girl In My Dreams . . . . Cliques
Glendora . . . . Perry Como
On The Street Where You Live . . . . Eddie Fisher
I'm In Love Again . . . . Fontane Sisters
Graduation Day. . . . . Four Freshmen
You're The Apple of My Eye. . . . . Four Lovers[1]
Kiss Me Another . . . . Georgia Gibbs

[1]The Four Lovers changed their name to the Four Seasons.

Free . . . . Tommy Leonetti
Standing on the Corner . . . . Dean Martin
Treasure of Love . . . . Clyde McPhatter
Standing on the Corner . . . . Mills Brothers
Transfusion. Nervous Norvis
I Want You, I Need You,
   I Love You . . . . Elvis Presley
Money Honey . . . . Elvis Presley
My Baby Left Me . . . . Elvis Presley
Graduation Day . . . . Rover Boys
Second Fiddle . . . . Kay Starr
Corina Corina . . . . Joe Turner

JUNE
Roll Over Beethoven. . . . . Chuck Berry
Love Love Love . . . . Clovers
That's All There Is To That. . . . . Nat "King" Cole
More . . . . Perry Como
Whatever Will Be, Will Be . . . . Doris Day
Love Love Love . . . . Diamonds
Soft Summer Breeze . . . . Eddie Heywood
Stranded in the Jungle. . . . . Jayhawks
Ready Teddy. Little Richard
Rip It Up . . . . Little Richard
Fever . . . . Little Willie John
Allegheny Moon. . . . . Patti Page
* My Prayer . . . . Platters
Wayward Wind . . . . Tex Ritter
Be-Bop-A-Lula. . . . . Gene Vincent
Woman Love . . . . Gene Vincent
You Don't Know Me . . . . Jerry Vale
Canadian Sunset. . . . . Hugo Winterhalter

JULY
The Flying Saucer . . . . Buchanan &
                                             Goodman
Stranded in the Jungle. . . . . Cadets
Ghost Town . . . . Don Cherry
The Fool . . . . Sanford Clark
Somebody Up There Likes Me . . . . Perry Como
Oh What a Night . . . . Dells
When My Dreamboat Comes Home . . . . . . Fats Domino
Heartbreak Hotel. . . . . Stan Freberg
Ka-Ding-Dong. . . . . G-Clefs

Stranded in the Jungle. . . . . Gadabouts
After the Lights Go Down Low . . . . Al Hibbler
Give Us This Day. . . . . Joni James
I Promise to Remember. . . . . Frankie Lymon &
the Teenagers
Song For a Summer Night . . . . Mitch Miller
Ape Call . . . . Nervous Norvus
Tonight You Belong To Me. . . . . Patience &
Prudence
Heaven on Earth . . . . Platters
Hound Dog . . . . Elvis Presley
Theme From the Proud Ones . . . . Nelson Riddle
A Casual Look. . . . . Six Teens
Fabulous Character. . . . . Sarah Vaughn

AUGUST
Happiness Street . . . . Tony Bennett
True Love . . . . Bing Crosby &
Grace Kelly
Ka-Ding-Dong. . . . . Diamonds
Honky Tonk . . . . Bill Doggett
In the Still of the Nite . . . . Five Satins
A House With Love In It . . . . Four Lads
The Bus Stop Song . . . . Four Lads
The Fool . . . . Gallahads
Happiness Street . . . . Georgia Gibbs
Rip It Up. . . . . Bill Haley & the
Comets
The Old Philosopher. . . . . Eddie Lawrence
In the Middle of the House. . . . . Vaughn Monroe
See Saw. . . . . Moonglows
True Love . . . . Jane Powell
* Don't Be Cruel . . . . Elvis Presley
Just Walking in the Rain. . . . . Johnnie Ray
Miracle of Love . . . . Eileen Rodgers
Let the Good Times Roll . . . . Shirley & Lee
The Italian Theme . . . . Cyril Stapleton
When the White Lilacs Bloom Again . . . . . . Billy Vaughn
St. Therese of the Roses . . . . Billy Ward & the
Dominoes
Canadian Sunset. . . . . Andy Williams
When the White Lilacs Bloom Again . . . . . . Florian Zabach
When the White Lilacs Bloom Again . . . . . . Helmut Zacharias

SEPTEMBER

Chains of Love . . . . Pat Boone
Friendly Persuasion. . . . . Pat Boone
I Walk the Line . . . . Johnny Cash
Tonight You Belong To Me . . . . Karen Chandler &
              Jimmy Wakely
Lay Down Your Arms . . . . Chordettes
Soft Summer Breeze . . . . Diamonds
Blueberry Hill . . . . Fats Domino
In the Middle of the House . . . . Rusty Draper
Out of Sight, Out of Mind . . . . Five Keys
Ka-Ding-Dong . . . . Hilltoppers
Tonight You Belong To Me . . . . Lennon Sisters
* The Green Door . . . . Jim Lowe
It Isn't Right . . . . Platters
You'll Never Never Know . . . . Platters
Blue Moon . . . . Elvis Presley

OCTOBER

Blueberry Hill . . . . Louis Armstrong
Slow Walk . . . . Sil Austin
Jamaica Farewell . . . . Harry Belefonte[1]
Mutual Admiration Society . . . . Teresa Brewer
Night Lights . . . . Nat "King" Cole
I Miss You So . . . . Chris Conner
Priscilla . . . . Eddie Cooley &
              the Dimples
Cindy, Oh Cindy . . . . Eddie Fisher
Rudy's Rock . . . . Bill Haley & the
              Comets
A Rose and a Baby Ruth. . . . . George Hamilton
              IV
City of Angels . . . . Highlights
Petticoats of Portugal . . . . Dick Jacobs
A.B.C.'s of Love . . . . Frankie Lymon &
              the Teenagers
Cindy, Oh Cindy . . . . Vince Martin &
              the Tarriers
* Singing the Blues . . . . Guy Mitchell
Two Different Worlds . . . . Jayne Morgan &
              Roger Williams
Mama from the Train . . . . Patti Page

[1]This song introduced the "Calypso" sound.

Anyway You Want Me . . . . Elvis Presley
I Don't Care If the Sun Don't Shine . . . . . . Elvis Presley
* Love Me Tender . . . . Elvis Presley[1]
Singing the Blues . . . . Marty Robbins
Two Different Worlds . . . . Don Rondo
Garden of Eden . . . . Joe Valino

NOVEMBER
Goodnight My Love . . . . Jessie Belvin
Since I Met You Baby . . . . Mindy Carson
There You Go . . . . Johnny Cash
Slow Walk . . . . Bill Doggett
Tra La La . . . . Georgia Gibbs
I Put a Spell On You . . . . Screamin' Jay
                                                  Hawkins
Since I Met You Baby . . . . Ivory Joe Hunter
I Dreamed . . . . Betty Johnson
Confidential . . . . Sonny Knight
Moonlight Gambler . . . . Frankie Laine
Rock-a-Bye Your Baby With a Dixie Melody . . Jerry Lewis
Goodnight My Love . . . . McGuire Sisters
Gonna Get Along Without Ya Now . . . . Patience &
                                                  Prudence
The Money Tree . . . . Patience &
                                                  Prudence
Love Me . . . . Elvis Presley
When My Blue Moon Turns To Gold Again . . Elvis Presley
Armen's Theme . . . . Joe Reisman
Love Me Tender . . . . Henri Rene
Auctioneer . . . . Leroy Van Dyke
The Money Tree . . . . Margaret Whiting
Baby Doll . . . . Andy Williams

DECEMBER
Jim Dandy . . . . Lavern Baker
Anastasia . . . . Pat Boone
* Don't Forbid Me . . . . Pat Boone
I Love My Baby . . . . Jill Corey
Blue Monday . . . . Fats Domino
Wisdom of a Fool . . . . Five Keys
The Banana Boat Song . . . . Fontane Sisters
Written On the Wind . . . . Four Aces

[1]Title song from Elvis' first movie.

Dreamy Eyes . . . . Four Preps
A Thousand Miles Away . . . . Heartbeats[1]
Ain't Got No Home . . . . Clarence
"Frogman"
Henry
Young Love . . . . Sonny James
The Banana Boat Song . . . . Vince Martin &
the Tarriers
Love Is Strange . . . . Mickey & Sylvia
On My Word of Honor . . . . Platters
One In a Million . . . . Platters
How Do You Think I Feel . . . . Elvis Presley
How's the World Treating You . . . . Elvis Presley
Paralyzed . . . . Elvis Presley
Old Shep . . . . Elvis Presley
Poor Boy . . . . Elvis Presley
Armen's Theme . . . . David Seville
I Feel Good . . . . Shirley & Lee
The Banana Boat Song . . . . Sarah Vaughn

[1]Lead singer "Shep" Sheppard later formed the group Shep & the Limelites and, in 1961, recorded "Daddy's Home."

1957

Rock 'n' roll received one of its biggest and most important boosts in 1957. A.B.C. Television presented a show called American Bandstand. Hosted by Dick Clark, the show featured music of the day, with personal appearances by the artists popular at the time, the playing of pop records and dancing by the studio audience, consisting, of course, of teen-agers. Along with Alan Freed, the D.J. who coined the phrase rock 'n' roll and promoted it in the early years, American Bandstand and Dick Clark are probably as responsible for rock 'n' roll's success as the artists and music themselves.

We consider 1957 to be the biggest year for super oldies. The evidence of this may be seen in Section 6, where our selection of "Songs of the Year" was limited to ten songs for any given year. In 1957, however, it was impossible to select any less than twenty-five songs.

The year 1957 marked the rise of Johnny Mathis, who was to become the most outstanding romantic symbol of the oldie era. With such songs as "It's Not for Me to Say" and "Wonderful, Wonderful," he won the hearts of young lovers across the country.

Pat Boone and Elvis continued to dominate the charts, along with the Everly Brothers. Chuck Berry enjoyed one of his most successful years in '57.

A shy young man named Buddy Holly was a rising star. His 1957 recording "Peggy Sue" became a hit. Believed by many to be the first legitimate threat to Elvis Presley's position at the top, Buddy Holly was destined to have a great career. Another destiny stepped in, however, when he, along with Ritchie Valens and the Big Bopper, was killed in a plane crash. So popular was this trio that Tommy Dee recorded "Three Stars" in tribute to them and it became a smash hit.

The year produced a one-hit group, Tom & Jerry, with a song called "Hey! School Girl." Though not too successful as oldie artists, they later achieved superstardom as Simon & Garfunkel.

Jerry Lee Lewis, one of the most dynamic performers ever, had his first and biggest hit, "Whole Lot of Shakin' Going On," in '57. He is still a big star today in country music.

Little Richard maintained his star status with "Lucille," "Jenny Jenny" and "Keep a Knockin.' "

Outside the music world, the U.S.S.R. launched the first satellite, Sputnik I.

The "beat" generation was represented by the publication of Jack Kerouac's "On The Road." On Broadway, *West Side Story* was playing. It was the year of the sack dress (in '58 Gerry Granahan was to record "No Chemise, Please").

26

"Stuffing" was a big fad of 1957. College students stuffed as many bodies as possible into Volkswagens, phone booths, etc.

JANUARY

Cinco Robles	Russell Arms[1]
The Banana Boat Song	Harry Belefonte
Ballerina	Nat "King" Cole
Young Love	Crew Cuts
Who Needs You	Four Lads
Marianne	Terry Gilkyson & the Easy Riders
Wringle Wrangle	Bill Hayes
Marianne	Hilltoppers
*Young Love	Tab Hunter
Bad Boy	Jive Bombers
The Banana Boat Song	Steve Lawrence
The Girl Can't Help It	Little Richard[2]
Wonderful, Wonderful	Johnny Mathis[3]
Without Love (There Is Nothing)	Clyde McPhatter
Knee Deep in the Blues	Guy Mitchell
Wringle Wrangle	Fess Parker
Cinco Robles	Les Paul & Mary Ford
Playing for Keeps	Elvis Presley
Too Much	Elvis Presley
Look Homeward Angel	Johnnie Ray
You Don't Owe Me a Thing	Johnnie Ray

FEBRUARY

I'm Stickin' With You	Jimmy Bowen[4]
Lucky Lips	Ruth Brown
Walkin' After Midnight	Patsy Cline
*Round and Round	Perry Como
Come Go With Me	Del Vikings
I'm Walkin'	Fats Domino
So Rare	Jimmy Dorsey
Fools Fall in Love	Drifters

[1]Russell Arms was a star of T.V.'s "Your Hit Parade."

[2]From the movie of the same name starring Jayne Mansfield.

[3]Mathis' album, "Johnny's Greatest Hits," stayed on the charts for more than eight years.

[4]Bowen's group, which included Buddy Knox, was known as the Rhythm Orchids.

Butterfly	Charlie Gracie
Only One Love	George Hamilton IV
Gone	Ferlin Husky
Party Doll	Buddy Knox[1]
Party Doll	Steve Lawrence
Your Wild Heart	Joy Layne
Little By Little	Micki Marlo
Tricky	Ralph Marterie
A Poor Man's Roses	Patti Page
Just Because	Lloyd Price
Teen-age Crush	Tommy Sands
Almost Paradise	Lou Stein
*Butterfly	Andy Williams
Almost Paradise	Roger Williams

MARCH

School Day	Chuck Berry
I'm Waiting Just For You	Pat Boone
Why Baby Why	Pat Boone
Empty Arms	Teresa Brewer
Sittin' In the Balcony	Eddie Cochran
Pledge of Love	Ken Copeland
Sittin' in the Balcony	Johnny Dee
Little Darlin'	Diamonds
Little Darlin'	Gladiolas
Ninety-Nine Ways	Tab Hunter
First Date, First Kiss, First Love	Sonny James
Love Is a Golden Ring	Frankie Laine
Lucille	Little Richard
Rock-a-Billy	Guy Mitchell
He's Mine	Platters
I'm Sorry	Platters
*All Shook Up	Elvis Presley
After School	Randy Starr

APRIL

Banana Boat	Stan Freberg
Dark Moon	Bonnie Guitar
Empty Arms	Ivory Joe Hunter
Little White Lies	Betty Johnson
It's Not For Me to Say	Johnny Mathis

[1]Knox's group, which included Jimmy Bowen, was known as the Rhythm Orchids.

Shish-Kebab	Ralph Marterie
Peace in the Valley	Elvis Presley
That's When Your Heartaches Begin	Elvis Presley
Yes Tonight, Josephine	Johnny Ray
Four Walls	Jim Reeves
A White Sport Coat	Marty Robbins
Dark Moon	Gale Storm
Pledge of Love	Mitchell Torok
C.C. Rider	Chuck Willis

MAY

Bernardine	Pat Boone
*Love Letters in the Sand	Pat Boone
Rang Tang Ding Dong	Cellos
Young Blood	Coasters
Searchin'	Coasters
The Girl With the Golden Braids	Perry Como
It's You I Love	Fats Domino
Valley of Tears	Fats Domino
Freight Train	Rusty Draper
Bye Bye Love	Everly Brothers
Shangri-La	Four Coins
I Just Don't Know	Four Lads
Fabulous	Charlie Gracie
Over the Mountain; Across the Sea	Johnnie & Joe
Rock Your Little Baby to Sleep	Buddy Knox
Four Walls	Jim Lowe
Talkin' to the Blues	Jim Lowe
Just to Hold My Hand	Clyde McPhatter
Queen of the Senior Prom	Mills Brothers
Start Movin'	Sal Mineo
A Teenager's Romance	Ricky Nelson[1]
I'm Walking	Ricky Nelson
Old Cape Cod	Patti Page
Wondering	Patti Page
My Dream	Platters
Gonna Find Me a Bluebird	Marvin Rainwater
With All My Heart	Jodie Sands
Goin' Steady	Tommy Sands
I Like Your Kind of Love	Andy Williams

[1]Nelson grew up in the public eye, as a co-star of T.V.'s "Ozzie and Harriet."

Johnny Mathis *(Columbia)*

Sam Cooke *(R.C.A.)*

I'm Gonna Sit Right Down
  and Write Myself a Letter . . . . Billy Williams
Around the World . . . . Victor Young

JUNE

Tammy . . . . Ames Brothers
Let the Four Winds Blow . . . . Roy Brown
Send for Me . . . . Nat "King" Cole
Whispering Bells . . . . Del Vikings
Rainbow . . . . Russ Hamilton
Susie-Q . . . . Dale Hawkins
Whole Lot of Shakin' Going On . . . . Jerry Lee Lewis
Jenny Jenny . . . . Little Richard
Around the World . . . . Mantovani
A Fallen Star. . . . . Jimmy Newman
*(Let Me Be Your) Teddy Bear. . . . . Elvis Presley
Loving You. . . . . Elvis Presley
Everyone's Laughing. . . . . Spaniels
Star Dust . . . . Billy Ward & the
                                                Dominoes
Short Fat Fannie . . . . Larry Williams

JULY

Diana . . . . Paul Anka[1]
In the Middle of an Island . . . . Tony Bennett
Farther Up the Road. . . . . Bobby Bland
Mr. Lee. . . . . Bobbettes
White Silver Sands . . . . Owen Bradley
                                                Quintet
Flying Saucer the 2nd . . . . Buchanan &
                                                Goodman
Love Me to Pieces . . . . Jill Corey
Cool Shake. . . . . Del Vikings
Think . . . . "5" Royales
To the Aisle . . . . Five Satins
White Silver Sands . . . . Dave Gardner
Fraulein. Bobby Helms
Goody Goody . . . . Frankie Lymon &
                                                the Teenagers

[1]Anka also wrote such hits as "She's a Lady" for Tom Jones, "My Way" for Frank Sinatra, the score for the motion picture *The Longest Day* and the theme song for the "Tonight" show.

*Tammy . . . . Debbie Reynolds
White Silver Sands . . . . Don Rondo

AUGUST
Long Lonely Nights . . . . Lee Andrews &
                                                 the Hearts
Black Slacks . . . . Joe Bennett & the
                                                 Sparkletones
Remember You're Mine . . . . Pat Boone
There's a Gold Mine in the Sky . . . . Pat Boone
That'll Be the Day . . . . Crickets[1]
Just Between You & Me . . . . Chordettes
When I See You . . . . Fats Domino
June Night . . . . Jimmy Dorsey
Bon Voyage . . . . Janice Harper
Rebel . . . . Carol Jarvis
Hula Love . . . . Buddy Knox
Tonite Tonite . . . . Mello Kings
Lasting Love . . . . Sal Mineo
You're My One and Only Love . . . . Ricky Nelson
Moonlight Swim . . . . Nick Noble
And That Reminds Me . . . . Della Reese
*Honeycomb . . . . Jimmie Rodgers
Rocking Pneumonia &
    the Boogie Woogie Flu . . . . Huey "Piano"
                                                 Smith
Lotta Lovin' . . . . Gene Vincent

SEPTEMBER
Melodie D'Amour . . . . Ames Brothers
With You On My Mind . . . . Nat "King" Cole
*Wake Up Little Susie . . . . Everly Brothers
My One Sin . . . . Four Coins
Peanuts . . . . Little Joe & the
                                                 Thrillers
Keep a Knockin' . . . . Little Richard
Chances Are . . . . Johnny Mathis
Be-Bop Baby . . . . Ricky Nelson
Have I Told You Lately
    That I Love You . . . . Ricky Nelson
Plaything . . . . Ted Newman
Honest I Do . . . . Jimmy Reed

[1]The Crickets' lead singer was Buddy Holly.

Back to School Again. . . . . Timmie Rogers
Alone . . . . Shepherd Sisters
Happy Happy Birthday Baby. . . . . Tune Weavers
Deep Purple. . . . . Billy Ward & the
Dominoes
Lips of Wine. . . . . Andy Williams

OCTOBER

Boys Do Cry. . . . . Joe Bennett & the
Sparkletones
*April Love . . . . Pat Boone
Just Born . . . . Perry Como
*You Send Me. . . . . Sam Cooke
Soft . . . . Bill Doggett
Wait and See. . . . . Fats Domino
Could This Be Magic. . . . . Dubs
Little Bitty Pretty One . . . . Thurston Harris
My Special Angel. . . . . Bobby Helms
The Twelfth of Never . . . . Johnny Mathis
I'll Remember Today. . . . . Patti Page
Moonlight Swim. . . . . Tony Perkins
*Jailhouse Rock . . . . Elvis Presley
Treat Me Nice. Elvis Presley
Daddy Cool . . . . Rays
Silhouettes . . . . Rays
All the Way . . . . Frank Sinatra
Plaything. . . . . Nick Todd[1]
Til . . . . Roger Williams
Reet Petite. . . . . Jackie Wilson

NOVEMBER

Tear Drops. . . . . Lee Andrews &
the Hearts
Rock & Roll Music . . . . Chuck Berry
You Send Me . . . . Teresa Brewer
Oh Boy!. . . . . Crickets
*At the Hop . . . . Danny & the
Juniors
Sometimes . . . . Danny & the
Juniors
Little Bitty Pretty One . . . . Bobby Day
Put a Light in the Window . . . . Four Lads
Wun'erful, Wun'erful. . . . . Stan Freberg

[1]Nick Todd is Pat Boone's brother.

34

Raunchy . . . . Ernie Freeman
Why Don't They Understand. . . . . George Hamilton
       IV
The Joker. . . . . Hilltoppers
Peggy Sue . . . . Buddy Holly
Buzz Buzz Buzz. . . . . Hollywood Flames
Raunchy . . . . Bill Justis
Great Balls of Fire . . . . Jerry Lee Lewis
The Joker. . . . . Billy Myles
The Story of My Life. . . . . Marty Robbins
Kisses Sweeter Than Wine . . . . Jimmie Rodgers
Raunchy . . . . Billy Vaughn
Dance to the Bop. . . . . Gene Vincent
Bony Moronie . . . . Larry Williams
You Bug Me Baby . . . . Larry Williams

DECEMBER
You Can Make It If You Try . . . . Gene Allison
I Love You Baby . . . . Paul Anka
La Dee Dah . . . . Billy & Lillie
Santa & the Satellite . . . . Buchanan &
       Goodman
I'll Come Running Back To You . . . . Sam Cooke
(I Love You)
  For Sentimental Reasons . . . . Sam Cooke
Oh Julie. . . . . Crescendos
Little Sandy Sleighfoot. . . . . Jimmy Dean
Henrietta. . . . . Jimmy Dee
The Stroll. . . . . Diamonds
The Big Beat. . . . . Fats Domino
Tell Me Why. . . . . Norman Fox & the
       Rob Roys
Jingle Bell Rock. . . . . Bobby Helms
No Love . . . . Johnny Mathis
Wild is the Wind . . . . Johnny Mathis
Sugartime . . . . McGuire Sisters
Stood Up . . . . Ricky Nelson
Waitin' in School . . . . Ricky Nelson
Hey! School Girl. . . . . Tom & Jerry[1]
Sail Along Silvery Moon . . . . Billy Vaughn
Hard Times (The Slop). . . . . Noble Watts

[1]Tom & Jerry later recorded under their real names, Simon & Garfunkel.

1958

The United States launched its first satellite, Explorer I, in '58. Conway Twitty launched his biggest hit ever, "It's Only Make Believe."

President Eisenhower signed the bill for Alaska's statehood and postal rates increased to 4¢ for regular mail and 7¢ for air mail.

One of the biggest fads ever to infect the nation did so in '58. The Hula Hoop hit the market, with over 30 million sales.

Aside from its share of great songs, 1958 brought forth two more oldie superstars. Ricky Nelson, who began his recording career in 1957 while appearing on his parents' "Ozzie and Harriet" show, recorded such songs as "Poor Little Fool" in 1958 and went on to enjoy an even more successful career. Connie Francis recorded "Who's Sorry Now" and that led to her becoming the most successful by far of all the female artists of the rock 'n' roll generation.

Throughout the rock 'n' roll years, the standard singers remained prominent. Some examples in 1958 were Perry Como with "Catch a Falling Star," Dean Martin with "Return to Me" and the Ames Brothers with "A Very Precious Love."

Women's Lib was heard from in '58 with the publishing of the book, *The Decline of the American Male*. Another noted book in 1958 was *Lolita*.

In sports, Sugar Ray Robinson regained the middleweight boxing crown for an incredible fifth time.

The country was experiencing a recession, but the recording business was flourishing.

By now, certain artists had established themselves as stars and had a number of hits year in and year out. In '58, Paul Anka had five, Pat Boone six, the Everly Brothers seven and Elvis Presley eight.

One of the few folk songs to make it big in the pop field, "Tom Dooley" by the Kingston Trio, reached #1 in the nation in 1958.

The Platters had two #1 songs in '58, "Twilight Time" and "Smoke Gets In Your Eyes."

JANUARY

Walkin' with Mr. Lee	Lee Allen
You Are My Destiny	Paul Anka
De De Dinah	Frankie Avalon
Ballad of a Teenage Queen	Johnny Cash
Maybe	Chantels
Angel Smile	Nat "King" Cole
Catch a Falling Star	Perry Como

Magic Moments . . . . Perry Como
Yellow Dog Blues . . . . Joe Darensbourg
                                                  & the Dixie
                                                  Flyers
26 Miles. . . . . Four Preps
Don't Let Go . . . . Roy Hamilton
The Swingin' Shepherd Blues. . . . . Moe Koffman
                                                  Quartet
March From the River Kwai and Colonel
  Bogey. . . . . Mitch Miller
Belonging to Someone . . . . Patti Page
Swinging Shepherd Blues . . . . Johnny Pate
                                                  Quintet
Jo-Ann. . . . . Playmates
*Don't. . . . . Elvis Presley
I Beg of You . . . . Elvis Presley
Short Shorts . . . . Royal Teens
*Get a Job . . . . Silhouettes
Betty & Dupree. . . . . Chuck Willis
She's Neat . . . . Dale Wright

FEBRUARY
Sweet Little Sixteen . . . . Chuck Berry
Reelin' & Rockin'. . . . . Chuck Berry
A Wonderful Time Up There. . . . . Pat Boone
It's Too Soon to Know . . . . Pat Boone
So Tough . . . . Casuals
*Tequila . . . . Champs
Maybe Baby . . . . Crickets
Rock & Roll Is Here to Stay . . . . Danny & the
                                                  Juniors
Click-Clack. . . . . Dickey Doo & the
                                                  Don'ts
This Little Girl of Mine . . . . Everly Brothers
Who's Sorry Now . . . . Connie Francis
7–11. . . . . Gone All-Stars
The Little Blue Man . . . . Betty Johnson
So Tough . . . . Kuf-Linx
Breathless . . . . Jerry Lee Lewis
Good Golly, Miss Molly . . . . Little Richard
Come To Me. . . . . Johnny Mathis
The Walk. Jimmy McCracklin
Pretty Little Girl . . . . Monarchs
Been So Long . . . . Pastels

Tequila . . . . Eddie Platt
We Belong Together . . . . Robert & Johnny
Oh-Oh I'm Falling in Love Again . . . . Jimmie Rodgers
Sing Boy Sing . . . . Tommy Sands
Bad Motorcycle . . . . Storey Sisters
Are You Sincere. . . . . Andy Williams

MARCH
Every Night . . . . Chantels
Lollipop. . . . . Chordettes
Lonely Island . . . . Sam Cooke
You Were Made For Me. . . . . Sam Cooke
There's Only One of You . . . . Four Lads
Oh Lonesome Me. . . . . Don Gibson
Now and For Always. . . . . George Hamilton
                                                          IV
Billy . . . . Kathy Linden
Talk to Me, Talk to Me . . . . Little Willie John
He's Got the Whole World
  (In His Hands). . . . . Laurie London
Return to Me . . . . Dean Martin
Book of Love . . . . Monotones
Lazy Mary . . . . Lou Monte
Believe What You Say . . . . Ricky Nelson
My Bucket's Got a Hole In It. . . . . Ricky Nelson
*Twilight Time . . . . Platters
Lollipop. . . . . Ronald & Ruby
Tumbling Tumbleweeds. . . . . Billy Vaughn
Dinner With Drac . . . . John Zacherle

APRIL
A Very Precious Love . . . . Ames Brothers
Crazy Love. . . . . Paul Anka
Let the Bells Keep Ringing. . . . . Paul Anka
You . . . . Aquatones
Johnny B. Goode . . . . Chuck Berry
Sugar Moon . . . . Pat Boone
Torero. . . . . Renato Carosone
Looking Back . . . . Nat "King" Cole
Kewpie Doll . . . . Perry Como
High Sign. . . . . Diamonds
Sick and Tired. . . . . Fats Domino
Ne Ne Na Na Na Na Nu Nu . . . . Dickey Doo & the
                                                          Don'ts[1]

[1]Lead singer Gerry Granahan had a solo hit, "No Chemise, Please" in May, 1958.

38

*All I Have To Do Is Dream . . . . Everly Brothers
Claudette. . . . . Everly Brothers
Big Man. . . . . Four Preps
Skinny Minnie. . . . . Bill Haley & the
                                     Comets
All the Time . . . . Johnny Mathis
Teacher, Teacher . . . . Johnny Mathis
Wear My Ring Around Your Neck. . . . . . . Elvis Presley
Doncha' Think It's Time. . . . . Elvis Presley
Just Married . . . . Marty Robbins
Secretly. . . . . Jimmie Rodgers
Alligator Wine. . . . . Screamin' Jay
                                     Hawkins
*Witch Doctor. . . . . David Seville
I Met Him on a Sunday . . . . Shirelles
Chanson d'Amour. . . . . Art & Dotty Todd
For Your Love. . . . . Ed Townsend
Wishing For Your Love . . . . Voxpoppers
Hang Up My Rock & Roll Shoes . . . . Chuck Willis
To Be Loved. . . . . Jackie Wilson
Rumble . . . . Link Wray

MAY
Try the Impossible . . . . Lee Andrews &
                                     the Hearts
Padre . . . . Toni Arden
Guess Things Happen That Way. . . . . Johnny Cash
El Rancho Rock . . . . Champs
Zorro . . . . Chordettes
*Yakety Yak . . . . Coasters
I Wonder Why . . . . Dion & the
                                     Belmonts
I'm Sorry I Made You Cry . . . . Connie Francis
Do You Want to Dance . . . . Bobby Freeman
(It's Been a Long Time)
  Pretty Baby . . . . Gino & Gina
You Need Hands . . . . Eydie Gorme
No Chemise, Please. . . . . Gerry Granahan
Rave On . . . . Buddy Holly
Jennie Lee . . . . Jan & Arnie
High School Confidential . . . . Jerry Lee Lewis
Come What May . . . . Clyde McPhatter
Ooh! My Soul . . . . Little Richard
Endless Sleep . . . . Jody Reynolds

Make Me a Miracle . . . . Jimmie Rodgers
Leroy . . . . Jack Scott
What Am I Living For . . . . Chuck Willis
*The Purple People Eater . . . . Sheb Wooley

JUNE
For Your Precious Love . . . . Jerry Butler
I Love You So . . . . Chantels
Got a Match . . . . Daddy-O's
One Summer Night . . . . Danleers
Splish Splash . . . . Bobby Darin
Rebel Rouser . . . . Duane Eddy
Enchanted Island . . . . Four Lads
Got a Match . . . . Frank Gallop
Blue Blue Day . . . . Don Gibson
When . . . . Kalin Twins
A Certain Smile . . . . Johnny Mathis
*Poor Little Fool . . . . Ricky Nelson
Willie and the Hand Jive . . . . Johnny Otis
Left Right Out of Your Heart . . . . Patti Page
Don't Go Home . . . . Playmates
*Patricia . . . . Prez Prado
Don't Ask Me Why . . . . Elvis Presley[1]
Hard Headed Woman . . . . Elvis Presley
My True Love . . . . Jack Scott
The Bird on My Head . . . . David Seville

JULY
Midnight . . . . Paul Anka
Ginger Bread . . . . Frankie Avalon
Delicious . . . . Jim Bakus &
                                                        Friend
If Dreams Came True . . . . Pat Boone
That's How Much I Love You . . . . Pat Boone
Just a Dream . . . . Jimmy Clanton
Moon Talk . . . . Perry Como
Think It Over . . . . Crickets
Everybody Loves a Lover . . . . Doris Day
*Little Star . . . . Elegants
Stupid Cupid . . . . Connie Francis
Fever . . . . Peggy Lee
Angel Baby . . . . Dean Martin

[1]First song to be released after Elvis went into the army.

40

Western Movies	Olympics
Born Too Late	Poni-Tails
Early in the Morning	Rinky Dinks[1]
The Freeze	Tony & Joe

AUGUST

Carol	Chuck Berry
Chantilly Lace	Big Bopper
The Ways of a Woman in Love	Johnny Cash
Summertime Blues	Eddie Cochran
Topsy II	Cozy Cole
Win Your Love For Me	Sam Cooke
Over and Over	Bobby Day
Rock-in Robin	Bobby Day
No One Knows	Dion & the Belmonts
Tea for Two Cha-Cha	Tommy Dorsey
Ramrod	Duane Eddy
*It's All in the Game	Tommy Edwards
Bird Dog	Everly Brothers
Devoted To You	Everly Brothers
Lazy Summer Night	Four Preps
Betty Lou Got a New Pair of Shoes	Bobby Freeman
Crazy Eyes For You	Bobby Hamilton
La-Do-Dada	Dale Hawkins
Itchy Twitchy Feeling	Bobby Hendricks
Early in the Morning	Buddy Holly
Sumertime; Sumertime	Jamies
Somebody Touched Me	Buddy Knox
Tears on My Pillow	Little Anthony & the Imperials
Two Kinds of People in the World	Little Anthony & the Imperials
Susie Darlin'	Robin Luke
Dance Everyone Dance	Betty Madigan
Volare	Dean Martin
*Nel Blu Di Pinto Di Blu	Domenico Modugno
Put a Ring On My Finger	Les Paul & Mary Ford

[1]Rinky Dinks was the group name, but Bobby Darin was the artist.

41

Down the Aisle of Love . . . . Quin-Tones
She Was Only Seventeen . . . . Marty Robbins
Treasure of Your Love . . . . Eileen Rodgers
Are You Really Mine . . . . Jimmie Rodgers
The Wizard . . . . Jimmie Rodgers
You Cheated . . . . Shields
You Cheated . . . . Slades
The Green Mosquito . . . . Tune Rockers
La Paloma . . . . Billy Vaughn
How the Time Flies . . . . Jerry Wallace
Promise Me Love . . . . Andy Williams
Near You . . . . Roger Williams

SEPTEMBER
Mexican Hat Rock . . . . Apple Jacks
Firefly . . . . Tony Bennett
For My Good Fortune . . . . Pat Boone
Gee, But It's Lonely . . . . Pat Boone
This Little Girl's Gone Rockin' . . . . Ruth Brown
Topsy I . . . . Cozy Cole
It's So Easy . . . . Crickets
Hideaway . . . . Four Esquires
The End . . . . Earl Grant
Ten Commandments of Love . . . . Harvey & the
                                                Moonglows
There Goes My Heart . . . . Joni James
The Secret . . . . Gordon MacRae
The Ballad of Thunder Road . . . . Robert Mitchum
The Day the Rains Came . . . . Jane Morgan
*To Know Him Is to Love Him . . . . Teddy Bears
*It's Only Make Believe . . . . Conway Twitty
Come On, Let's Go . . . . Ritchie Valens

OCTOBER
Pussy Cat . . . . Ames Brothers
I'll Wait For You . . . . Frankie Avalon
The Hula Hoop Song . . . . Teresa Brewer
A Letter To An Angel . . . . Jimmy Clanton
Love Makes the World Go Round . . . . Perry Como
Queen of the Hop . . . . Bobby Darin
Please Love Me Forever . . . . Tommy Edwards
The Blob . . . . Five Blobs[1]

[1]One of Burt Bacharach's early efforts as a songwriter.

Fallin'	Connie Francis
The Hula Hoop Song	Georgia Gibbs
Give Myself a Party	Don Gibson
Forget Me Not	Kalin Twins
*Tom Dooley	Kingston Trio
Call Me	Johnny Mathis
A Lover's Question	Clyde McPhatter
I Got a Feeling	Ricky Nelson
Lonesome Town	Ricky Nelson
Need You	Donnie Owens
Poor Boy	Royaltones
With Your Love	Jack Scott

NOVEMBER

I'll Remember Tonight	Pat Boone
A Part Of Me	Jimmy Clanton
C'mon Everybody	Eddie Cochran
Love You Most of All	Sam Cooke
16 Candles	Crests
Walking Along	Diamonds
Whole Lotta Lovin'	Fats Domino
Cannonball	Duane Eddy
Love Is All We Need	Tommy Edwards
Problems	Everly Brothers
Love of My Life	Everly Brothers
The World Outside	Four Coins
The Mockingbird	Four Lads
Gotta Travel On	Billy Grammer
The Day the Rains Came	Raymond LeFevre
Philadelphia U.S.A.	Nu-Tornados
*Smoke Gets In Your Eyes	Platters
Beep Beep	Playmates
I Got Stung	Elvis Presley
One Night	Elvis Presley
That Old Black Magic	Louis Prima & Keely Smith
Bimbombey	Jimmie Rodgers
Believe Me	Royal Teens
Dreamy Eyes	Johnny Tillotson
Donna	Ritchie Valens
The Wedding	June Valli
Lonely Teardrops	Jackie Wilson

43

DECEMBER

Wiggle Wiggle. . . . . Accents
(All of a Sudden)
  My Heart Sings. . . . . Paul Anka
The Teen Commandments . . . . Paul Anka—
                         George
                         Hamilton IV—
                         Johnny Nash

Rocka-Conga. Applejacks
I Cried a Tear. . . . . Lavern Baker
Big Bopper's Wedding. . . . . Big Bopper
Lucky Ladybug. . . . . Billy & Lillie
Try Me . . . . James Brown
Peek-A-Boo. Cadillacs
The Closer You Are . . . . Channels
*The Chipmunk Song . . . . Chipmunks
Pretty Girls Everywhere. . . . . Eugene Church
Nobody But You . . . . Dee Clark
Turvy II. . . . . Cozy Cole
Don't Pity Me. . . . . Dion & the
                         Belmonts
My Happiness . . . . Connie Francis
Manhattan Spiritual. . . . . Reg Owen
The All American Boy. . . . . Bill Parsons
*Stagger Lee. Lloyd Price
Teasin' . . . . Quaker City Boys
Donde Esta Santa Claus . . . . Augie Rios
Goodbye Baby. . . . . Jack Scott
The Diary . . . . Neil Sedaka
Don't You Just Know It . . . . Huey "Piano"
                         Smith

Conway Twitty *(MCA)*

Duane Eddy *(R.C.A.)*

Bobby Darin *(Dona Kay)*   Isely Brothers *(R.C.A.)*

1959

Names in the news in 1959 included politicians and oldie artists.

In politics, Vice-President Richard Nixon visited Russia and Khrushchev visited America; John Foster Dulles died. Congress made Hawaii the 50th state.

In music, big names included Paul Anka and Frankie Avalon. Anka produced four hits, including the #1-ranked "Lonely Boy," and Avalon had a fantastic year with six hit records, including two #1's ("Venus," "Why"). Connie Francis' popularity reached new heights and Bobby Darin made his mark on musical history with two greats, "Mack the Knife" and "Dream Lover." Darin's death in 1973 ended a brilliant career. Paul Anka had become a star in 1957 at the age of fifteen. His recording of "Diana" has become a classic to oldie lovers. But Paul was to go on to become a major star of the rock years, and continues to be a top recording artist today. He is also one of the most sought-after nightclub performers in the country. Paul's talent includes the writing of most of his own songs such as "Diana" and "Puppy Love," as well as major hits for the biggest stars, including "My Way" for Frank Sinatra and "She's a Lady" for Tom Jones; in addition, Paul wrote the score for the movie *The Longest Day* and the theme song of the "Tonight" show. Paul Anka is recognized as a giant in the rock 'n' roll field, as well as music in general.

The Fleetwoods accomplished a giant feat in 1959 by producing two #1 songs, "Come Softly to Me" and "Mr. Blue."

Other oldies from '59 that made it big were "Kansas City" (Wilbert Harrison), "The Battle of New Orleans" (Johnny Horton) and Marty Robbins' saga, "El Paso."

JANUARY

Red River Rose	Ames Brothers
Tall Paul	Annette
Peter Gunn	Ray Anthony
Petite Fleur	Chris Barber's Jazz Band
With the Wind & the Rain In Your Hair	Pat Boone
Don't Take Your Guns to Town	Johnny Cash
The Bluebird, the Buzzard & the Oriole	Bobby Day
The Lonely One	Duane Eddy
I'm a Man	Fabian

Lovers Never Say Goodbye	Flamingos
Heartbeat.	Buddy Holly
There Must Be a Way	Joni James
Let's Love	Johnny Mathis
You Are Beautiful.	Johnny Mathis
May You Always.	McGuire Sisters
The Children's Marching Song	Mitch Miller
The Children's Marching Song	Cyril Stapleton
The Little Space Girl.	Jessie Lee Turner
La Bamba	Ritchie Valens
Blue Hawaii	Billy Vaughn
Hawaiian Wedding Song.	Andy Williams
Nola	Billy Williams

FEBRUARY

*Venus	Frankie Avalon
I've Had It	Bell Notes
It's Just a Matter of Time	Brook Benton
Alvin's Harmonica	The Chipmunks
Charlie Brown.	Coasters
Plain Jane	Bobby Darin
She Say (Oom Dooby Doom)	Diamonds
Please Mr. Sun.	Tommy Edwards
Sea Cruise	Frankie Ford
The Shag	Billy Graves
Ambrose (Part 5)	Linda Laurie
I Got a Wife	Mark IV
Moonlight Serenade	Rivieras
The Hanging Tree	Marty Robbins
Since I Don't Have You	Skyliners
Pink Shoe Laces.	Dodie Stevens
The Story of My Love	Conway Twitty
Tragedy.	Thomas Wayne
Raw-Hide.	Link Wray

MARCH

Bunny Hop.	Applejacks
This Should Go on Forever	Rod Bernard
For a Penny	Pat Boone
Heavenly Lover.	Teresa Brewer
No Other Arms, No Other Lips	Chordettes
Tomboy.	Perry Como
Everybody Likes to Cha Cha Cha	Sam Cooke

48

*The Happy Organ . . . . Dave "Baby"
                                              Cortez
Six Nights a Week . . . . Crests
The Morning Side of the Mountain . . . . Tommy Edwards
*Come Softly To Me . . . . Fleetwoods
If I Didn't Care . . . . Connie Francis
It Doesn't Matter Anymore . . . . Buddy Holly
Sorry (I Ran All the Way Home) . . . . Impalas
Come To Me . . . . Marv Johnson
Someone . . . . Johnny Mathis
It's Late . . . . Ricky Nelson
Never Be Anyone Else But You . . . . Ricky Nelson
Enchanted . . . . Platters
A Fool Such As I . . . . Elvis Presley
Where Were You
  (On Our Wedding Day) . . . . Lloyd Price
The Beat . . . . Rockin' R's
I'm Never Gonna Tell . . . . Jimmie Rodgers
I Go Ape . . . . Neil Sedaka
Tell Him No . . . . Travis & Bob
Guitar Boogie Shuffle . . . . Virtues
That's Why . . . . Jackie Wilson

APRIL
I Miss You So . . . . Paul Anka
Jo-Jo the Dog Faced Boy . . . . Annette
I Waited Too Long . . . . Laverne Baker
Guess Who . . . . Jessie Belvin[1]
Endlessly . . . . Brook Benton
Almost Grown . . . . Chuck Berry
Kookie, Kookie
  (Lend Me Your Comb) . . . . Edward Byrnes[2]
Dream Lover . . . . Bobby Darin
Three Stars . . . . Tommy Dee
Quiet Village . . . . Martin Denny
A Teenager in Love . . . . Dion & the
                                              Belmonts
My Heart Is an Open Book . . . . Carl Dobkins, Jr.
Yep . . . . Duane Eddy
Poor Jenny . . . . Everly Brothers

[1]Belvin was formerly with the Shields of "You Cheated" fame.
[2]Edward Byrnes' character in the T.V. series "77 Sunset Strip" was named Kookie.
The female voice on the record belonged to Connie Stevens.

Take a Message to Mary . . . . Everly Brothers
Turn Me Loose . . . . Fabian
You're So Fine . . . . Falcons
So Fine . . . . Fiestas
*Kansas City . . . . Wilbert Harrison
Raining in my Heart . . . . Buddy Holly
Rockin' Crickets . . . . Hot-Toddys
Goodbye Jimmy, Goodbye . . . . Kathy Linden
Only You . . . . Frank Pourcel
I Need Your Love Tonight . . . . Elvis Presley
Lonely For You . . . . Gary Stites
I've Come of Age . . . . Billy Storm
That's My Little Susie . . . . Ritchie Valens

MAY
A Boy Without a Girl . . . . Frankie Avalon
Bobby Sox to Stockings . . . . Frankie Avalon
Robbin' the Cradle . . . . Tony Bellus
So Close . . . . Brook Benton
Tallahassee Lassie . . . . Freddy Cannon
The Class . . . . Chubby Checker
Just Keep It Up . . . . Dee Clark
Along Came Jones . . . . Coasters
Gidget . . . . James Darren
I'm Ready . . . . Fats Domino
My Melancholy Baby . . . . Tommy Edwards
Bongo Rock . . . . Preston Epps
Graduation's Here . . . . Fleetwoods
Frankie . . . . Connie Francis
Lipstick On Your Collar . . . . Connie Francis
*Battle of New Orleans . . . . Johnny Horton
Waterloo . . . . Stonewall Jackson
Crossfire . . . . Johnny & the
                                                      Hurricanes
There Is Something On Your Mind . . . . Big Jay McNeely
Little Dipper . . . . Mickey Mozart
                                                      Quintet
Hushabye . . . . Mystics
The Wonder of You . . . . Ray Peterson
Personality . . . . Lloyd Price
Tall Cool One . . . . Wailers
What a Difference a Day Makes . . . . Dinah Washington

50

JUNE

*Lonely Boy	Paul Anka
Back in the USA	Chuck Berry
Twixt Twelve & Twenty	Pat Boone
Only Sixteen	Sam Cooke
There Goes My Baby	Drifters
Forty Miles of Bad Road	Duane Eddy
Tiger	Fabian
I Only Have Eyes For You	Flamingos
Mona Lisa	Carl Mann
Small World	Johnny Mathis
Since You've Been Gone	Clyde McPhatter
Remember When	Platters
Like Young	Andre Previn
Ring-a-Ling-a-Lario	Jimmie Rodgers
Wonderful You	Jimmie Rodgers
It Was I	Skip & Flip
High Hopes	Frank Sinatra[1]
This I Swear	Skyliners
Lavender-Blue	Sammy Turner
I'll Be Satisfied	Jackie Wilson

JULY

Lonely Guitar	Annette
Thank You Pretty Baby	Brook Benton
Till There Was You	Anita Bryant
What'd I Say	Ray Charles
Ragtime Cowboy Joe	Chipmunks
The Quiet Three	Duane Eddy
Here Comes Summer	Jerry Keller
Just a Little Too Much	Ricky Nelson
Sweeter Than You	Ricky Nelson
Sea of Love	Phil Phillips
What Is Love	Playmates
*A Big Hunk O' Love	Elvis Presley
My Wish Came True	Elvis Presley
Makin' Love	Floyd Robinson
Kissin' Time	Bobby Rydell
Linda Lu	Ray Sharpe
The Way I Walk	Jack Scott
Ten Thousand Drums	Carl Smith

[1]From the movie *Hole in the Head*, starring Frank Sinatra and co-starring Eddie Hodges, who later recorded "I'm Gonna Knock on Your Door."

51

To a Soldier Boy . . . . Tassels
See You in September . . . . Tempos
Mona Lisa . . . . Conway Twitty
Broken-Hearted Melody . . . . Sarah Vaughan

AUGUST
Just As Much As Ever . . . . Bob Becham
*The Three Bells . . . . Browns
Like I Love You. . . . . Edward Byrnes
I Got Stripes. . . . . Johnny Cash
Miami. . . . . Eugene Church
My Own True Love . . . . Jimmy Clanton
Hey Little Girl . . . . Dee Clark
Poison Ivy . . . . Coasters
The Angels Listened In . . . . Crests
*Mack the Knife . . . . Bobby Darin
I Want To Walk You Home. . . . . Fats Domino
I'm Gonna Be a Wheel Someday. . . . . Fats Domino
'Til I Kissed You. . . . . Everly Brothers
Poco-Loco . . . . Gene & Eunice
Mary Lou. . . . . Ronnie Hawkins
Baby Talk . . . . Jan & Dean
Red River Rock . . . . Johnny & the
                                                  Hurricanes
The Mummy. . . . . Bob McFadden
With Open Arms . . . . Jayne Morgan
I Ain't Never. . . . . Webb Pierce
I'm Gonna Get Married . . . . Lloyd Price
Morgen. . . . . Ivo Robic
*Sleep Walk . . . . Santo & Johnny
True True Happiness. . . . . Johnny Tillotson
Caribbean . . . . Mitchell Torok
Primrose Lane. . . . . Jerry Wallace

SEPTEMBER
Put Your Head On My Shoulder. . . . . Paul Anka
Just Ask Your Heart . . . . Frankie Avalon
Two Fools . . . . Frankie Avalon
The Fool's Hall of Fame. . . . . Pat Boone
Love Potion No. 9 . . . . Clovers
I'm a Hog For You . . . . Coasters
Say Man . . . . Bo Diddley
Seven Little Girls Sitting
    in the Back Seat . . . . Paul Evans

Come On and Get Me . . . . Fabian
In the Mood . . . . Ernie Fields
You Were Mine . . . . Fireflies
*Mr. Blue . . . . Fleetwoods
The Three Bells . . . . Dick Flood
You're Gonna Miss Me . . . . Connie Francis
Battle of Kookamonga . . . . Homer & Jethro
Shout . . . . Isley Brothers
Breaking Up Is Hard To Do . . . . Jivin' Gene
Deck of Cards . . . . Wink Martindale
Teen Beat . . . . Sandy Nelson
Don't You Know . . . . Della Reese
Tucumcari . . . . Jimmie Rodgers
Lonely Street . . . . Andy Williams
You Better Know It . . . . Jackie Wilson

OCTOBER
So Many Ways . . . . Brook Benton
Dance With Me . . . . Drifters
High School USA . . . . Tommy Facenda[1]
Torquay . . . . Fireballs
Enchanted Island . . . . Islanders
If I Give My Heart To You . . . . Kitty Kallen
Misty . . . . Johnny Mathis
*Heartaches By the Number . . . . Guy Mitchell
Just To Be With You . . . . Passions
*Running Bear . . . . Johnny Preston
Midnight Stroll . . . . Revels
Living Doll . . . . Cliff Richard
Woo-Hoo . . . . Rock-a-Teens
I Dig Girls . . . . Bobby Rydell
We Got Love . . . . Bobby Rydell
Oh! Carol . . . . Neil Sedaka
It Happened Today . . . . Skyliners
The Clouds . . . . Spacemen
Danny Boy . . . . Conway Twitty
Unforgettable . . . . Dinah Washington

[1]Over forty versions were recorded, so that the schools mentioned in the song would match the area in which the record was to be released.

NOVEMBER

It's Time To Cry	Paul Anka
First Name Initial	Annette
*Why	Frankie Avalon
Scarlet Ribbons	Browns
Way Down Yonder in New Orleans	Freddy Cannon
I'm Movin' On	Ray Charles
The Enchanted Sea	Martin Denny
Be My Guest	Fats Domino
I've Been Around	Fats Domino
True Love, True Love	Drifters
Some Kind-a Earthquake	Duane Eddy
Hound Dog Man	Fabian
This Friendly World	Fabian
The Big Hurt	Miss Toni Fisher
Among My Souvenirs	Connie Francis
Marina	Rocco Granata
Sandy	Larry Hall
Reveille Rock	Johnny & the Hurricanes
You Got What It Takes	Marv Johnson
Pretty Blue Eyes	Steve Lawrence
Uh! Oh! Part 2	Nutty Squirrels
Goodnight My Love	Ray Peterson
Come Into My Heart	Lloyd Price
Won't 'Cha Come Home	Lloyd Price
*El Paso	Marty Robbins
Always	Sammy Turner
Talk That Talk	Jackie Wilson

DECEMBER

Singin' On a Rainbow	Frankie Avalon
Smokie, Part 2	Bill Black's Combo
Go, Jimmy, Go	Jimmy Clanton
How About That	Dee Clark
Run Red Run	Coasters
The Happy Reindeer	Dancer, Prancer & Nervous
*Teen Angel	Mark Dinning
Lucky Devil	Carl Dobkins, Jr.
If I Had a Girl	Rod Lauren
Sweet Nothin's	Brenda Lee

54

1960

1960 was the year of the payola investigation by Congress, culminating with the arrest of a number of disc jockeys.

A strike by Actors' Equity closed all Broadway theaters for twelve days.

In politics, John F. Kennedy and Richard M. Nixon both announced their intention to run for president.

In sports, Floyd Patterson became the first boxer to regain the heavyweight title, and Arnold Palmer, at age thirty, was voted Golfer of the Year by the P.G.A.

The year 1960 produced a new recording star, together with perhaps the most popular dance craze ever, when Chubby Checker infected the country with "The Twist," a song Hank Ballard had written and also recorded. One of the most popular oldie instrumentals, "The Theme from a Summer Place," also hit the charts in '60.

Novelty songs, which had been big since the days of "The Flying Saucer," "The Witch Doctor" and "The Purple People Eater," had a good year in 1960, with "Alley Oop" and "Mr. Custer," both #1 songs.

Brenda Lee was beginning to rival Connie Francis' popularity. Her 1960 releases of "I'm Sorry" and "I Want To Be Wanted," both #1 songs, helped make her the second most successful female artist of the oldie era.

In 1960, a singer named Charlie Rich recorded "Lonely Weekends," which became a hit. In '65 he had "Mohair Sam." Moderately successful as an oldie artist, Charlie came back in 1973 with "The Most Beautiful Girl in the World," and today "The Silver Fox" is one of the biggest names in both country and pop music.

Other hits of 1960 included "Handy Man" by Jimmy Jones and "Stay" by Maurice Williams & the Zodiacs.

Elvis had another tremendous year in '60, with six songs making the Top 40, three reaching #1.

JANUARY

Crazy Arms	Bob Becham
Baby (You've Got What It Takes)	Brook Benton & Dinah Washington
Too Much Tequila	Champs
Beyond the Sea	Bobby Darin
Where or When	Dion & the Belmonts

56

Bonnie Came Back . . . . Duane Eddy
Midnite Special . . . . Paul Evans
Let It Be Me. Everly Brothers
*The Theme From a Summer Place . . . . . . Percy Faith
Bulldog . . . . Fireballs
Down By the Station. . . . . Four Preps
Little Things Mean a Lot . . . . Joni James
Handy Man . . . . Jimmy Jones
Darling Lorraine . . . . Knockouts
Forever. . . . . Little Dippers
Harbor Lights . . . . Platters
He'll Have To Go. . . . . Jim Reeves
Am I That Easy To Forget . . . . Debbie Reynolds
T.L.C. Tender Love and Care . . . . Jimmie Rodgers
Waltzing Matilda . . . . Jimmie Rodgers
Tracy's Theme. . . . . Spencer Ross
What in the World's Come
   Over You . . . . Jack Scott
Rockin' Little Angel . . . . Ray Smith
Why Do I Love You So . . . . Johnny Tillotson
Lonely Blue Boy . . . . Conway Twitty
Harlem Nocturne. . . . . Viscounts
Little Coco Palm . . . . Jenny Wallace

FEBRUARY
China Doll . . . . Ames Brothers
Puppy Love . . . . Paul Anka
O Dio Mio . . . . Annette
Let the Little Girl Dance . . . . Billy Bland
New Lovers . . . . Pat Boone
Green Fields. Brothers Four
Fannie Mae . . . . Buster Brown
Tall Oak Tree . . . . Dorsey Burnette
Chattanooga Shoe Shine Boy . . . . Freddy Cannon
Alvin's Orchestra . . . . Chipmunks
Time and the River. . . . . Nat "King" Cole
Country Boy. Fats Domino
This Magic Moment . . . . Drifters
String Along . . . . Fabian
Angela Jones. Johnny Ferguson
Outside My Window . . . . Fleetwoods
Mama . . . . Connie Francis
Beatnick Fly . . . . Johnny & the
                                                   Hurricanes

Hully Gully.	Olympics
Gloria	Passions
Lady Luck	Lloyd Price
Baby What You Want Me To Do	Jimmy Reed
Little Bitty Girl	Bobby Rydell
Wild One.	Bobby Rydell
Sixteen Reasons	Connie Stevens
Lawdy Miss Clawdy	Gary Stites
Money.	Barret Strong
Bad Boy.	Marty Wilde

MARCH

Don't Throw Away All Those Teardrops	Frankie Avalon
White Silver Sands	Bill Black's Combo
The Old Lamplighter	Browns
Step By Step	Crests
Clementine.	Bobby Darin
Mountain of Love.	Harold Dorman
About This Thing Called Love	Fabian
Teddy.	Connie Francis
Just One Time.	Don Gibson
Sink the Bismarck.	Johnny Horton
I Love the Way You Love.	Marv Johnson
Summer Set	Monty Kelly
Footsteps.	Steve Lawrence
Starbright.	Johnny Mathis
Lonely Weekends.	Charlie Rich[1]
Big Iron.	Marty Robbins
Caravan.	Santo & Johnny
Apple Green.	June Valli
Night	Jackie Wilson

APRIL

Adam & Eve.	Paul Anka
The Ties That Bind.	Brook Benton
The Madison.	Al Brown's Tunetoppers
Paper Roses	Anita Bryant
Madison Time	Ray Bryant
*Cathy's Clown	Everly Brothers
Nobody Loves Me Like You	Flamingos
Got a Girl	Four Preps

[1]The same Charlie Rich who became a star of the '70's.

58

Ooh Poo Pah Doo—Part II . . . . Jessie Hill
Love You So . . . . Ron Holden
Good Timin' . . . . Jimmy Jones
Mr. Lucky . . . . Henry Mancini
Fame & Fortune . . . . Elvis Presley
*Stuck On You . . . . Elvis Presley
Cradle of Love . . . . Johnny Preston
Burning Bridges. . . . . Jack Scott
Stairway to Heaven. . . . . Neil Sedaka
Cherry Pie . . . . Skip & Flip
Barbara . . . . Temptations
What Am I Living For . . . . Conway Twitty
Doggin' Around . . . . Jackie Wilson

MAY
My Home Town. . . . . Paul Anka
Finger Poppin' Time . . . . Hank Ballard &
the Midnighters
Clap Your Hands . . . . Beau Marks
A Rockin' Good Way . . . . Brook Benton &
Dinah
Washington
He'll Have to Stay . . . . Jeannie Black
Dutchman's Gold . . . . Walter Brennan
Think . . . . James Brown
Jump Over . . . . Freddy Cannon
Another Sleepless Night . . . . Jimmy Clanton
Wonderful World . . . . Sam Cooke
Theme From the Unforgiven. . . . . Don Costa
Won't You Come Home Bill Bailey . . . . Bobby Darin
When You Wish Upon a Star . . . . Dion & the
Belmonts
Because They're Young . . . . Duane Eddy
I Really Don't Want to Know. . . . . Tommy Edwards
Happy-Go-Lucky Me . . . . Paul Evans
Theme for Young Lovers . . . . Percy Faith
Mule Skinner Blues. . . . . Fendermen
Mack the Knife . . . . Ella Fitzgerald
Runaround . . . . Fleetwoods
*Everybody's Somebody's Fool. . . . . Connie Francis
Jealous Of You. . . . . Connie Francis
All I Could Do Was Cry . . . . Etta James
Please Help Me, I'm Falling . . . . Hank Locklin
Young Emotions. . . . . Ricky Nelson

Big Boy Pete. Olympics
For Love . . . . Lloyd Price
No If's—No And's. . . . . Lloyd Price
Hot Rod Lincoln . . . . Charlie Ryan
Ding-a-Ling . . . . Bobby Rydell
Swingin' School . . . . Bobby Rydell
Oh, Little One. . . . . Jack Scott
Pennies From Heaven . . . . Skyliners

JUNE
Train of Love . . . . Annette
Where Are You . . . . Frankie Avalon
Mission Bell . . . . Donnie Brooks
Hey Little One . . . . Dorsey Burnette
Trouble in Paradise. . . . . Crests
Alley-Oop. . . . . Dante & the
                                                    Evergreens
Walking to New Orleans. . . . . Fats Domino
When Will I Be Loved. . . . . Everly Brothers
Look for a Star . . . . Dean Hawley
*Alley-Oop. . . . . Hollywood Argyles
*I'm Sorry . . . . Brenda Lee
That's All You Gotta Do. . . . . Brenda Lee
Heartbreak. . . . . Little Willie John
There's Something on Your Mind . . . . Bobby Marchan
Maria . . . . Johnny Mathis
Look For a Star . . . . Garry Miles
Look For a Star . . . . Gary Mills
Only the Lonely. . . . . Roy Orbison
One of Us . . . . Patti Page
Tell Laura I Love Her . . . . Ray Peterson
Feel So Fine . . . . Johnny Preston
I'm Gettin' Better. . . . . Jim Reeves
Is There Any Chance. . . . . Marty Robbins
Image of a Girl . . . . Safaris
Heartbreak (It's Hurtin' Me) . . . . Jon Thomas
Is a Blue Bird Blue . . . . Conway Twitty
Look For a Star . . . . Billy Vaughn
This Bitter Earth . . . . Dinah Washington

JULY
The Twist . . . . Hank Ballard &
                                                    the Midnighters
Josephine. . . . . Bill Black's Combo

I Shot Mr. Lee. . . . . Bobbettes
In My Little Corner of
 the World . . . . Anita Bryant
Dreamin'. . . . . Johnny Burnette
Sticks and Stones . . . . Ray Charles
I'll Be There. . . . . Bobby Darin
Over the Rainbow . . . . Dimensions
In the Still of the Night . . . . Dion & the
 Belmonts
Don't Come Knockin' . . . . Fats Domino
Theme From the Apartment . . . . Ferrante &
 Teicher
*Itsy Bitsy Teenie Weenie
 Yellow Polka Dot Bikini. . . . . Brian Hyland
Ta Ta . . . . Clyde McPhatter
A Mess of Blues. . . . . Elvis Presley
*It's Now or Never . . . . Elvis Presley
Question . . . . Lloyd Price
Volare. . . . . Bobby Rydell
One Boy . . . . Joanie Sommers
Walk—Don't Run. . . . . Ventures
All My Love . . . . Jackie Wilson
A Woman, A Lover, A Friend . . . . Jackie Wilson

AUGUST
Hello Young Lovers . . . . Paul Anka
I Love You In the Same Old Way . . . . Paul Anka
Pineapple Princess . . . . Annette
Kiddio. . . . . Brook Benton
The Same One . . . . Brook Benton
Hot Rod Lincoln . . . . Johnny Bond
Any More. . . . . Teresa Brewer
A Kookie Little Paradise. . . . . Jo-Ann Campbell
A Million To One. . . . . Jimmy Charles
*The Twist. Chubby Checker
You're Looking Good. . . . . Dee Clark
Chain Gang . . . . Sam Cooke
Never On Sunday. . . . . Don Costa
(I Can't Help You)
 I'm Falling Too. . . . . Skeeter Davis
*My Heart Has a Mind Of Its Own . . . . . . Connie Francis
(I Do the) Shimmy Shimmy. . . . . Bobby Freeman
Honest I Do . . . . Innocents[1]

[1]The same Innocents recorded "A Thousand Stars" in October 1960 with Kathy Young.

61

Yogi	Ivy Three
Diamonds and Pearls	Paradons
Red Sails in the Sunset	Platters
It Only Happened Yesterday	Jack Scott
Run Samson Run	Neil Sedaka
You Mean Everything To Me	Neil Sedaka
Devil or Angel	Bobby Vee

SEPTEMBER

Togetherness	Frankie Avalon
Let's Go Let's Go Let's Go	Hank Ballard & the Midnighters
Don't Be Cruel	Bill Black's Combo
Twistin' U.S.A.	Danny & the Juniors
Three Nights a Week	Fats Domino
*Save the Last Dance For Me	Drifters
Lucille	Everly Brothers
North to Alaska	Johnny Horton
Let's Have a Party	Wanda Jackson
My Dearest Darling	Etta James
Move Two Mountains	Marv Johnson
You Talk Too Much	Joe Jones
*I Want To Be Wanted	Brenda Lee
Sleep	Little Willie John
Let's Think About Living	Bob Luman
I'm Not Afraid	Ricky Nelson
Yes Sir, That's My Baby	Ricky Nelson
Shimmy Like Kate	Olympics
Blue Angel	Roy Orbison
Tonight's the Night	Shirelles
A Fool In Love	Ike & Tina Turner
*Mr. Custer	Larry Verne

OCTOBER

Summer's Gone	Paul Anka
My Hero	Blue Notes
New Orleans	Gary "U.S." Bonds
*Georgia On My Mind	Ray Charles
The Hucklebuck	Chubby Checker
Last Date	Floyd Cramer
I'll Save the Last Dance For You	Damita Jo
Artificial Flowers	Bobby Darin

62

Lonely Teenager . . . . Dion
My Girl Josephine. . . . . Fats Domino
Peter Gunn . . . . Duane Eddy
Just a Little . . . . Brenda Lee
Sailor . . . . Lolita
To Each His Own. . . . . Platters
Wait For Me. . . . . Playmates
Am I Losing You . . . . Jim Reeves
Ballad of the Alamo . . . . Marty Robbins
Poetry in Motion . . . . Johnny Tillotson
Love Walked In. . . . . Dinah Washington
Last Date. . . . . Lawrence Welk
*Stay. . . . . Maurice Williams
                                          & the Zodiacs
Alone at Last . . . . Jackie Wilson
Am I The Man. . . . . Jackie Wilson
A Thousand Stars . . . . Kathy Young &
                                          the Innocents

NOVEMBER
Bumble Bee . . . . Lavern Baker
Fools Rush In . . . . Brook Benton
Wonderland By Night . . . . Anita Bryant
You're Sixteen. . . . . Johnny Burnette
He Will Break Your Heart . . . . Jerry Butler
Ruby. . . . . Ray Charles
Once In a While . . . . Chimes
Natural Born Lover. . . . . Fats Domino
Like Strangers. . . . . Everly Brothers
Exodus . . . . Ferrante &
                                          Teicher
Many Tears Ago. . . . . Connie Francis
Don't Go To Strangers. . . . . Etta Jones
*Wonderland By Night . . . . Bert Kaempfert
Exodus . . . . Mantovani
Ruby Duby Du . . . . Tobin Mathews
Corina, Corina. . . . . Ray Peterson
* Are You Lonesome Tonight . . . . Elvis Presley
I Gotta Know . . . . Elvis Presley
Wonderland By Night . . . . Louis Prima
Sway. . . . . Bobby Rydell
* Will You Love Me Tomorrow . . . . Shirelles
Perfidia . . . . Ventures
Ruby Duby Du . . . . Charles Wolcott

63

DECEMBER

The Hoochi Coochi Coo	Hank Ballard & the Midnighters
Blue Tango.	Bill Black's Combo
Doll House	Donnie Brooks
The Magnificent Seven	Al Caiola
Rudolph the Red Nosed Reindeer	Chipmunks
Sad Mood.	Sam Cooke
My Last Date With You	Skeeter Davis
Little Miss Blue	Dion
I Count the Tears.	Drifters
Pepe.	Duane Eddy
Utopia.	Frank Gari
Wings of a Dove	Ferlin Husky
My Last Date	Joni James
Lovey Dovey	Buddy Knox
Rockin' Around the Christmas Tree.	Brenda Lee
Dance By the Light of the Moon	Olympics
I'm Hurtin'.	Roy Orbison
Shop Around.	Smokey Robinson & the Miracles
Angel Baby.	Rosie & the Originals
Calendar Girl	Neil Sedaka
Baby Oh Baby.	Shells
Rubber Ball	Bobby Vee
* Calcutta	Lawrence Welk

1961

In 1961 Joan Sutherland made her American debut at the Metropolitan Opera. Ernest Hemingway died and the American Medical Association was beginning to express its anti-smoking attitude.

Surfing was taking hold as a major sport and pastime. Within two years, "surfin" music" would become a major part of the rock 'n' roll scene. Groups like Jan & Dean and the Beach Boys would become idols of the surfing set.

Another top oldie, "Runaway," was recorded by Del Shannon in '61. Roy Orbison emerged as a top star with the help of such songs as "Running Scared."

Elvis Presley was still The King, and 1961 brought about a subtle change from the typical rock sound with "Surrender."

Tony Orlando's oldie career consisted of two great songs in 1961, "Halfway to Paradise" and "Bless You." Tony was not to remain an oldie star; his return in the '70's as Tony Orlando and Dawn established him as a superstar.

Adam Wade scored three times in '61 with "Take Good Care of Her," "The Writing on the Wall" and "As If I Didn't Know."

Ricky Nelson had his biggest hit ever, "Travelin' Man," in 1961.

An unusual sound, that of Gary "U.S." Bonds, appeared in 1960 with "New Orleans," and in '61 Gary enjoyed huge success with "Quarter to Three," "School Is Out" and "School Is In."

JANUARY

The Story of My Love	Paul Anka
Lost Love	H. B. Barnum
All In My Mind	Maxine Brown
There's a Moon Out Tonight	Capris[1]
* Pony Time	Chubby Checker
Baby Sittin' Boogie	Buzz Clifford
Ginnie Bell	Paul Dino
Ain't That Just Like a Woman	Fats Domino
What a Price	Fats Domino
Angel On My Shoulder	Shelby Flint
No One	Connie Francis
Where the Boys Are	Connie Francis
Apache	Jorgen Ingmann
Spanish Harlem	Ben E. King

[1]Although released in 1958, this song first became a hit in 1961.

65

Emotions . . . . Brenda Lee
Don't Believe Him Donna . . . . Lenny Miles
You Are the Only One. . . . . Ricky Nelson
If I Didn't Care . . . . Platters
(Ghost Riders) in the Sky . . . . Ramrods
Good Time Baby . . . . Bobby Rydell
Dedicated To the One I Love . . . . Shirelles
Wheels . . . . String-a-Longs
Jimmy's Girl . . . . Johnny Tillotson
C'est Si Bon . . . . Conway Twitty
Ram-Bunk-Shush . . . . Ventures
There She Goes . . . . Jerry Wallace
My Empty Arms . . . . Jackie Wilson
The Tear of the Year. . . . . Jackie Wilson

FEBRUARY
Let's Go Again . . . . Hank Ballard &
the Midnighters
For My Baby. Brook Benton
Think Twice . . . . Brook Benton
Hearts of Stone . . . . Bill Black's Combo
Little Boy Sad . . . . Johnny Burnette
Your Friends. Dee Clark
Wait a Minute . . . . Coasters
Lazy River . . . . Bobby Darin
Don't Let Him Shop Around . . . . Debbie Dean
Honky Tonk (Part 2) . . . . Bill Doggett
Ebony Eyes . . . . Everly Brothers
Walk Right Back . . . . Everly Brothers
You Can Have Her . . . . Roy Hamilton
But I Do . . . . Clarence
"Frogman"
Henry
I Don't Want to Cry . . . . Chuck Jackson
Asia Minor . . . . Kokomo
I'm Learning About Love . . . . Brenda Lee
Model Girl . . . . Johnny Maestro
To be Loved (Forever). . . . . Pentagons
(I Wanna) Love My Life Away . . . . Gene Pitney
* Surrender . . . . Elvis Presley
Don't Worry . . . . Marty Robbins
Once Upon a Time . . . . Rochell & the
Candles
Gee Whiz. . . . . Carla Thomas

66

Wheels . . . . Billy Vaughn
Stayin' In . . . . Bobby Vee
Watusi. . . . . Vibrations
Bye Bye Baby . . . . Mary Wells
Happy Birthday Blues . . . . Kathy Young &
                                            the Innocents

MARCH
Tonight My Love Tonight. . . . . Paul Anka
Bewildered. . . . . James Brown
Find Another Girl . . . . Jerry Butler
Please Love Me Forever. . . . . Cathy Jean & the
                                              Roommates
One Mint Julep . . . . Ray Charles
That's It—I Quit—I'm Movin' On . . . . Sam Cooke
On the Rebound . . . . Floyd Cramer
Fell in Love on Monday. . . . . Fats Domino
Shu Rah. . . . . Fats Domino
Some Kind of Wonderful . . . . Drifters
Baby Blue . . . . Echoes
Theme From Dixie. . . . . Duane Eddy
Trust In Me . . . . Etta James
Hide Away. . . . . Freddy King
Portrait Of My Love . . . . Steve Lawrence
* Blue Moon. Marcels
A Hundred Pounds of Clay . . . . Gene McDaniels
Just For Old Times Sake. . . . . McGuire Sisters
Lonely Man . . . . Elvis Presley
I've Told Every Little Star . . . . Linda Scott
* Runaway . . . . Del Shannon
Tonight I Fell In Love. . . . . Tokens[1]
Take Good Care Of Her. . . . . Adam Wade
Please Tell Me Why . . . . Jackie Wilson
Your One and Only Love . . . . Jackie Wilson

APRIL
Saved . . . . Lavern Baker
I'm a Fool To Care . . . . Joe Barry
The Continental Walk . . . . Hank Ballard &
                                          the Midnighters
Bumble Boogie . . . . B. Bumble & the
                                          Stingers

[1]The Tokens were originally formed by Neil Sedaka.

Funny. . . . . Maxine Brown
Bonanza . . . . Al Caiola
Dance the Mess Around. . . . . Chubby Checker
I'm In the Mood For Love . . . . Chimes
Little Egypt . . . . Coasters
Girl of My Best Friend. . . . . Ral Donner
Three Hearts In a Tangle . . . . Roy Drusky
Tragedy. . . . . Fleetwoods
Breakin' In a Brand New
   Broken Heart. . . . . Connie Francis
Underwater . . . . Frogmen
Lullabye of Love . . . . Frank Gari
Triangle. . . . . Janie Grant
Exodus . . . . Eddie Harris
* Mother-In-Law . . . . Ernie K-Doe
You Can Depend On Me . . . . Brenda Lee
Tossin' & Turnin'. . . . . Bobby Lewis
What'd I Say. Jerry Lee Lewis
What a Surprise. . . . . Johnny Maestro
Peanut Butter . . . . Marathons
* Travelin' Man . . . . Ricky Nelson
* Running Scared. . . . . Roy Orbison
Jura . . . . Les Paul & Mary
                                      Ford
Flaming Star. Elvis Presley
Be My Boy. . . . . Paris Sisters
Glory Of Love. . . . . Roommates[1]
Daddy's Home. . . . . Shep & the
                                      Limelites[2]
Mama Said . . . . Shirelles
Better Tell Him No. . . . . Starlets
Brass Buttons . . . . String-a-Longs
The Bilbao Song. . . . . Andy Williams
Hello Walls. . . . . Faron Young

MAY
Tell Me Why. Belmonts
The Boll Weevil Song . . . . Brook Benton
* Quarter To Three . . . . Gary "U.S." Bonds

[1]The same Roommates that recorded this song did "Please Love Me Forever" a month earlier with Cathy Jean.

[2]Lead singer James "Shep" Sheppard was also the lead singer with the Heartbeats in 1956, when they recorded "A Thousand Miles Away."

```
* Moody River. . . . . . . . . . . . . . . . . . Pat Boone
Raindrops. . . . . . . . . . . . . . . . . . . . Dee Clark
Heart and Soul . . . . . . . . . . . . . . . . . Cleftones
I Fall To Pieces . . . . . . . . . . . . . . . . Patsy Cline
It Keeps On Rainin' . . . . . . . . . . . . . . Fats Domino
Count Every Star . . . . . . . . . . . . . . . . Donnie & the
                                                   Dreamers
Rama Lama Ding Dong . . . . . . . . . . . . Edsels
You Always Hurt the One
   You Love . . . . . . . . . . . . . . . . . . . Clarence
                                                   "Frogman"
                                                   Henry
Stand By Me. . . . . . . . . . . . . . . . . . . Ben E. King
Every Beat of My Heart. . . . . . . . . . . . Pips
Those Oldies But Goodies. . . . . . . . . . . Little Caesar &
                                                   the Romans
Hello Mary Lou . . . . . . . . . . . . . . . . . Ricky Nelson
Halfway to Paradise . . . . . . . . . . . . . . Tony Orlando[1]
I Feel So Bad . . . . . . . . . . . . . . . . . Elvis Presley
Barbara-Ann . . . . . . . . . . . . . . . . . . Regents
That Old Black Magic . . . . . . . . . . . . . Bobby Rydell
Little Devil. . . . . . . . . . . . . . . . . . . Neil Sedaka
The Writing On the Wall . . . . . . . . . . . Adam Wade
```

JUNE

```
Dance On Little Girl. . . . . . . . . . . . . . Paul Anka
Ole Buttermilk Sky. . . . . . . . . . . . . . . Bill Black's Combo
Sacred. . . . . . . . . . . . . . . . . . . . . . Castels
No No No . . . . . . . . . . . . . . . . . . . . Chanters
Let's Twist Again . . . . . . . . . . . . . . . Chubby Checker
Never On Sunday. . . . . . . . . . . . . . . . Chordettes
Cupid . . . . . . . . . . . . . . . . . . . . . . Sam Cooke
San Antonio Rose . . . . . . . . . . . . . . . Floyd Cramer
Nature Boy. . . . . . . . . . . . . . . . . . . Bobby Darin
Please Stay . . . . . . . . . . . . . . . . . . . Drifters
Temptation. . . . . . . . . . . . . . . . . . . Everly Brothers
Sea of Heartbreak. . . . . . . . . . . . . . . Don Gibson
Rainin' In My Heart . . . . . . . . . . . . . . Slim Harpo
I'm Gonna Knock On Your Door . . . . . . . Eddie Hodges
Right Or Wrong. . . . . . . . . . . . . . . . . Wanda Jackson
I Like It Like That . . . . . . . . . . . . . . . Chris Kenner
Dum Dum . . . . . . . . . . . . . . . . . . . . Brenda Lee
```

[1]Later became Tony Orlando & Dawn.

Yellow Bird . . . . Arthur Lyman
My Kind of Girl . . . . Matt Munro
Wild In the Country . . . . Elvis Presley
Hats Off to Larry . . . . Del Shannon
You Can't Sit Down—Part II . . . . Phil Upchurch
                                                    Combo
How Many Tears . . . . Bobby Vee
Tonight (Could Be the Night). . . . . Velvets
I'm Comin' On Back To You . . . . Jackie Wilson

JULY
I Just Don't Understand . . . . Ann-Margaret
The Switch-a-Roo . . . . Hank Ballard &
                                                    the Midnighters
School Is Out . . . . Gary "U.S." Bonds
I'm a Telling You . . . . Jerry Butler
One Summer Night. . . . . Diamonds
Let the Four Winds Blow . . . . Fats Domino
You Don't Know What You've Got . . . . Ral Donner
* Wooden Heart. . . . . Joe Dowell
Quite a Party . . . . Fireballs
Together . . . . Connie Francis
Princess. . . . . Frank Gari
Nag . . . . Halos
* Michael. . . . . Highwaymen
Heart and Soul . . . . Jan & Dean
The Astronaut . . . . Jose Jiminez
My True Story. . . . . Jive Five
I'll Be There. . . . . Damita Jo
Pretty Little Angel Eyes. . . . . Curtis Lee
Eventually . . . . Brenda Lee
Last Night . . . . Mar-Keys
A Tear . . . . Gene McDaniels
Runaround . . . . Regents
I Dreamed Of a Hill-Billy Heaven. . . . . . . Tex Ritter
The Fish . . . . Bobby Rydell
Don't Bet Money Honey . . . . Linda Scott
Starlight, Starbright. . . . . Linda Scott
Ready For Your Love . . . . Shep & the
                                                    Limelights
A Thing Of the Past . . . . Shirelles
What a Sweet Thing That Was. . . . . Shirelles
Water Boy . . . . Don Shirley Trio
That's What Girls Are Made For. . . . . Spinners

As If I Didn't Know . . . . Adam Wade
I Don't Want To Take a Chance. . . . . Mary Wells
Hurt. . . . . Timi Yuro

AUGUST
Frankie & Johnny. . . . . Brook Benton
Lover's Island . . . . Blue Jays
Big Cold Wind. . . . . Pat Boone
Transistor Sister . . . . Freddy Cannon
The Mountain's High. . . . . Dick & Dee Dee
Does Your Chewing Gum
   Lose Its Flavor . . . . Lonnie Donegan
When We Get Married . . . . Dreamlovers
More Money For You and Me . . . . Four Preps[1]
Let Me Belong To You. . . . . Brian Hyland
Don't Cry Baby . . . . Etta James
A Little Bit of Soap. . . . . Jarmels
Amor . . . . Ben E. King
Wizard of Love . . . . Ly-Dells
Who Put the Bomp. . . . . Barry Mann
Mexico . . . . Bob Moore
Candy Man. Roy Orbison
Crying. . . . . Roy Orbison
Bless You . . . . Tony Orlando
Missing You . . . . Ray Peterson
Every Breath I Take . . . . Gene Pitney
I'll Never Smile Again . . . . Platters
Little Sister. Elvis Presley
Jeremiah Peabody's Poly Unsaturated
   Quick Dissolving Fast Acting Pleasant
   Tasting Green and Purple Pills . . . . Ray Stevens
Without You . . . . Johnny Tillotson
It's Gonna Work Out Fine . . . . Ike & Tina Turner
* Take Good Care Of My Baby . . . . Bobby Vee
Years From Now . . . . Jackie Wilson

SEPTEMBER
Kissin' On the Phone. . . . . Paul Anka
Just Out of Reach. . . . . Solomon Burke
Look In My Eyes . . . . Chantels
* Hit The Road, Jack. . . . . Ray Charles

[1]In this song, the Four Preps imitated several oldie groups singing their hits.

71

You Must Have Been A
  Beautiful Baby . . . . Bobby Darin
Ya Ya . . . . Lee Dorsey
Bristol Stomp . . . . Dovells
Sweets For My Sweet . . . . Drifters
Stick Shift . . . . Duals
You're the Reason . . . . Bobby Edwards
Foot Stompin'—Part I . . . . Flares
I Understand (Just How You Feel) . . . . G-Clefs
Human . . . . Tommy Hunt
The Way You Look Tonight . . . . Lettermen
One Track Mind . . . . Bobby Lewis
* Please Mr. Postman . . . . Marvelettes
Let's Get Together . . . . Haley Mills
Juke Box Saturday Night. . . . . Nino & the Ebb
                                                Tides
I Love How You Love Me . . . . Paris Sisters
Marie's the Name of
  His Latest Flame . . . . Elvis Presley
So Long Baby . . . . Del Shannon
This Time . . . . Troy Shondell
Sad Movies (Make Me Cry) . . . . Sue Thompson

OCTOBER
'Til. . . . . Angels
School Is In . . . . Gary "U.S." Bonds
God, Country & My Baby. . . . . Johnny Burnette
Moon River . . . . Jerry Butler
The Fly. . . . . Chubby Checker
Crazy . . . . Patsy Cline
Goodbye Cruel World . . . . James Darren
*Big Bad John . . . . Jimmy Dean
*Runaround Sue. . . . . Dion
What a Party. . . . . Fats Domino
Please Don't Go. . . . . Ral Donner
Don't Blame Me . . . . Everly Brothers
Tonight . . . . Ferrante &
                                                Teicher
He's My Dreamboat . . . . Connie Francis
Gypsy Woman. . . . . Impressions
In the Middle of a Heartache. . . . . Wanda Jackson
Anybody But Me . . . . Brenda Lee
Fool #1 . . . . Brenda Lee
Sad Movies. Lennon Sisters

Moon River . . . . Henry Mancini
Heartaches . . . . Marcels
Tower of Strength . . . . Gene McDaniels
A Wonder Like You . . . . Ricky Nelson
Everlovin' . . . . Ricky Nelson
I Wanna Thank You . . . . Bobby Rydell
Three Steps To the Altar . . . . Shep & the
                                       Limelites
Big John . . . . Shirelles
Soothe Me . . . . Sims Twins
I Really Love You . . . . Stereos
September In the Rain . . . . Dinah Washington

NOVEMBER
Revenge . . . . Brook Benton
Johnny Will . . . . Pat Boone
Well I Told You . . . . Chantels
There's No Other . . . . Crystals
*Peppermint Twist . . . . Joey Dee & the
                                       Starliters
Your Ma Said You Cried
   In Your Sleep Last Night . . . . Kenny Dino
Funny How Time Slips Away . . . . Jimmy Elledge
When the Boy in Your Arms . . . . Connie Francis
I Know . . . . Barbara George
The Gypsy Rover . . . . Highwaymen
Gee Whiz . . . . Innocents
When I Fall in Love . . . . Lettermen
Language of Love . . . . John D.
                                       Loudermilk
Let There Be Drums . . . . Sandy Nelson
Town Without Pity . . . . Gene Pitney
If You Gotta Make a Fool
   of Somebody . . . . James Raye
I Don't Know Why . . . . Linda Scott
Happy Birthday, Sweet Sixteen . . . . Neil Sedaka
*The Lion Sleeps Tonight . . . . Tokens
Walk On By . . . . Leroy Van Dyke
Run To Him . . . . Bobby Vee
Up a Lazy River . . . . Si Zentner

DECEMBER

Twist-Her . . . . Bill Black's Combo
Turn On Your Love Light . . . . Bobby Bland
Dear Lady Twist . . . . Gary "U.S." Bonds
Tuff . . . . Ace Cannon
Unchain My Heart . . . . Ray Charles
Smoky Places . . . . Corsairs
Irresistible You . . . . Bobby Darin
Multiplication . . . . Bobby Darin
The Majestic . . . . Dion
The Wanderer . . . . Dion
I Hear You Knocking . . . . Fats Domino
Jambalaya . . . . Fats Domino
She's Everything . . . . Ral Donner
Do-Re-Mi . . . . Lee Dorsey
Cotton Fields . . . . Highwaymen
A Little Bitty Tear . . . . Burl Ives
Letter Full of Tears . . . . Gladys Knight &
the Pips
Small Sad Sam . . . . Phil McLean
Can't Help Falling In Love . . . . Elvis Presley
Rock-a-Hula Baby . . . . Elvis Presley
Jingle Bell Rock . . . . Bobby Rydell &
Chubby Checker
Hey! Little Girl . . . . Del Shannon
Baby It's You . . . . Shirelles
Tears From An Angel . . . . Troy Shondell
Flying Circle . . . . Frank Slay
Norman . . . . Sue Thompson
Poor Fool . . . . Ike & Tina Turner

1962

1962 was a big year in government, art, sports, show business and music.

The Cuban Missile Crisis occurred in '62, and John Glenn became the first astronaut to orbit the earth. He made three orbits in the Friendship 7.

And 1962 ushered in a new baseball team, the New York Mets, whose debut was something less than memorable. A young golfer joined the P.G.A. tour in '62: his name was Jack Nicklaus. One of the greatest jockeys of all time, Eddie Arcaro, retired from horse racing.

A new art form, "Pop Art," featured soup cans and the like as subjects.

On the show-biz scene, *Lawrence of Arabia* was the Academy Award movie of the year; the romance of the year was shared by Elizabeth Taylor and Richard Burton. One of the biggest box-office draws of the fifties, a legendary show business personality, Marilyn Monroe, died.

In fashion, wigs and boots became popular for women.

A new group hit the music scene in '62 and brought with them a whole new sound. "Sherry" and "Big Girls Don't Cry" introduced the Four Seasons, featuring Frankie Valli. Their popularity endured throughout the sixties. Today Frankie Valli is a popular solo artist.

Carole King had "It Might As Well Rain Until September" in '62. She became a bigger star in the seventies. Carole's most important contribution to the oldie scene was her songwriting along with her husband, which included such hits as "Will You Still Love Me Tomorrow" (Shirelles), "Take Good Care of My Baby" (Bobby Vee) and "Loco-Motion" (Little Eva).

Some of the biggest hits of 1962 were "Johnny Angel," "Duke of Earl" and David Rose's instrumental "The Stripper."

Another novelty song, "Monster Mash," by Bobby (Boris) Pickett, made #1 in 1962. It was brought back in 1973 and became a hit all over again.

JANUARY

Shadrack	Brook Benton
Percolator	Billy Joe & the Checkmates
I'll See You in My Dreams	Pat Boone
*Duke of Earl	Gene Chandler
*Hey! Baby.	Bruce Channel
She's Got You	Patsy Cline

Chattanooga Choo Choo. . . . . Floyd Cramer
Dear Ivan . . . . Jimmy Dean
The Cajun Queen. . . . . Jimmy Dean
To a Sleeping Beauty. . . . . Jimmy Dean
Do the New Continental . . . . Dovells
My Boomerang Won't Come Back. . . . . . . Charlie Drake
Crying In the Rain . . . . Everly Brothers
Jamie . . . . Eddie Holland
I'm Blue . . . . Ikettes[1]
Break It To Me Gently. . . . . Brenda Lee
Surfer's Stomp. . . . . Marketts
Twistin' Postman . . . . Marvelettes
Chip Chip . . . . Gene McDaniels
Lizzie Borden . . . . Chad Mitchell
  Trio[2]
He Knows I Love Him Too Much . . . . Paris Sisters
What's So Good About Goodbye. . . . . Smokey Robinson
  & the Miracles
Let Me In . . . . Sensations
The Greatest Hurt . . . . Jackie Wilson

FEBRUARY
You Better Move On. . . . . Arthur Alexander
Love Me Warm & Tender . . . . Paul Anka
Midnight In Moscow . . . . Kenny Ball
Walk On the Wild Side . . . . Brook Benton
Twistin' The Night Away . . . . Sam Cooke
Soul Twist . . . . King Curtis
Her Royal Majesty . . . . James Darren
Hey, Let's Twist. . . . . Joey Dee & the
  Starliters
You Win Again . . . . Fats Domino
What's Your Name . . . . Don & Juan
When My Little Girl Is Smiling . . . . Drifters
Dear One. . . . . Larry Finnegan
*Don't Break The Heart
  That Loves You. . . . . Connie Francis
Something's Got a Hold On Me . . . . Etta James
Love Letters. Ketty Lester
Come Back Silly Girl. . . . . Lettermen

[1]The Ikettes were the backup group for Ike and Tina Turner.
[2]After Chad Mitchell left the group, a then unknown singer joined the group. His name was John Denver.

Drums Are My Beat	Sandy Nelson
Dream Baby	Roy Orbison
I've Got Bonnie	Bobby Rydell
Please Don't Ask About Barbara	Bobby Vee

MARCH

Cry Baby Cry	Angels
You Are Mine	Frankie Avalon
*Stranger On the Shore	Mr. Acker Bilk
Twist Twist Senora	Gary "U.S." Bonds
Nut Rocker.	B. Bumble & the Stingers
Slow Twistin'.	Chubby Checker
The Alvin Twist.	Chipmunks
Caterina	Perry Como
Patti Ann.	Johnny Crawford
Uptown.	Crystals
What'd I Say.	Bobby Darin
P.T. 109.	Jimmy Dean
Shout	Joey Dee & the Starliters
Tell Me.	Dick & Dee Dee
*Johnny Angel.	Shelly Fabares[1]
The Jam	Bobby Gregg & His Friends
Ginny Come Lately	Brian Hyland
She Cried.	Jay & the Americans
Lollipops & Roses.	Jack Jones
Shout! Shout! (Knock Yourself Out)	Ernie Maresca
Lover Please.	Clyde McPhatter
Johnny Jingo.	Hayley Mills
Young World.	Ricky Nelson
She Can't Find Her Keys	Paul Peterson[2]
Anything That's Part Of You	Elvis Presley
*Good Luck Charm.	Elvis Presley
I Wish That We Were Married.	Ronnie & the Hi-Lites
Cinderella	Jack Ross
King of Clowns	Neil Sedaka

[1]Shelly played Donna Reed's daughter on T.V.'s "Donna Reed Show."
[2]Paul played Donna Reed's son on the same show.

Mashed Potato Time . . . . Dee Dee Sharp
*Soldier Boy . . . . Shirelles
Twistin' Matilda . . . . Jimmy Soul
Two Of a Kind . . . . Sue Thompson
If a Woman Answers . . . . Leroy Van Dyke
The One Who Really Loves You . . . . Mary Wells

APRIL
I Sold My Heart To
   the Junkman . . . . Blue Belles
Old Rivers . . . . Walter Brennan
Night Train . . . . James Brown
Blues Stay Away From Me . . . . Ace Cannon
So This Is Love . . . . Castels
Hide 'Nor Hair . . . . Ray Charles
Conscience . . . . James Darren
Lovers Who Wander . . . . Dion
Funny Way of Laughin' . . . . Burl Ives
Any Day Now . . . . Chuck Jackson
Don't Play That Song . . . . Ben E. King
Everybody Loves Me But You . . . . Brenda Lee
Teach Me Tonight . . . . George Maharis
Village of Love . . . . Nathaniel Mayer
Most People Get Married . . . . Patti Page
(The Man Who Shot)
   Liberty Valance . . . . Gene Pitney
Itty Bitty Pieces . . . . James Ray
Count Every Star . . . . Linda Scott
I Love You . . . . Volumes

MAY
Where Have You Been . . . . Arthur Alexander
A Steel Guitar &
   a Glass of Wine . . . . Paul Anka
Hit Record . . . . Brook Benton
Palisades Park . . . . Freddy Cannon
Limbo Rock . . . . Champs
Born To Lose . . . . Ray Charles
*I Can't Stop Loving You . . . . Ray Charles
Having a Party . . . . Sam Cooke
Cindy's Birthday . . . . Johnny Crawford[1]
Fortune Teller . . . . Bobby Curtola

[1]Johnny costarred on T.V.'s "The Rifleman" and was a former Mousketeer.

My Real Name. . . . . Fats Domino
Bristol Twistin' Annie . . . . Dovells
That's Old Fashioned. . . . . Everly Brothers
West Of the Wall . . . . Miss Toni Fisher
Snap Your Fingers . . . . Joe Henderson
Wolverton Mountain . . . . Claude King
Playboy . . . . Marvelettes
Al Di La . . . . Emelio Pericoli
Follow That Dream. . . . . Elvis Presley
I'll Try Something New . . . . Smokey Robinson
& the Miracles
*The Stripper . . . . David Rose
Walk On the Wild Side . . . . Jimmy Smith
Johnny Get Angry . . . . Joanie Sommers
Lipstick Traces . . . . Benny Spellman
It Keeps Right On A-Hurtin' . . . . Johnny Tillotson
Theme From Ben Casey. . . . . Valjean
Sharing You . . . . Bobby Vee
Where Are You . . . . Dinah Washington

JUNE
Seven Day Weekend. . . . . Gary "U.S." Bonds
Speedy Gonzales . . . . Pat Boone
Theme From Dr. Kildare . . . . Richard
Chamberlin
Dancin' Party . . . . Chubby Checker
Party Lights . . . . Claudine Clark
Bring It On Home To Me. . . . . Sam Cooke
Mary's Little Lamb. . . . . James Darren
Little Red Rented Rowboat. . . . . Joe Dowell
Johnny Loves Me . . . . Shelly Fabares
I Need Your Loving . . . . Don Gardner &
Dee Dee Ford
(Girls, Girls, Girls)
Made To Love . . . . Eddie Hodges
Sealed With a Kiss . . . . Brian Hyland
Twist & Shout. . . . . Isley Brothers
It Started All Over Again . . . . Brenda Lee
*The Loco-Motion . . . . Little Eva
Bongo Stomp . . . . Little Joey & the
Flips
You'll Lose a Good Thing . . . . Barbara Lynn
Little Bitty Pretty One . . . . Clyde McPhatter
I Don't Love You No More . . . . Jimmy Norman

The Crowd. . . . . Roy Orbison
The Wah Watusi . . . . Orlons
Route 66 Theme . . . . Nelson Riddle
I'll Never Dance Again . . . . Bobby Rydell
*Breaking Up Is Hard To Do. . . . . Neil Sedaka
Gravy. . . . . Dee Dee Sharp
Welcome Home Baby . . . . Shirelles
Ahab the Arab. . . . . Ray Stevens
Have a Good Time . . . . Sue Thompson
*Roses Are Red . . . . Bobby Vinton
Baby Elephant Walk . . . . Lawrence Welk
Stranger On the Shore. . . . . Andy Williams

JULY
Shame On Me. . . . . Bobby Bare
Come On Little Angel. . . . . Belmonts
Alley Cat . . . . Bent Fabric
Till Death Do Us Part . . . . Bob Braun
Make It Easy On Yourself. . . . . Jerry Butler
You Don't Know Me . . . . Ray Charles
Rinky Dink. . . . . Dave "Baby"
                                                Cortez
Things. . . . . Bobby Darin
Little Diane . . . . Dion
The Ballad of Paladin . . . . Duane Eddy
Vacation . . . . Connie Francis
Call Me Mr. In-Between. . . . . Burl Ives
Stop The Wedding . . . . Etta James
Heart In Hand. . . . . Brenda Lee
Devil Woman . . . . Marty Robbins
*Sheila . . . . Tommy Roe[1]
A Swingin' Safari . . . . Billy Vaughn
What's a Matter Baby . . . . Timi Yuro

AUGUST
Surfin' Safari. Beach Boys
Lie To Me . . . . Brook Benton
Green Onions . . . . Booker T. & the
                                                MG's
I'm the Girl From
   Wolverton Mountain. . . . . Jo-Ann Campbell
Venus In Blue Jeans . . . . Jimmy Clanton

[1]This song captured the same sound that Buddy Holly displayed on "Peggy Sue."

80

Ramblin' Rose . . . . Nat "King" Cole
Do You Love Me . . . . Contours
Your Nose Is Gonna Grow . . . . Johnny Crawford
What Kind of Love Is This . . . . Joey Dee & the
                  Starliters
Hully Gully Baby . . . . Dovells
You Belong To Me . . . . Duprees
*Sherry . . . . Four Seasons
Hide And Go Seek . . . . Bunker Hill
It Might As Well Rain
 Until September . . . . Carole King[1]
Patches . . . . Dickey Lee
A Wonderful Dream . . . . Majors
Beechwood 4–5789 . . . . Marvelettes
Point Of No Return . . . . Gene McDaniels
Let's Dance . . . . Chris Montez
Teenage Idol. Ricky Nelson
Just Tell Her Jim Said Hello . . . . Elvis Presley
She's Not You . . . . Elvis Presley
Papa-Oom-Mow-Mow . . . . Rivingtons
Silver Threads & Golden Needles . . . . Springfields[2]
Mr. Songwriter . . . . Connie Stevens
Send Me the Pillow That
 You Dream On . . . . Johnny Tillotson
I Love You the Way You Are. . . . . Bobby Vinton
Rain Rain Go Away. . . . . Bobby Vinton
You Beat Me To the Punch . . . . Mary Wells

SEPTEMBER
Don't Go Near the Indians . . . . Rex Allen
Limbo Rock . . . . Chubby Checker
Popeye the Hitchhiker. . . . . Chubby Checker
Close to Cathy. . . . . Mike Clifford
Nothing Can Change This Love . . . . Sam Cooke
*He's A Rebel . . . . Crystals
If a Man Answers . . . . Bobby Darin
Little Black Book . . . . Jimmy Dean
He's the Great Imposter. . . . . Fleetwoods
Warmed Over Kisses. . . . . Brian Hyland

 [1]Carole became a bigger recording star in the seventies. In the fifties and sixties she and her husband co-authored such hits as "The Loco-Motion," "Take Good Care of My Baby" and "Will You Still Love Me Tomorrow."
 [2]Dusty Springfield went on to become a solo success in 1964.

81

I Remember You . . . . Frank Ifield
Torture . . . . Kris Jensen
All Alone Am I . . . . Brenda Lee
Gina . . . . Johnny Mathis
Workin' For the Man. . . . . Roy Orbison
*Monster Mash . . . . Bobby (Boris)
                                                   Pickett[1]
If I Didn't Have a Dime. . . . . Gene Pitney
Only Love Can Break a Heart . . . . Gene Pitney
King of the Whole Wide World . . . . Elvis Presley
No One Will Ever Know . . . . Jimmie Rodgers
Stop the Music. . . . . Shirelles
James (Hold the Ladder Steady) . . . . Sue Thompson
Punish Her. . . . . Bobby Vee
Don't You Believe It . . . . Andy Williams

OCTOBER
Anna . . . . Arthur Alexander
The Lonely Bull. . . . . Herb Alpert & the
                                                   Tijuana Brass
Mama Sang a Song . . . . Bill Anderson
409. . . . . Beach Boys
Bobby's Girl . . . . Marcie Blaine
Mama Sang a Song . . . . Walter Brennan
Love Me Tender . . . . Richard
                                                   Chamberlain
Wiggle Wobble . . . . Les Cooper
My Own True Love . . . . Duprees
Dance With the Guitar Man . . . . Duane Eddy
Lovers By Night, Strangers By Day . . . . . . Fleetwoods
*Big Girls Don't Cry . . . . Four Seasons
I Was Such a Fool. . . . . Connie Francis
Mama Sang a Song . . . . Stan Kenton
That Stranger Used to
   Be My Girl . . . . Trade Martin
I've Got a Woman . . . . Jimmy McGriff
Leah. . . . . Roy Orbison
Don't Hang Up . . . . Orlons
Release Me. . . . . Little Esther
                                                   Phillips
Return to Sender . . . . Elvis Presley

[1]The song became a hit again by Pickett in 1973.

82

Susie Darlin' . . . . Tommy Roe[2]
The Cha Cha Cha. . . . . Bobby Rydell
Next Door To an Angel . . . . Neil Sedaka
Ride . . . . Dee Dee Sharp
Pop Pop Pop-Pie . . . . Sherrys
I Can't Help It . . . . Johnny Tillotson

NOVEMBER
Eso Beso . . . . Paul Anka
Hotel Happiness. . . . . Brook Benton
Zip-A-Dee-Doo-Dah . . . . Bob B. Soxx & the
                                                                                    Blue Jeans
You Are My Sunshine . . . . Ray Charles
Your Cheating Heart. . . . . Ray Charles
Dear Lonely Hearts . . . . Nat "King" Cole
Chains. . . . . Cookies
Rumors . . . . Johnny Crawford
Love Came To Me . . . . Dion
Up On the Roof. . . . . Drifters
Coney Island Baby . . . . Excellents
That's Life . . . . Gabriel & the
                                                                                    Angels
Mary Ann Regrets . . . . Burl Ives
*Go Away Little Girl. . . . . Steve Lawrence
Keep Your Hands Off My Baby . . . . Little Eva
Spanish Lace. Gene McDaniels
My Dad. . . . . Paul Peterson
Ruby Ann . . . . Marty Robbins
Let's Go . . . . Routers
*Telstar . . . . Tornadoes
The Push & the Kick. . . . . Mark Valentino
Shutters and Boards . . . . Jerry Wallace

DECEMBER
See See Rider . . . . Lavern Baker
He's Sure the Boy I Love . . . . Crystals
Remember Then . . . . Earls
Tell Him . . . . Exciters
The Ballad of Jed Clampett. . . . . Flatt & Scruggs
Santa Claus Is Coming To Town . . . . Four Seasons
I'm Gonna Be Warm This Winter . . . . Connie Francis

[2]A much bigger hit in 1958 by Robin Luke.

Cast Your Fate to the Wind. . . . . Vince Guaraldi
                                                 Trio
Fly Me To the Moon Bossa Nova . . . . Joe Harnell
My Coloring Book . . . . Kitty Kallen
I Saw Linda Yesterday. . . . . Dickey Lee
Lovesick Blues. . . . . Frank Ifield
From a Jack To a King. . . . . Ned Miller
Pepino the Italian Mouse . . . . Lou Monte
It's Up To You. . . . . Ricky Nelson
Cinnamon Cinder. . . . . Pastel Six
*Hey Paula. Paul & Paula
Monster's Holiday. . . . . Bobby (Boris)
                                                 Pickett
Half Heaven-Half Heartache . . . . Gene Pitney
Wild Weekend. . . . . Rebels
You Really Got a Hold On Me . . . . Smoky Robinson &
                                                 the Miracles
Little Town Flirt . . . . Del Shannon
Everybody Loves a Lover. . . . . Shirelles
My Coloring Book . . . . Sandy Stewart
Loop De Loop. . . . . Johnny Thunder
The Night Has a Thousand Eyes. . . . . Bobby Vee
Let's Kiss and Make Up . . . . Bobby Vinton
Trouble Is My Middle Name . . . . Bobby Vinton
Two Lovers . . . . Mary Wells
Shake Me I Rattle. . . . . Marion Worth

1963

President John F. Kennedy was assassinated on November 22, 1963. Kennedy was loved by many, many Americans. A year earlier, Jimmy Dean had produced a Top 10 song depicting the deeds of Kennedy during the war. The song, of course, was "P.T. 109."

The Hootenanny, a gathering of folks to play and sing folk music, was represented by a group known as the Glencoves, who, in 1963, broke into the Top 40 with their recording of "Hootenanny."

In the sports world, Stan "the Man" Musial retired from baseball, and Arnold Palmer became the first golfer to win more than $100,000 in a single year.

The best picture of the year was *Tom Jones,* and the most expensive picture ever, *Cleopatra,* made its debut.

Headlines for '63 included the kidnapping of Frank Sinatra, Jr., and the Freedom March to Washington, D.C., by more than 200,000 people.

Headlines were also being made in pop music; a sound that began in 1962 known as surfin' music dominated 1963. A number of groups recorded surfin' music, including Jan and Dean ("Surf City"). But when surfin' music was mentioned, it was generally called the sound of the Beach Boys. They dominated much of 1963, '64 and '65, and established a link with the past, as their music survived beyond the great oldie era. A surprise success of 1963 was the recording by the Singing Nun of "Dominique" which went on to become #1 in the nation.

A young man, blind since birth, had the first of many great hits in '63. Little Stevie Wonder, with "Fingertips—Part 2," began a career which is bigger today than ever before. Bobby Vinton had four hits in '63; two of them reached #1.

The year 1963 was to be the last "pure" oldie year; the country was to be infected with "Beatlemania" in 1964, and the "invasion" of the British sound was to signal the end of an era. A different kind of rock was about to be born.

JANUARY

Everyday I Have to Cry . . . . Steve Alaimo
Puddin 'n Tain . . . . Alley Cats
Love Makes the World Go Round . . . . Paul Anka
Call On Me . . . . Bobby Bland
Mama Didn't Lie . . . . Jan Bradley
Rhythm of the Rain . . . . Cascades

The Gypsy Cried . . . . Lou Christie
Send Me Some Lovin' . . . . Sam Cooke
Proud . . . . Johnny Crawford
You're the Reason I'm Living. . . . . Bobby Darin
The End of the World . . . . Skeeter Davis
Ruby Baby . . . . Dion
*Walk Like a Man . . . . Four Seasons
Hitch Hike . . . . Marvin Gaye
Blame It On the Bossa Nova . . . . Eydie Gorme
Your Used To Be . . . . Brenda Lee
Days of Wine & Roses . . . . Henry Mancini
What Will Mary Say . . . . Johnny Mathis
*Walk Right In . . . . Rooftop Singers

FEBRUARY
Why Do Lovers Break Each
   Others' Hearts . . . . Bob B. Soxx & the
                     Blue Jeans
All I Have To Do Is Dream. . . . . Richard
                     Chamberlain
Don't Set Me Free . . . . Ray Charles
Let's Limbo Some More. . . . . Chubby Checker
Twenty Miles . . . . Chubby Checker
*He's So Fine . . . . Chiffons
Mr. Bass Man . . . . Johnny Cymbal
Boss Guitar. . . . . Duane Eddy
Tell Him I'm Not Home. . . . . Chuck Jackson
Linda . . . . Jan & Dean
Let's Turkey Trot. . . . . Little Eva
In Dreams . . . . Roy Orbison
South Street . . . . Orlons
One Broken Heart For Sale. . . . . Elvis Presley
Our Winter Love . . . . Bill Pursell
Yakety Sax . . . . Boots Randolph
*Our Day Will Come. . . . . Ruby & the
                     Romantics
Butterfly Baby. . . . . Bobby Rydell
Alice in Wonderland . . . . Neil Sedaka
The Dog . . . . Rufus Thomas
Laughing Boy . . . . Mary Wells

MARCH

Surfin' U.S.A...	Beach Boys
I Got What I Wanted	Brook Benton
Pipeline.	Chantays
Two Faces Have I	Lou Christie
Don't Say Nothin' Bad	Cookies
Hot Pastrami with Mashed Potatoes.	Joey Dee & the Starliters
Young & in Love	Dick & Dee Dee
Sandy	Dion
On Broadway	Drifters
Follow the Boys.	Connie Francis
Little Band of Gold.	James Gilreath
Don't Be Afraid, Little Darlin'	Steve Lawrence
*I Will Follow Him	Little Peggy March
I Got a Woman	Ricky Nelson
Young Lovers	Paul & Paula
Mecca.	Gene Pitney
The Bird's the Word	Rivingtons
A Love She Can Count On	Smokey Robinson & the Miracles
Killer Joe.	Rocky Fellers
Watermelon Man	Mongo Santamaria
Do the Bird	Dee Dee Sharp
Foolish Little Girl.	Shirelles
*If You Wanna Be Happy	Jimmy Soul
Out of my Mind.	Johnny Tillotson
Charms	Bobby Vee
Over the Mountain, Across the Sea.	Bobby Vinton[1]
That's How Heartaches are Made	Baby Washington
Can't Get Used To Losing You.	Andy Williams
Days of Wine & Roses	Andy Williams
Baby Workout.	Jackie Wilson

APRIL

Still	Bill Anderson
Remember Diana.	Paul Anka
El Watusi.	Ray Barreto
Shut Down.	Beach Boys
Prisoner of Love	James Brown

[1]Originally done in 1957 by Johnnie & Joe.

If You Need Me . . . . Solomon Burke
Take These Chains from My Heart . . . . Ray Charles
Another Saturday Night . . . . Sam Cooke
Da Doo Ron Ron . . . . Crystals
Hot Pastrami. Dartels
This Little Girl . . . . Dion
You Can't Sit Down . . . . Dovells
Ain't That a Shame . . . . Four Seasons
Pushover . . . . Etta James
The Love of My Man. . . . . Theola Kilgore
Losing You . . . . Brenda Lee
Today I Met the Boy
  I'm Gonna Marry. . . . . Darlene Love[1]
Come & Get These Memories . . . . Martha & the
                                              Vandellas
I Love You Because . . . . Al Martino
The Bounce . . . . Olympics
What a Guy . . . . Raindrops
Let's Go Steady Again . . . . Neil Sedaka

MAY
Birdland . . . . Chubby Checker
Those Lazy-Hazy-Crazy Days
  of Summer. Nat "King" Cole
18 Yellow Roses . . . . Bobby Darin
Shake a Tail Feather . . . . Five Du-Tones
If My Pillow Could Talk . . . . Connie Francis
Pride & Joy . . . . Marvin Gaye
Needles & Pins . . . . Jackie DeShannon
*It's My Party . . . . Lesley Gore
Poor Little Rich Girl . . . . Steve Lawrence
Hello Stranger. . . . . Barbara Lewis
I'm Movin' On. . . . . Matt Lucas
Every Step of the Way. . . . . Johnny Mathis
String Along . . . . Ricky Nelson
Little Latin Lupe Lu . . . . Righteous Brothers
My Summer Love. . . . . Ruby & the
                                              Romantics
Wildwood Days . . . . Bobby Rydell
*Sukiyaki . . . . Kyu Sakamoto
Blue on Blue. Bobby Vinton
Your Old Stand-by . . . . Mary Wells

[1]Before becoming a soloist, she was a member of the Blossoms and sang the lead for the Crystals' hit, "He's a Rebel."

JUNE

Not Too Young to Get Married.	Bob B. Soxx & the Blue Jeans
Detroit City	Bobby Bare
My True Confession	Brook Benton
Ring of Fire	Johnny Cash
No One.	Ray Charles
Without Love	Ray Charles
One Fine Day.	Chiffons
Till Then	Classics
I Love You and Don't You Forget It	Perry Como
Six Days on the Road.	Dave Dudley
*Easier Said Than Done.	Essex
Goodnight My Love	Fleetwoods
Mockingbird	Inez Foxx
On Top of Spaghetti	Tom Glazer & the Children's Chorus
Hootenanny	Glencoves
Abilene	George Hamilton IV
Tie Me Kangaroo Down, Sport.	Rolf Harris
*Surf City.	Jan & Dean
I (Who Have Nothing)	Ben E. King
Memphis	Lonnie Mack
I Wish I Was a Princess	Little Peggy March
Green Green.	New Christy Minstrels
Falling	Roy Orbison
Not Me	Orlons
First Quarrel.	Paul & Paula
(You're the) Devil in Disguise	Elvis Presley
Denise	Randy & the Rainbows
Don't Say Goodnight and Mean Goodbye	Shirelles
Harry the Hairy Ape.	Ray Stevens
Wipe Out.	Surfaris
Just One Look.	Doris Troy
*So Much In Love	Tymes
Be True to Yourself.	Bobby Vee
Hopeless	Andy Williams
*Fingertips—Part 2.	Little Stevie Wonder

Dion *(Columbia)*

Little Peggy March *(R.C.A.)*

JULY

It Hurts to be Sixteen	Andrea Carroll
Twist It Up	Chubby Checker
Frankie & Johnny	Sam Cooke
Candy Girl	Four Seasons
Marlena	Four Seasons
Judy's Turn to Cry	Lesley Gore
The Monkey Time	Major Lance
I Want to Stay Here	Steve Lawrence & Eydie Gorme
I Wonder	Brenda Lee
My Whole World Is Falling Down	Brenda Lee
Wait 'Til My Bobby Gets Home	Darlene Love
Painted Tainted Rose	Al Martino
Danke Schoen	Wayne Newton
True Love Never Runs Smooth	Gene Pitney
Hey Girl	Freddy Scott
The Dreamer	Neil Sedaka
Shake, Shake, Shake	Jackie Wilson
More	Kai Winding
Make the World Go Away	Timi Yuro

AUGUST

* My Boyfriend's Back	Angels
Little Deuce Coupe	Beach Boys
Surfer Girl	Beach Boys
That Sunday That Summer	Nat "King" Cole
Then He Kissed Me	Crystals
Why Don't You Believe Me	Duprees
A Walkin' Miracle	Essex
Drownin' My Sorrows	Connie Francis
Only In America	Jay & the Americans
Sally Go 'Round the Roses	Jaynetts
Heat Wave	Martha & the Vandellas
Cry Baby	Garnett Mimms & the Enchanters
The Lonely Surfer	Jack Nitzsche
Birthday Party	Pixies Three
The Kind of Boy You Can't Forget	Raindrops
Martian Hop	Ran-Dells
Please Don't Talk to the Lifeguard	Diane Ray

Mickey's Monkey . . . . Smoky Robinson &
the Miracles
Be My Baby . . . . Ronettes
Hey There Lonely Boy . . . . Ruby & the
Romantics
Hello Mudduh, Hello Faddah. . . . . Allan Sherman
Surfer Joe. . . . . Surfaris
Part Time Love . . . . Little Johnnie
Taylor
You Can Never Stop Me Loving You . . . . . . Johnny Tillotson
Wonderful Wonderful . . . . Tymes
* Blue Velvet . . . . Bobby Vinton

SEPTEMBER
Two Tickets to Paradise . . . . Brook Benton
Bust Out . . . . Busters
Busted. . . . . Ray Charles
A Love So Fine . . . . Chiffons
I Can't Stay Mad at You . . . . Skeeter Davis
Donna the Prima Donna . . . . Dion
Down at Papa Joe's. . . . . Dixiebelles
Red Sails in the Sunset. . . . . Fats Domino
I'll Take You Home. . . . . Drifters
*Sugar Shack. . . . . Jimmy Gilmer &
the Fireballs
She's a Fool . . . . Lesley Gore
Cry To Me . . . . Betty Harris
It's All Right . . . . Impressions
Honolulu Lulu. . . . . Jan & Dean
Down the Aisle . . . . Patty Labelle &
the Bluebelles
The Grass is Greener. . . . . Brenda Lee
Hello Heartache, Goodbye Love. . . . . Little Peggy
March
Maria Elena . . . . Los Indios
Trabajaras
Fools Rush In . . . . Ricky Nelson
Blue Bayou. Roy Orbison
Mean Woman Blues . . . . Roy Orbison
Cross Fire . . . . Orlons
My Babe . . . . Righteous Brothers
What Does a Girl Do. . . . . Shirelles
Talk To Me. Sunny & the
Sunglows

*Deep Purple . . . . Nino Tempo &
                                              April Stevens[1]
Washington Square . . . . Village Stompers
You Lost the Sweetest Boy . . . . Mary Wells

OCTOBER
I Adore Him . . . . Angels
500 Miles from Home . . . . Bobby Bare
I Wonder What She's
    Doing Tonight . . . . Barry & the
                                              Tamerlanes
Little Red Rooster . . . . Sam Cooke
*I'm Leaving It Up To You . . . . Dale & Grace
New Mexico Rose . . . . Four Seasons
Your Other Love . . . . Connie Francis
Can I Get a Witness . . . . Marvin Gaye
Hey Little Girl . . . . Major Lance
Walking Proud . . . . Steve Lawrence
Living a Lie . . . . Al Martino
Twenty-Four Hours from Tulsa . . . . Gene Pitney
Bossa Nova Baby . . . . Elvis Presley
Witchcraft . . . . Elvis Presley
Misty . . . . Lloyd Price
Everybody . . . . Tommy Roe
Wild . . . . Dee Dee Sharp
Walking the Dog . . . . Rufus Thomas
Since I Fell for You . . . . Lenny Welch
What's Easy for Two Is
    So Hard for One . . . . Mary Wells
Workout Stevie, Workout . . . . Little Stevie
                                              Wonder

NOVEMBER
Be True to Your School . . . . Beach Boys
In My Room . . . . Beach Boys
Need To Belong . . . . Jerry Butler
You Don't Have To Be a Baby To Cry . . . . . Caravelles
Loddy Lo . . . . Chubby Checker
I Have a Boyfriend . . . . Chiffons
Girls Grow Up Faster Than Boys . . . . Cookies
Tra La La La Suzy . . . . Dean & Jean

[1]Nino & April are brother and sister.

94

Turn Around. Dick & Dee Dee
Drip Drop . . . . Dion
Have You Heard . . . . Duprees
Misery. . . . . Dynamics
The Nitty Gritty. . . . . Shirley Ellis
Wives & Lovers. . . . . Jack Jones
Long Tall Texan. . . . . Murry Kellum
Louie Louie . . . . Kingsmen
Quicksand . . . . Martha & the
                                          Vandellas
Baby Don't You Weep. . . . . Garnett Mimms &
                                          the Enchanters
For Your Precious Love . . . . Garnett Mimms &
                                          the Enchanters
Marvelous Toy. . . . . Chad Mitchell Trio
Popsicles & Icicles . . . . Murmaids
Midnight Mary . . . . Joey Powers
I Gotta Dance To Keep from Crying . . . . . . Smokey Robinson
                                          & the Miracles
I Got a Woman . . . . Freddy Scott
The Boy Next Door. . . . . Secrets
Bad Girl . . . . Neil Sedaka
*Dominique . . . . Singing Nun
Talk Back Trembling Lips. . . . . Johnny Tillotson
*There! I've Said It Again . . . . Bobby Vinton
Wonderful Summer. . . . . Robin Ward

DECEMBER
Harlem Shuffle. . . . . Bob & Earl
That Lucky Old Sun . . . . Ray Charles
Hooka Tooka. . . . . Chubby Checker
Daisy Petal Pickin' . . . . Jimmy Gilmer &
                                          the Fireballs
You Don't Own Me. . . . . Lesley Gore
Drag City. . . . . Jan & Dean
As Usual . . . . Brenda Lee
Out of Limits . . . . Marketts
For You. . . . . Ricky Nelson
Pretty Paper. . . . . Roy Orbison
It's All in the Game . . . . Cliff Richard
Hey Little Cobra . . . . Rip Chords
Baby I Love You . . . . Ronettes
What Kind of Fool
  (Do You Think I Am) . . . . Tams

95

1964

In terms of music, 1964 should be called a year of changes.

The Beatles' arrival on the music scene in 1964 signaled the end of the oldie era. A new age was about to begin. Still, the oldies fared well. The Beach Boys and the Four Seasons both had great years in '64 with such hits as "Fun Fun Fun" and "I Get Around" (Beach Boys) and "Dawn" and "Rag Doll" (Four Seasons). The Drifters, a group dating back to the rhythm & blues days, had one of the biggest hits of their career, "Under the Boardwalk."

Many other of the big stars had great oldie hits in this transitional year; Chuck Berry had three songs in the Top 40; Roy Orbison had two smash hits, "Pretty Woman" and "It's Over." Elvis was still riding high, producing such '64 hits as "Kissin' Cousins," "Viva Las Vegas" and "Such a Night." Bobby Vinton had one of his biggest years, including the #1 song, "Mr. Lonely."

Outside the music world, '64 caused a lot of other changes.

Johnson and Humphrey were put in the White House; the most populous state changed from New York to California; Cassius Clay "arrived" and singlehandedly changed the boxing world; discotheques were "in"; the Surgeon General announced that cigarette smoking could be harmful to your health.

Of all the changes that occurred in '64, none was more significant than that of the new sound of music.

It is indeed a tribute to the greatness of the oldie sound that so many oldie hits existed during the first year of the Beatles, a year totally flooded by British sounds.

JANUARY

Going, Going, Gone	Brook Benton
Good News	Sam Cooke
Stop & Think It Over	Dale & Grace
Southtown USA	Dixiebelles
Java	Al Hirt
Talking About My Baby	Impressions
Um Um Um Um Um Um	Major Lance
Puppy Love	Barbara Lewis
Navy Blue	Diane Renay
California Sun	Rivieras
Come On	Tommy Roe
Who Do You Love	Sapphires
I Only Want to Be With You	Dusty Springfield
A Fool Never Learns	Andy Williams

FEBRUARY

Miller's Cave	Bobby Bare
Fun Fun Fun	Beach Boys
Abigail Beecher	Freddy Cannon
Understand Your Man	Johnny Cash
Baby Don't You Cry	Ray Charles
My Heart Cries For You	Ray Charles
Hey Jean Hey Dean	Dean & Jean
The Shoop Shoop Song	Betty Everett
Dawn	Four Seasons
Stay	Four Seasons
Blue Winter	Connie Francis
Live Wire	Martha & the Vandellas
I Love You More & More Every Day	Al Martino
He Walks Like a Man	Jody Miller
It Hurts Me	Elvis Presley
Kissin' Cousins	Elvis Presley
Suspicion	Terry Stafford
Star Dust	Nino Tempo & April Stevens
The Way You Do the Things You Do	Temptations
Worried Guy	Johnny Tillotson
Bird Dance Beat	Trashmen
Hi-Heel Sneakers	Tommy Tucker
My Heart Belongs to Only You	Bobby Vinton

MARCH

Nadine	Chuck Berry
Hey Bobba Needle	Chubby Checker
Shangri-La	Vic Dana
Forever	Pete Drake
You're a Wonderful One	Marvin Gaye
That's the Way Boys Are	Lesley Gore
Dead Man's Curve	Jan & Dean
The New Girl in School	Jan & Dean
The Matador	Major Lance
Think	Brenda Lee
Shangri-La	Robert Maxwell
Stay Awhile	Dusty Springfield
Hippy Hippy Shake	Swinging Blue Jeans
Wish Someone Would Care	Irma Thomas
My Girl Sloopy	Vibrations

98

Ebb Tide . . . . Lenny Welch
White on White . . . . Danny Williams

APRIL
Diane . . . . Bachelors
Goodbye Baby, Goodbye . . . . Solomon Burke
Love Me with All Your Heart . . . . Ray Charles
                                            Singers
Ronnie . . . . Four Seasons
Cotton Candy . . . . Al Hirt
I'm So Proud. Impressions
In My Lonely Room . . . . Martha & the
                                              Vandellas
The Very Thought of You. . . . . Ricky Nelson
Today . . . . New Christy
                                              Minstrels
It's Over . . . . Roy Orbison
(Just Like) Romeo & Juliet . . . . Reflections
Kiss Me Sailor . . . . Diane Renay
Three Window Coupe . . . . Rip Chords
The Best Part of Breakin' Up. . . . . Ronettes
*My Guy . . . . Mary Wells
Wrong For Each Other . . . . Andy Williams

MAY
*I Get Around. Beach Boys
Don't Worry Baby . . . . Beach Boys
No Particular Place to Go. . . . . Chuck Berry
*Chapel of Love. . . . . Dixie Cups
Be Anything (But Be Mine). . . . . Connie Francis
What's the Matter with You Baby . . . . Marvin Gaye &
                                              Mary Wells
I Don't Want to be a Loser . . . . Lesley Gore
Every Little Bit Hurts . . . . Brenda Holloway
Tears & Roses . . . . Al Martino
Kiss Me Quick. . . . . Elvis Presley
Viva Las Vegas . . . . Elvis Presley
What'd I Say. Elvis Presley
Memphis . . . . Johnny Rivers
My Boy Lollipop . . . . Millie Small
I'll Touch a Star. . . . . Terry Stafford
I'll Be in Trouble . . . . Temptations
I Rise, I Fall . . . . Johnny Tillotson
Tell Me Why. Bobby Vinton

JUNE
I Believe . . . . Bachelors
Lazy Elsie Molly . . . . Chubby Checker
Good Times . . . . Sam Cooke
Tennessee Waltz . . . . Sam Cooke
Under the Boardwalk . . . . Drifters
Alone . . . . Four Seasons
*Rag Doll. Four Seasons
Once Upon a Time . . . . Marvin Gaye &
Mary Wells
Keep on Pushing . . . . Impressions
The Little Old Lady (From Pasadena) . . . . . Jan & Dean
I Like It Like That . . . . Smokey Robinson
& the Miracles
Do I Love You . . . . Ronettes

JULY
You're My World . . . . Cilla Black
Just Be True . . . . Gene Chandler
She's the One . . . . Chartbusters
Deserie . . . . Charts
People Say . . . . Dixie Cups
Say You . . . . Ronnie Dove
C'Mon and Swim . . . . Bobby Freeman
Maybe I Know. . . . . Lesley Gore
It Hurts to be in Love . . . . Gene Pitney
Such a Night. . . . . Elvis Presley
Handyman . . . . Del Shannon
Walk Don't Run '64 . . . . Ventures
In the Misty Moonlight . . . . Jerry Wallace

AUGUST
You Never Can Tell . . . . Chuck Berry
Out of Sight . . . . James Brown
Save it for Me . . . . Four Seasons
Baby I Need Your Loving. . . . . Four Tops
Funny. . . . . Joe Hinton
I'm on the Outside
  (Looking In). . . . . Little Anthony &
the Imperials
Dancing in the Street . . . . Martha & the
Vandellas
Bread & Butter . . . . Newbeats
*Pretty Woman . . . . Roy Orbison

100

Maybelline . . . . Johnny Rivers
G.T.O.. . . . . Ronny & the
                                     Daytonas
Remember (Walkin' in the Sand) . . . . Shangri-Las
Haunted House . . . . Jumpin' Gene
                                     Simmons
Sweet William . . . . Millie Small
Clinging Vine . . . . Bobby Vinton

SEPTEMBER
I Wouldn't Trade You
  for the World . . . . Bachelors
When I Grow Up . . . . Beach Boys
Bless Our Love . . . . Gene Chandler
Cousin of Mine . . . . Sam Cooke
Mercy Mercy . . . . Don Covay
I've Got Sand in my Shoes . . . . Drifters
Let it be Me . . . . Betty Everett &
                                     Jerry Butler
Little Honda . . . . Hondells
You Must Believe Me . . . . Impressions
Ride the Wild Surf . . . . Jan & Dean
Come a Little Bit Closer . . . . Jay & the
                                     Americans
*Do Wah Diddy Diddy . . . . Manfred Mann
The Door Is Still Open To My Heart . . . . . . Dean Martin
That's What Love Is Made Of . . . . Smokey Robinson
                                     & the Miracles
Why You Wanna Make Me Blue . . . . Temptations
On the Street Where You Live. . . . . Andy Williams
Last Kiss . . . . J. Frank Wilson &
                                     the Cavaliers

OCTOBER
Wendy . . . . Beach Boys
Oh No Not My Baby . . . . Maxine Brown
You Should Have Seen the Way
  He Looked At Me . . . . Dixie Cups
Right Or Wrong. . . . . Ronnie Dove
Gone Gone Gone . . . . Everly Brothers
*Ringo . . . . Lorne Greene
Sidewalk Surfin' . . . . Jan & Dean
Is It True . . . . Brenda Lee
Everything's Alright . . . . Newbeats

I'm Gonna Be Strong. . . . . Gene Pitney
Ain't That Loving You Baby . . . . Elvis Presley
Ask Me . . . . Elvis Presley
Mountain of Love. . . . . Johnny Rivers
Walking in the Rain . . . . Ronettes
*Leader of the Pack . . . . Shangri-Las
She Understands Me . . . . Johnny Tillotson
*Mr. Lonely . . . . Bobby Vinton
Slaughter on Tenth Avenue. . . . . Ventures

NOVEMBER
Dance Dance Dance . . . . Beach Boys
One More Time. . . . . Ray Charles
                                              Singers
Thou Shalt Not Steal . . . . Dick & Dee Dee
Saturday Night at the Movies. . . . . Drifters
Big Man in Town . . . . Four Seasons
Amen . . . . Impressions
Dear Heart. . . . . Jack Jones
The Jerk . . . . Larks
Goin' Out of My Head . . . . Little Anthony &
                                              the Imperials
Sha La La . . . . Manfred Mann
Too Many Fish in the Sea. . . . . Marvelettes
Walk Away. . . . . Matt Munro
The Wedding . . . . Julie Rogers
Forget Him . . . . Bobby Rydell
Keep Searchin' . . . . Del Shannon
Dear Heart. . . . . Andy Williams

DECEMBER
No Arms Can Ever Hold You. . . . . Bachelors
What Now . . . . Gene Chandler
Leader of the Laundromat . . . . Detergents
The Name Game . . . . Shirley Ellis
How Sweet It Is. . . . . Marvin Gaye
Let's Lock the Door . . . . Jay & the
                                              Americans
Wild One. Martha & the
                                              Vandellas
*You've Lost That Lovin' Feelin' . . . . Righteous Brothers
Give Him a Great Big Kiss . . . . Shangri-Las

1965

Along with the dramatic change in music came a change in fashion, attitude and philosophy. The young people were entering the age of "do your own thing."

Bell-bottom trousers became the style. Men's hair, influenced by the Beatles, grew longer and longer. The "unisex" look was in.

Although the oldie era had officially ended, and the British invasion was in full bloom, the oldie sound hung on. The Beach Boys had a #1 with "Help Me Rhonda." Jay and the Americans had a great oldie, "Cara Mia."

Rock 'n' roll was gone but not forgotten. Through movies, television, the stage, oldie concerts and new artists recording old songs, rock 'n' roll lives on. Elvis Presley has changed, but is still on top of the charts.

Today, in the seventies, rock 'n' roll music is enjoying a great deal of popularity. Within the last year or two, there have been two major motion pictures, a television series, a Broadway play and countless concerts centering around rock 'n' roll. More and more of today's artists are recording hits of the fifties; a number of the oldie artists continue to enjoy successful careers.

Perhaps Danny and the Juniors said it best with their 1958 smash oldie, "Rock & Roll Is Here to Stay. . . ."

JANUARY

Boy from New York City . . . . Ad Libs
Birds and the Bees . . . . Jewel Akens
A Change Is Gonna Come . . . . Sam Cooke
Shake . . . . Sam Cooke
Bye Bye Baby . . . . Four Seasons
Break Away . . . . Newbeats
My Girl . . . . Temptations
Paper Tiger . . . . Sue Thompson
Use Your Head . . . . Mary Wells

FEBRUARY

Do You Wanna Dance . . . . Beach Boys
People Get Ready . . . . Impressions
Hurt So Bad . . . . Little Anthony &
        the Imperials
No Where to Run . . . . Martha & the
        Vandellas
Goodnight . . . . Roy Orbison

I Must Be Seeing Things. . . . . Gene Pitney
Do the Clam. Elvis Presley
Born to be Together . . . . Ronettes
Stranger in Town . . . . Del Shannon

MARCH
Got to Get You Off My Mind. . . . . Solomon Burke
One Kiss for Old Time's Sake . . . . Ronnie Dove
The Clapping Song . . . . Shirley Ellis
Ooo Baby Baby . . . . Smokey Robinson
                                               & the Miracles
Cast Your Fate to the Wind. . . . . Sounds Orchestral
Long Lonely Nights . . . . Bobby Vinton

APRIL
*Help Me Rhonda . . . . Beach Boys
Nothing Can Stop Me . . . . Gene Chandler
I Gotta Woman . . . . Ray Charles
Do the Freddie . . . . Chubby Checker
Dream on Little Dreamer. . . . . Perry Como
Iko Iko . . . . Dixie Cups
Crying in the Chapel. . . . . Elvis Presley[1]
Just Once in My Life. . . . . Righteous Brothers
Wooly Bully . . . . Sam the Sham &
                                               the Pharohs
She's About a Mover . . . . Sir Douglas
                                               Quintet
It's Growing . . . . Temptations

MAY
*I Can't Help Myself. . . . . Four Tops
You Really Know How to Hurt a Guy . . . . . Jan & Dean
Too Many Rivers . . . . Brenda Lee
Laurie. . . . . Dickey Lee
(Remember Me) I'm the One
   Who Loves You. . . . . Dean Martin
I'll Keep Holding On. . . . . Marvelettes
Yes I'm Ready. . . . . Barbara Mason
Last Chance to Turn Around. . . . . Gene Pitney
Give Us Your Blessings. . . . . Shangri-Las
Boo-Ga-Loo . . . . Tom & Jerrio
L-O-N-E-L-Y. Bobby Vinton

[1] One of the first true oldies; recorded by both Sonny Til & the Orioles and June Valli in 1953.

JUNE

Marie . . . . Bachelors
Hold Me, Thrill Me, Kiss Me . . . . Mel Carter
A Little Bit of Heaven . . . . Ronnie Dove
Don't Just Stand There . . . . Patty Duke
Girl Come Running. . . . . Four Seasons
Sunshine, Lollipops
    and Rainbows . . . . Lesley Gore
Theme From a Summer Place . . . . Lettermen
Cara Mia . . . . Jay & the
                                                       Americans
Baby I'm Yours . . . . Barbara Lewis
Take Me Back . . . . Little Anthony &
                                                       the Imperials
(Such An) Easy Question . . . . Elvis Presley

JULY

California Girls . . . . Beach Boys
Papa's Got a Brand New Bag . . . . James Brown
Sugar Dumpling. . . . . Sam Cooke
Ride Your Pony . . . . Lee Dorsey
It's the Same Old Song . . . . Four Tops
You're My Girl . . . . Roy Orbison
Looking Through the Eyes of Love . . . . Gene Pitney
Unchained Melody . . . . Righteous Brothers
The Tracks of My Tears . . . . Smokey Robinson
                                                       & the Miracles
Down in the Boondocks . . . . Billy Joe Royal

AUGUST

Action. . . . . Freddy Cannon
Liar Liar . . . . Castaways
I'll Make All Your Dreams Come True . . . . . Ronnie Dove
You've Been in Love Too Long . . . . Martha & the
                                                       Vandellas
Sad, Sad Girl. . . . . Barbara Mason
Ride Away . . . . Roy Orbison
I'm Yours. . . . . Elvis Presley
Mohair Sam . . . . Charlie Rich
Heartaches By the Number . . . . Johnny Tillotson

SEPTEMBER

Taste of Honey . . . . Herb Alpert & the
                                                       Tijuana Brass
Keep On Dancing . . . . Gentrys

Some Enchanted Evening. . . . . Jay & the
Americans
Make Me Your Baby . . . . Barbara Lewis
I Knew You When . . . . Billy Joe Royal
A Lover's Concerto. . . . . Toys
What Color Is a Man . . . . Bobby Vinton

OCTOBER
Make the World Go Away. . . . . Eddy Arnold
Chapel in the Moonlight. . . . . Bachelors
Rescue Me . . . . Fontella Bass
(All of a Sudden) My Heart Sings . . . . Mel Carter
Say Something Funny . . . . Patty Duke
Let's Hang On. . . . . Four Seasons
I Found a Girl. . . . . Jan & Dean
Rusty Bells. . . . . Brenda Lee
I Miss You So . . . . Little Anthony &
the Imperials
Run, Baby Run . . . . Newbeats
My Girl Has Gone . . . . Smokey Robinson
& the Miracles

NOVEMBER
The Little Girl I Once Knew. . . . . Beach Boys
Kiss Away . . . . Ronnie Dove
Sunday and Me . . . . Jay & the
Americans
Princess in Rags. . . . . Gene Pitney
Puppet on a String . . . . Elvis Presley
I Can Never Go Home Anymore . . . . Shangri-Las

DECEMBER
Tijuana Taxi . . . . Herb Alpert & the
Tijuana Brass
Zorba the Greek . . . . Herb Alpert & the
Tijuana Brass
Recovery . . . . Fontella Bass
Crying Time. . . . . Ray Charles
Lightning Strikes . . . . Lou Christie
Spanish Eyes. . . . . Al Martino
Ebb Tide . . . . Righteous Brothers
Sandy . . . . Ronny & the
Daytonas
Satin Pillows . . . . Bobby Vinton

2
AUTHORS' TOP 100

Bill Haley and the Comets *(MCA)*

The following list, in our opinion, represents the super oldies of all time. This has been compiled with consideration given to impact, popularity and "classic" sound.

Many songs never made it big statistically, but enjoyed tremendous popularity and had a huge impact on the music world. For example, "In the Still of the Nite," by the Five Satins, never scored high on the charts, but we consider it to be one of the greatest all-time hits.

After the Top 100 is a list of "extras," songs the authors consider classics, that didn't make the Top 100.

Following our Top 100 is a statistical Top 100. This one was done with no other consideration than statistics. It is interesting to compare the two.

NO.	SONG	ARTIST
1.	Rock Around the Clock	Bill Haley & the Comets
2.	Don't Be Cruel/Hound Dog	Elvis Presley
3.	The Great Pretender	Platters
4.	Diana	Paul Anka
5.	Little Darlin'.	Diamonds
6.	Heartbreak Hotel	Elvis Presley
7.	At the Hop	Danny & the Juniors
8.	In the Still of the Nite	Five Satins
9.	All Shook Up.	Elvis Presley
10.	Runaway	Del Shannon
11.	It's Only Make Believe.	Conway Twitty
12.	Blueberry Hill	Fats Domino
13.	Love Letters in the Sand	Pat Boone
14.	Wake Up Little Susie.	Everly Brothers
15.	Love Me Tender	Elvis Presley
16.	Kansas City.	Wilbert Harrison
17.	You Send Me	Sam Cooke
18.	Young Love	Sonny James

NO.	SONG	ARTIST
19.	Tossin' & Turnin'	Bobby Lewis
20.	Venus	Frankie Avalon
21.	It's Not For Me To Say	Johnny Mathis
22.	Whole Lot of Shakin' Goin On	Jerry Lee Lewis
23.	My Prayer	Platters
24.	I Want You, I Need You, I Love You	Elvis Presley
25.	Come Go With Me	Del Vikings
26.	Dream Lover	Bobby Darin
27.	Peggy Sue	Buddy Holly
28.	School Day	Chuck Berry
29.	The Lion Sleeps Tonight	Tokens
30.	Only You	Platters
31.	Come Softly to Me	Fleetwoods
32.	(Let Me Be Your) Teddy Bear	Elvis Presley
33.	The Green Door	Jim Lowe
34.	Searchin'	Coasters
35.	Donna	Ritchie Valens
36.	The Wayward Wind	Gogi Grant
37.	Little Star	Elegants
38.	All I Have To Do Is Dream	Everly Brothers
39.	The Twist	Chubby Checker
40.	Everybody's Somebody's Fool	Connie Francis
41.	Silhouettes	Rays
42.	Memories Are Made of This	Dean Martin
43.	Mr. Blue	Fleetwoods
44.	Bye Bye Love	Everly Brothers
45.	Mack the Knife	Bobby Darin
46.	Chantilly Lace	Big Bopper
47.	The Battle of New Orleans	Johnny Horton
48.	Why Do Fools Fall in Love	Frankie Lymon & the Teenagers
49.	Chances Are	Johnny Mathis
50.	A White Sport Coat	Marty Robbins
51.	It's Almost Tomorrow	Dream Weavers
52.	Jailhouse Rock	Elvis Presley
53.	That'll Be the Day	Crickets
54.	Book of Love	Monotones
55.	Handy Man	Jimmy Jones
56.	Blue Suede Shoes	Carl Perkins
57.	Sherry	Four Seasons
58.	Don't Forbid Me	Pat Boone
59.	Save the Last Dance For Me	Drifters

NO.	SONG	ARTIST
60.	Don't	Elvis Presley
61.	Honeycomb	Jimmie Rodgers
62.	Personality	Lloyd Price
63.	Please Mr. Postman.	Marvelettes
64.	Sixteen Tons	Ernie Ford
65.	Tears On My Pillow	Little Anthony & the Imperials
66.	Be-Bop-a-Lula	Gene Vincent
67.	Lonely Boy.	Paul Anka
68.	Duke of Earl.	Gene Chandler
69.	Sweet Little Sixteen	Chuck Berry
70.	Are You Lonesome Tonight.	Elvis Presley
71.	Party Doll	Buddy Knox
72.	Over the Mountain; Across the Sea	Johnnie & Joe
73.	Tammy	Debbie Reynolds
74.	Singing the Blues	Guy Mitchell
75.	Earth Angel	Penguins
76.	Witch Doctor	David Seville
77.	El Paso	Marty Robbins
78.	Since I Don't Have You	Skyliners
79.	It's All in the Game	Tommy Edwards
80.	My Special Angel	Bobby Helms
81.	Runaround Sue	Dion
82.	Theme From a Summer Place	Percy Faith
83.	Get a Job.	Silhouettes
84.	What'd I Say.	Ray Charles
85.	Only the Lonely.	Roy Orbison
86.	Will You Love Me Tomorrow	Shirelles
87.	The Diary	Neil Sedaka
88.	You Cheated.	Shields
89.	Stagger Lee	Lloyd Price
90.	I'm Sorry	Brenda Lee
91.	Tequila	Champs
92.	You've Lost That Lovin' Feelin'	Righteous Brothers
93.	Butterfly	Andy Williams
94.	Mother-in-Law.	Ernie-K-Doe
95.	To Know Him Is To Love Him.	Teddy Bears
96.	Hey Paula	Paul & Paula
97.	Take Good Care of My Baby	Bobby Vee
98.	Happy Happy Birthday Baby.	Tune Weavers
99.	Travelin' Man	Ricky Nelson
100.	Blue Moon	Marcels

TOP 100 "EXTRAS" (ALPHABETICAL BY ARTIST)

Tear Drops	Lee Andrews & the Hearts
My Boyfriend's Back	Angels
I Get Around	Beach Boys
Rhythm of the Rain	Cascades
Hey! Baby	Bruce Channel
Maybe	Chantels
I Can't Stop Loving You	Ray Charles
Hearts of Stone	Charms
Just a Dream	Jimmy Clanton
Yakety Yak	Coasters
Round & Round	Perry Como
Sh-Boom	Crew Cuts
I'm Leaving It Up To You	Dale & Grace
Teen Angel	Mark Dinning
A Teenager in Love	Dion & the Belmonts
Chapel of Love	Dixie Cups
Honky Tonk	Bill Doggett
Mountain of Love	Harold Dorman
So Rare	Jimmy Dorsey
Johnny Angel	Shelly Fabares
Big Girls Don't Cry	Four Seasons
Rag Doll	Four Seasons
Who's Sorry Now	Connie Francis
Sugar Shack	Jimmy Gilmer & the Fireballs
It's My Party	Lesley Gore
Surf City	Jan & Dean
Sweet Nothin's	Brenda Lee
Poor Little Fool	Ricky Nelson
Pretty Woman	Roy Orbison
Running Scared	Roy Orbison
Sea of Love	Phil Phillips
Cherry Pink & Apple Blossom White	Prez Prado
A Big Hunk O' Love	Elvis Presley

112

Good Luck Charm . . . . Elvis Presley
It's Now or Never. . . . . Elvis Presley
Stuck on You. . . . . Elvis Presley
Surrender. . . . . Elvis Presley
Running Bear . . . . Johnny Preston
Sheila . . . . Tommy Roe
Our Day Will Come . . . . Ruby & the
                                            Romantics
Breaking Up Is Hard To Do . . . . Neil Sedaka
Soldier Boy. Shirelles
Dominique. Singing Nun
Rock & Roll Waltz . . . . Kay Starr
Sixteen Reasons . . . . Connie Stevens
Poetry In Motion . . . . Johnny Tillotson
La Bamba . . . . Ritchie Valens
Roses Are Red. . . . . Bobby Vinton
My Guy. . . . . Mary Wells
Stay . . . . Maurice Williams
                                            & the Zodiacs

Elvis *(R.C.A.)*

3

STATISTICAL TOP 100

In order to arrive at the all-time Top 100 oldies, the following rating system was used:

All oldies making the Top 40 were rated. For number of weeks on the charts, a song was given that number of points; for highest position the song reached, it was given from 1 to 40 points, a #1 song receiving 40 points, a #40 song receiving 1 point. The highest score was 77 points—39 points for a #2 song and 38 points for 38 weeks on the charts.

Those songs receiving the most points comprise the statistical Top 100. Songs with † were recorded by more than one artist at the same time. Artists shown had the biggest hit. Following the Top 100 is a list of "extras," songs that just missed making the Top 100.

NO.	SONG	ARTIST	POINTS
1.	So Rare	Jimmy Dorsey	77
2.	Love Letters in the Sand	Pat Boone	74
†3.	Tammy	Debbie Reynolds	71
4.	It's Not For Me To Say	Johnny Mathis	70
5.	All Shook Up	Elvis Presley	70
†6.	Canadian Sunset	Hugo Winterhalter	70
7.	Round and Round	Perry Como	69
8.	Rock Around the Clock	Bill Haley & the Comets	69
9.	Diana	Paul Anka	68
†10.	True Love	Bing Crosby & Grace Kelly	68
11.	Honky Tonk	Bill Doggett	68
†12.	The Wayward Wind	Gogi Grant	68
†13.	Lisbon Antigua	Nelson Riddle	68
14.	Honeycomb	Jimmie Rodgers	68
15.	Come Go With Me	Del-Vikings	67
16.	Whole Lot of Shakin' Going On	Jerry Lee Lewis	67
17.	Don't Be Cruel	Elvis Presley	67
18.	Heartbreak Hotel	Elvis Presley	67

NO.	SONG	ARTIST	POINTS
19.	Hound Dog	Elvis Presley	67
20.	Jailhouse Rock	Elvis Presley	67
21.	Running Bear	Johnny Preston	67
22.	Just Walking In the Rain	Johnnie Ray	67
†23.	Autumn Leaves	Roger Williams	67
24.	April Love	Pat Boone	66
†25.	You Send Me	Sam Cooke	66
†26.	Mack the Knife	Bobby Darin	66
27.	Whatever Will Be Will Be	Doris Day	66
28.	Bye Bye Love	Everly Brothers	66
29.	Wake Up Little Susie	Everly Brothers	66
30.	Moments To Remember	Four Lads	66
31.	The Green Door	Jim Lowe	66
†32.	Singing the Blues	Guy Mitchell	66
33.	Allegheny Moon	Patti Page	66
†34.	Moonglow & Theme From Picnic	Morris Stoloff	66
†35.	Little Darlin'	Diamonds	65
†36.	Love Is a Many Splendored Thing	Four Aces	65
37.	(Let Me Be Your) Teddy Bear	Elvis Presley	65
38.	Rock & Roll Waltz	Kay Starr	65
†39.	Poor People of Paris	Les Baxter	64
†40.	Blueberry Hill	Fats Domino	64
41.	Gone	Ferlin Husky	64
†42.	Memories Are Made of This	Dean Martin	64
43.	Chances Are	Johnny Mathis	64
†44.	The Yellow Rose of Texas	Mitch Miller	64
†45.	Only You	Platters	64
46.	The Great Pretender	Platters	64
47.	A White Sport Coat	Marty Robbins	64
48.	I Almost Lost My Mind	Pat Boone	63
49.	I'm Sorry	Brenda Lee	63
50.	Tossin' & Turnin'	Bobby Lewis	63
51.	Please Mr. Postman	Marvelettes	63
52.	Wonderful Wonderful	Johnny Mathis	63
53.	My Prayer	Platters	63
†54.	Love Me Tender	Elvis Presley	63
55.	To Know Him Is To Love Him	Teddy Bears	63

NO.	SONG	ARTIST	POINTS
56.	School Day	Chuck Berry	62
57.	Don't Forbid Me	Pat Boone	62
†58.	Limbo Rock	Chubby Checker	62
59.	Searchin'	Coasters	62
60.	Hot Diggity	Perry Como	62
61.	My Heart Is An Open Book	Carl Dobkins, Jr.	62
62.	It's All In the Game	Tommy Edwards	62
63.	Sixteen Tons	Ernie Ford	62
64.	No Not Much	Four Lads	62
†65.	Party Doll	Buddy Knox	62
66.	I Want You I Need You I Love You	Elvis Presley	62
67.	He'll Have To Go	Jim Reeves	62
68.	El Paso	Marty Robbins	62
69.	Sixteen Reasons	Connie Stevens	62
70.	Donna	Ritchie Valens	62
71.	Sail Along Silvery Moon	Billy Vaughn	62
†72.	Stranger on the Shore	Mr. Acker Bilk	61
†73.	The Twist	Chubby Checker	61
74.	Send For Me	Nat "King" Cole	61
75.	At The Hop	Danny & the Juniors	61
†76.	I'm Walkin'	Fats Domino	61
77.	Theme From a Summer Place	Percy Faith	61
†78.	He	Al Hibbler	61
79.	The Battle of New Orleans	Johnny Horton	61
†80.	Young Love	Tab Hunter	61
81.	Tom Dooley	Kingston Trio	61
82.	Sweet Nothin's	Brenda Lee	61
83.	Cherry Pink & Apple Blossom White	Prez Prado	61
84.	Stagger Lee	Lloyd Price	61
85.	It's Only Make Believe	Conway Twitty	61
86.	Finger Poppin' Time	Hank Ballard & the Midnighters	60¹
87.	Chantilly Lace	Big Bopper	60
88.	16 Candles	Crests	60
89.	That'll Be the Day	Crickets	60
90.	Rock-in-Robin	Bobby Day	60

¹Songs listed from 86–102 are all tied for last place in the top 100.

NO.	SONG	ARTIST	POINTS
†91.	Exodus	Ferrante & Teicher	60
92.	Mr. Blue	Fleetwoods	60
93.	Peggy Sue	Buddy Holly	60
94.	North to Alaska	Johnny Horton	60
95.	Moonlight Gambler	Frankie Laine	60
96.	Great Balls of Fire	Jerry Lee Lewis	60
97.	Heartaches by the Number	Guy Mitchell	60
†98.	Tonight You Belong To Me	Patience & Prudence	60
99.	Don't	Elvis Presley	60
100.	It's Now or Never	Elvis Presley	60
101.	I Hear You Knocking	Gale Storm	60
†102.	Butterfly	Andy Williams	60

STATISTICAL TOP
100 "EXTRAS"

SONG	ARTIST	POINTS
Mr. Lee	Bobbettes	59
Greenfields	Brothers Four	59
†Ivory Tower	Cathy Carr	59
†Tequila	Champs	59
Topsy II	Cozy Cole	59
†Last Date	Floyd Cramer	59
I'm In Love Again	Fats Domino	59
Who's Sorry Now	Connie Francis	59
Smoke Gets In Your Eyes	Platters	59
Will You Love Me Tomorrow	Shirelles	59
†Dark Moon	Gale Storm	59
†I'll Be Home	Pat Boone	58
I Can't Stop Loving You	Ray Charles	58
†Band of Gold	Don Cherry	58
He's a Rebel	Crystals	58
†On the Street Where You Live	Vic Damone	58
Peppermint Twist	Joey Dee & the Starliters	58
The Stroll	Diamonds	58
Teen Angel	Mark Dinning	58
Save the Last Dance For Me	Drifters	58
There Goes My Baby	Drifters	58
†Standing On the Corner	Four Lads	58
Everybody's Somebody's Fool	Connie Francis	58
†Raunchy	Bill Justis	58
He's Got the Whole World (In His Hands)	Laurie London	58
Return to Me	Dean Martin	58
†Blue Suede Shoes	Carl Perkins	58
Personality	Lloyd Price	58
Silhouettes	Rays	58
Sleep Walk	Santo & Johnny	58
I'm Gonna Sit Right Down and Write Myself a Letter	Billy Williams	58
Stay	Maurice Williams & the Zodiacs	58

4
TOP 100 OLDIE INSTRUMENTALS

While some of the songs listed contain a chorus or whistling or a small amount of vocal, they are considered instrumentals by the authors. These songs are rated in the same way as the statistical 100. Songs with † were recorded (as instrumentals) by more than one artist at the same time. Artists shown had the biggest hit. Following the Top 100 is a list of "extras."

NO.	SONG	ARTIST	POINTS
1.	So Rare	Jimmy Dorsey	77
†2.	Canadian Sunset	Hugo Winterhalter	70
3.	Honky Tonk	Bill Doggett	68
†4.	Lisbon Antigua	Nelson Riddle	68
†5.	Autumn Leaves	Roger Williams	67
6.	Cherry Pink & Apple Blossom White	Prez Prado	66
†7.	Moonglow & Theme from Picnic	Morris Stoloff	66
†8.	Poor People of Paris	Les Baxter	64
9.	Sail Along Silvery Moon	Billy Vaughn	62
†10.	Stranger on the Shore	Mr. Acker Bilk	61
11.	Theme from a Summer Place	Percy Faith	61
12.	Patricia	Prez Prado	61
†13.	Exodus	Ferrante & Teicher	60
†14.	Tequila	Champs	59
15.	Topsy II	Cozy Cole	59
†16.	Last Date	Floyd Cramer	59
†17.	Raunchy	Bill Justis	58
18.	Sleep Walk	Santo & Johnny	58
19.	The Happy Organ	Dave "Baby" Cortez	57
†20.	Wonderland by Night	Bert Kaempfert	57
21.	The Stripper	David Rose	57
22.	The Shifting Whispering Sands	Billy Vaughn	57
23.	Walk-Don't Run	Ventures	57
24.	Calcutta	Lawrence Welk	57

NO.	SONG	ARTIST	POINTS
25.	In the Mood	Ernie Fields	56
26.	Apache	Jorgen Ingmann	56
27.	Moon River	Henry Mancini	56
28.	Telstar	Tornadoes	56
29.	Wipe Out	Surfaris	55
30.	Fingertips Part 2	Little Stevie Wonder	55
31.	Green Onions	Booker T. & M.G.'s	54
32.	Tea for Two Cha Cha	Tommy Dorsey	54
33.	Soft Summer Breeze	Eddie Heywood	54
†34.	Wheels	String-a-Longs	54
35.	Midnight in Moscow	Kenny Ball	53
36.	Pipeline	Chantays	53
37.	Quiet Village	Martin Denny	53
38.	Java	Al Hirt	53
39.	Red River Rock	Johnny & the Hurricanes	53
40.	Teen Beat	Sandy Nelson	53
41.	Washington Square	Village Stompers	53
42.	Alley Cat	Bent Fabric	52
43.	Because They're Young	Duane Eddy	52
†44.	Theme From the Three Penny Opera (Moritat)	Dick Hyman Trio	52
45.	Out of Limits	Marketts	52
46.	Last Night	Mar-Keys	52
47.	The Happy Whistler	Don Robertson	52
48.	Guitar Boogie Shuffle	Virtues	52
49.	Petit Fleur	Chris Barber's Jazz Band	51
50.	Theme From the Apartment	Ferrante & Teicher	51
51.	A Taste of Honey	Herb Alpert & the Tijuana Brass	50
52.	Peter Gunn	Ray Anthony	50
53.	On the Rebound	Floyd Cramer	50
54.	Let There Be Drums	Sandy Nelson	50
55.	Wild Weekend	Rebels	50
56.	The Lonely Bull	Herb Alpert & the Tijuana Brass	49
57.	Maria Elena	Los Indios Trabajaras	49
58.	Yellow Bird	Arthur Lyman	49
59.	Memphis	Lonnie Mack	49
60.	March from the River Kwai & Colonel Bogey	Mitch Miller	49
61.	Mexico	Bob Moore	49
†62.	Around the World	Victor Young	49

126

NO.	SONG	ARTIST	POINTS
63.	Rebel Rouser	Duane Eddy	48
64.	Manhattan Spiritual	Reg Owen	48
65.	Only You	Frank Pourcell	48
66.	Near You	Roger Williams	48
67.	More	Kai Winding	48
68.	Forty Miles of Bad Road.	Duane Eddy	47
69.	Asia Minor	Kokomo	47
70.	One Mint Julep	Ray Charles	46
71.	Tonight	Ferrante & Teicher	46
72.	Our Winter Love	Bill Pursell	46
†73.	White Silver Sands	Bill Black's Combo	45
74.	Rinky Dink	Dave "Baby" Cortez	45
75.	San Antonio Rose	Floyd Cramer	45
76.	Cast Your Fate to the Wind	Sounds Orchestral	45
77.	Percolator	Billy Joe & the Checkmates	44
78.	Don't Be Cruel	Bill Black's Combo	43
†79.	Theme from the Man with the Golden Arm	Richard Maltby	43
80.	Zorba the Greek	Herb Alpert & the Tijuana Brass	42
81.	Tracy's Theme	Spencer Ross	42
82.	Watermelon Man	Mongo Santamaria	42
83.	Hot Pastrami	Dartells	41
84.	Poor Boy	Royal Tones	41
85.	Mexican Hat Rock	Applejacks	40
86.	Tuff	Ace Cannon	40
87.	Bongo Rock	Preston Epps	40
88.	Fly Me to the Moon—Bossa Nova	Joe Harnell	40
89.	A Swingin' Safari	Billy Vaughn	40
90.	Beatnik Fly	Johnny & the Hurricanes	39
91.	Perfidia	Ventures	39
92.	Rumble	Link Wray	39
93.	Never on Sunday	Don Costa	38
94.	Cannonball	Duane Eddy	38
95.	Woo-Hoo	Rock-a-Teens	37
†96.	Slow Walk	Sil Austin	36
97.	Smokie-Pt. 2	Bill Black's Combo	36
†98.	Almost Paradise	Roger Williams	35
99.	Petticoats of Portugal	Dick Jacobs	34
100.	Mr. Lucky	Henry Mancini	33

INSTRUMENTAL "EXTRAS"

SONG	ARTIST	POINTS
Bonanza	Al Caiola	32
Portuguese Washerwomen	Joe "Fingers" Carr	32
Crossfire	Johnny & the Hurricanes	32
The Lonely One	Duane Eddy	31
Foot Stompin' Pt. 1	Flares	31
Bumble Boogie	B. Bumble & the Stingers	30
The Italian Theme	Cyril Stapleton	30

5
NUMBER-ONE SONGS
1953-1965

Ever wonder how many songs made *Number One?* From over 2,700 oldies came only 166 that were #1 in the nation.

Shirelles *(courtesy Arlene Gallup)*

1953
The Song from Moulin Rouge . . . . Percy Faith (with
Felicia Sanders)

1954
Mr. Sandman . . . . Chordettes
Sh-Boom . . . . Crew Cuts
Secret Love . . . . Doris Day
Hearts of Stone . . . . Fontane Sisters
Little Things Mean a Lot . . . . Kitty Kallen
Sincerely . . . . McGuire Sisters
Let Me Go Lover . . . . Joan Weber

1955
Sixteen Tons . . . . Ernie Ford
Love is a Many Splendored Thing . . . . Four Aces
Melody of Love . . . . Four Aces
Rock Around the Clock . . . . Bill Haley & the
Comets
Ballad of Davey Crockett . . . . Bill Hayes
Memories are Made of This . . . . Dean Martin
The Yellow Rose of Texas . . . . Mitch Miller
The Great Pretender . . . . Platters
Cherry Pink & Apple Blossom White . . . . . . Prez Prado
Rock & Roll Waltz . . . . Kay Starr
Autumn Leaves . . . . Roger Williams

1956
The Poor People of Paris . . . . Les Baxter
I Almost Lost My Mind . . . . Pat Boone
Don't Forbid Me . . . . Pat Boone
The Wayward Wind . . . . Gogi Grant
The Green Door . . . . Jim Lowe
Singing the Blues . . . . Guy Mitchell
My Prayer . . . . Platters
Heartbreak Hotel . . . . Elvis Presley

Don't Be Cruel . . . . Elvis Presley
Love Me Tender . . . . Elvis Presley

1957
Love Letters in the Sand . . . . Pat Boone
April Love . . . . Pat Boone
Round & Round. . . . . Perry Como
You Send Me . . . . Sam Cooke
At the Hop. . . . . Danny & the
                                                        Juniors
Wake Up Little Susie. . . . . Everly Brothers
Young Love . . . . Tab Hunter
All Shook Up. . . . . Elvis Presley
(Let Me Be Your) Teddy Bear . . . . Elvis Presley
Jailhouse Rock. Elvis Presley
Tammy . . . . Debbie Reynolds
Honeycomb . . . . Jimmie Rodgers
Butterfly . . . . Andy Williams

1958
Tequila . . . . Champs
The Chipmunk Song . . . . Chipmunks
Yakety Yak. . . . . Coasters
It's All in the Game . . . . Tommy Edwards
Little Star . . . . Elegants
All I Have to Do Is Dream . . . . Everly Brothers
Tom Dooley . . . . Kingston Trio
Nel Blu Di Pinto Di Blu. . . . . Domenico
                                                        Modugno
Poor Little Fool. . . . . Ricky Nelson
Smoke Gets in Your Eyes . . . . Platters
Twilight Time. Platters
Patricia . . . . Prez Prado
Don't . . . . Elvis Presley
Stagger Lee . . . . Lloyd Price
Witch Doctor . . . . David Seville
Get a Job. . . . . Silhouettes
To Know Him Is to Love Him . . . . Teddy Bears
It's Only Make Believe. . . . . Conway Twitty
The Purple People Eater . . . . Sheb Wooley

1959
Lonely Boy. . . . . Paul Anka
Venus. . . . . Frankie Avalon

132

Why . . . . Frankie Avalon
The Three Bells . . . . Browns
The Happy Organ . . . . Dave "Baby"
                                                   Cortez
Mack the Knife . . . . Bobby Darin
Teen Angel . . . . Mark Dinning
Come Softly to Me . . . . Fleetwoods
Mr. Blue . . . . Fleetwoods
Kansas City . . . . Wilbert Harrison
The Battle of New Orleans . . . . Johnny Horton
Heartaches by the Number . . . . Guy Mitchell
A Big Hunk O' Love . . . . Elvis Presley
Running Bear . . . . Johnny Preston
El Paso . . . . Marty Robbins
Sleep Walk . . . . Santo & Johnny

1960
Georgia on My Mind . . . . Ray Charles
The Twist . . . . Chubby Checker
Save the Last Dance for Me . . . . Drifters
Cathy's Clown . . . . Everly Brothers
Theme from a Summer Place . . . . Percy Faith
Everybody's Somebody's Fool . . . . Connie Francis
My Heart Has a Mind of It's Own . . . . Connie Francis
Alley Oop . . . . Hollywood Argyles
Itsy Bitsy Teenie Weenie
    Yellow Polka Dot Bikini . . . . Brian Hyland
Wonderland by Night . . . . Bert Kaempfert
I'm Sorry . . . . Brenda Lee
I Want To Be Wanted . . . . Brenda Lee
Are You Lonesome Tonight . . . . Elvis Presley
It's Now or Never . . . . Elvis Presley
Stuck on You . . . . Elvis Presley
Will You Love Me Tomorrow . . . . Shirelles
Mr. Custer . . . . Larry Verne
Calcutta . . . . Lawrence Welk
Stay . . . . Maurice Williams
                                                   & the Zodiacs

1961
Quarter To Three . . . . Gary "U.S." Bonds
Moody River . . . . Pat Boone
Hit the Road, Jack . . . . Ray Charles
Pony Time . . . . Chubby Checker

133

Big Bad John. Jimmy Dean
The Peppermint Twist. . . . . Joey Dee & the
                                          Starliters
Runaround Sue . . . . Dion
Wooden Heart. . . . . Joe Dowell
Michael . . . . Highwaymen
Mother-in-Law. . . . . Ernie-K-Doe
Tossin' & Turnin'. . . . . Bobby Lewis
Blue Moon . . . . Marcels
Please Mr. Postman. . . . . Marvelettes
Travelin' Man . . . . Ricky Nelson
Running Scared . . . . Roy Orbison
Surrender. . . . . Elvis Presley
Runaway . . . . Del Shannon
The Lion Sleeps Tonight . . . . Tokens
Take Good Care of My Baby . . . . Bobby Vee

1962

Stranger on the Shore . . . . Mr. Acker Bilk
Duke of Earl. Gene Chandler
Hey! Baby . . . . Bruce Channel
I Can't Stop Loving You. . . . . Ray Charles
He's a Rebel . . . . Crystals
Johnny Angel . . . . Shelly Fabares
Big Girls Don't Cry. . . . . Four Seasons
Sherry. . . . . Four Seasons
Don't Break the Heart That Loves You . . . . Connie Francis
Go Away Little Girl . . . . Steve Lawrence
The Loco-Motion . . . . Little Eva
Hey Paula . . . . Paul & Paula
Monster Mash . . . . Bobby (Boris)
                                          Pickett
Good Luck Charm . . . . Elvis Presley
Sheila . . . . Tommy Roe
The Stripper. David Rose
Breaking Up Is Hard To Do . . . . Neil Sedaka
Soldier Boy. . . . . Shirelles
Telstar. . . . . Tornadoes
Roses Are Red. . . . . Bobby Vinton

1963

My Boyfriend's Back . . . . Angels
He's So Fine . . . . Chiffons
I'm Leaving It Up To You. . . . . Dale & Grace

134

Easier Said Than Done . . . . Essex
Walk Like a Man . . . . Four Seasons
Sugar Shack . . . . Jimmy Gilmer &
                                 the Fireballs
It's My Party. . . . . Lesley Gore
Surf City . . . . Jan & Dean
I Will Follow Him . . . . Little Peggy
                                 March
Walk Right In . . . . Rooftop Singers
Our Day Will Come . . . . Ruby & the
                                 Romantics
Sukiyaki. Kyu Sakamoto
Dominique . . . . Singing Nun
If You Wanna Be Happy. . . . . Jimmy Soul
Deep Purple. . . . . Nino Tempo &
                                 April Stevens
So Much in Love . . . . Tymes
Blue Velvet . . . . Bobby Vinton
There! I've Said It Again . . . . Bobby Vinton
Fingertips—Part 2 . . . . Little Stevie
                                 Wonder

1964
I Get Around . . . . Beach Boys
Chapel of Love . . . . Dixie Cups
Rag Doll . . . . Four Seasons
Ringo . . . . Lorne Greene
Do Wah Diddy Diddy . . . . Manfred Mann
Oh! Pretty Woman . . . . Roy Orbison
You've Lost That Lovin' Feelin' . . . . Righteous Brothers
Leader of the Pack . . . . Shangri-Las
Mr. Lonely . . . . Bobby Vinton
My Guy. . . . . Mary Wells

1965
Help Me Rhonda . . . . Beach Boys
I Can't Help Myself . . . . Four Tops

135

Beach Boys *(Capitol)*

6
ARTISTS OF THE YEAR
SONGS OF THE YEAR

Brenda Lee *(MCA)*

Each year produced a number of super hits and outstanding artists. The following compilations show some of these.

The classic oldies of each year are shown by the authors' selection of no more than ten "Songs of the Year." While some of the songs were done by more than one artist, the version shown is our choice.

"Artists of the Year" is intended to show our opinion of no more than three artists who topped them all.

The one noted exception is 1957, by far the biggest year for super oldies. It is impossible to list any fewer than four artists and twenty-five songs.

1953
Artists: Teresa Brewer
Dean Martin
Songs: The Song from Moulin Rouge (Percy Faith with Felicia Sanders)
That's Amore (Dean Martin)

1954
Artists: Crew Cuts
Bill Haley & the Comets
Songs: Hearts of Stone (Charms)
Sh-Boom (Crew Cuts)
Shake, Rattle and Roll (Bill Haley & the Comets)

1955
Artists: Bill Haley & the Comets
Platters
Songs: 16 Tons (Ernie Ford)
Rock Around the Clock (Bill Haley & the Comets)
Memories are Made of This (Dean Martin)
Only You (Platters)
The Great Pretender (Platters)
Cherry Pink & Apple Blossom White (Prez Prado)
Rock & Roll Waltz (Kay Starr)

1956

Artists: Fats Domino
Platters
Elvis Presley

Songs: Blueberry Hill (Fats Domino)
In the Still of the Nite (Five Satins)
The Wayward Wind (Gogi Grant)
The Green Door (Jim Lowe)
My Prayer (Platters)
Don't be Cruel/Hound Dog (Elvis Presley)
Heartbreak Hotel (Elvis Presley)
I Want You, I Need You, I Love You (Elvis Presley)
Love Me Tender (Elvis Presley)
Be-Bop-A-Lula (Gene Vincent)

1957

Artists: Chuck Berry
Pat Boone
Johnny Mathis
Elvis Presley

Songs: Diana (Paul Anka)
School Day (Chuck Berry)
Mr. Lee (Bobettes)
Love Letters in the Sand (Pat Boone)
Searchin' (Coasters)
Round & Round (Perry Como)
You Send Me (Sam Cooke)
At the Hop (Danny & the Juniors)
Come Go With Me (Del Vikings)
Little Darlin' (Diamonds)
So Rare (Jimmy Dorsey)
Bye Bye Love (Everly Brothers)
Wake Up Little Susie (Everly Brothers)
Peggy Sue (Buddy Holly)
Young Love (Tab Hunter or Sonny James)
Party Doll (Buddy Knox)
Whole Lot of Shakin' Going On (Jerry Lee Lewis)
It's Not for Me to Say (Johnny Mathis)
Chances Are (Johnny Mathis)
All Shook Up (Elvis Presley)
Jailhouse Rock (Elvis Presley)
(Let Me Be Your) Teddy Bear (Elvis Presley)
Tammy (Debbie Reynolds)
A White Sport Coat (Marty Robbins)
Honeycomb (Jimmie Rodgers)

1958

Artists: Everly Brothers
Ricky Nelson
Elvis Presley

Songs: Chantilly Lace (Big Bopper)
It's All in the Game (Tommy Edwards)
Little Star (Elegants)
All I Have to Do is Dream (Everly Brothers)
Who's Sorry Now (Connie Francis)
Poor Little Fool (Ricky Nelson)
Don't (Elvis Presley)
Stagger Lee (Lloyd Price)
It's Only Make Believe (Conway Twitty)
Donna (Ritchie Valens)

1959

Artists: Paul Anka
Bobby Darin
Connie Francis

Songs: Put Your Head on My Shoulder (Paul Anka)
Venus (Frankie Avalon)
Dream Lover (Bobby Darin)
Mack the Knife (Bobby Darin)
Mr. Blue (Fleetwoods)
Kansas City (Wilbert Harrison)
The Battle of New Orleans (Johnny Horton)
Running Bear (Johnny Preston)

1960

Artists: Connie Francis
Elvis Presley
Neil Sedaka

Songs: The Twist (Chubby Checker)
Save the Last Dance for Me (Drifters)
Theme from a Summer Place (Percy Faith)
Everybody's Somebody's Fool (Connie Francis)
Handyman (Jimmy Jones)
I'm Sorry (Brenda Lee)
It's Now or Never (Elvis Presley)
Will You Love Me Tomorrow (Shirelles)
16 Reasons (Connie Stevens)

1961

Artists: Brenda Lee
Roy Orbison
Songs: Big Bad John (Jimmy Dean)
Runaround Sue (Dion)
Mother-in-Law (Ernie-K-Doe)
Fool #1 (Brenda Lee)
Tossin' & Turnin' (Bobby Lewis)
Travelin' Man (Ricky Nelson)
Runaway (Del Shannon)

1962

Artists: Four Seasons
Elvis Presley
Shirelles
Songs: Duke of Earl (Gene Chandler)
Johnny Angel (Shelly Fabares)
Sherry (Four Seasons)
Hey Paula (Paul & Paula)
Monster Mash (Bobby Boris Pickett)
Soldier Boy (Shirelles)

1963

Artists: Beach Boys
Bobby Vinton
Songs: Surfin' U.S.A. (Beach Boys)
I'm Leaving It up to You (Dale & Grace)
Sugar Shack (Jimmy Gilmer & the Fireballs)
Surf City (Jan & Dean)
Dominique (Singing Nun)
Blue Velvet (Bobby Vinton)

1964

Artists: Beach Boys
Four Seasons
Bobby Vinton
Songs: I Get Around (Beach Boys)
Under the Boardwalk (Drifters)
Rag Doll (Four Seasons)
Pretty Woman (Roy Orbison)
You've Lost That Lovin' Feelin' (Righteous Brothers)
Mr. Lonely (Bobby Vinton)
My Guy (Mary Wells)

1965
Artists: Beach Boys
Jay & the Americans
Righteous Brothers
Songs: Help Me Rhonda (Beach Boys)
Cara Mia (Jay & the Americans)
A Lover's Concerto (Toys)

Ricky Nelson *(MCA)*

7
MOST PRODUCTIVE
ARTISTS

The Top 40 was the measure of success for every recording artist. Based on the total number of songs reaching the
national Top 40, the following are the most productive
male, female and group artists of the rock 'n' roll years.

Neil Sedaka *(R.C.A.)*

MALE

ARTIST	NUMBER OF SONGS IN TOP 40
Elvis Presley	70
Pat Boone	37
Fats Domino	36
Ricky Nelson	33
Sam Cooke	28
Paul Anka	23
Ray Charles	22
Chubby Checker	22
Brook Benton	21
Perry Como	21
Andy Williams	20
Roy Orbison	20
Jackie Wilson	20
Nat "King" Cole	19
Bobby Darin	19
Bobby Rydell	19
Bobby Vinton	17
Dion	14
Chuck Berry	13
Johnny Mathis	13
Gene Pitney	13
Neil Sedaka	13

FEMALE

ARTIST	NUMBER OF SONGS IN TOP 40
Connie Francis	35
Brenda Lee	27
Patti Page	13
Teresa Brewer	11

ARTIST	NUMBER OF SONGS IN TOP 40
Lesley Gore	10
Mary Wells	10
Lavern Baker	7
Georgia Gibbs	7
Etta James	7
Joni James	6
Gale Storm	6
Dinah Washington	6
Annette	5
Patsy Cline	5
Dee Dee Sharp	5
Sue Thompson	5
Sarah Vaughn	5
Anita Bryant	4
Skeeter Davis	4
Eydie Gorme	4
Barbara Lewis	4

GROUP

GROUP	NUMBER OF SONGS IN TOP 40
Everly Brothers	25
Platters	20
Four Seasons	18
Beach Boys	16
Drifters	16
Duane Eddy	15
Bill Haley & the Comets	15
Jan & Dean	13
Shirelles	12
Smokey Robinson & the Miracles	12
Diamonds	11
Four Lads	11
McGuire Sisters	11
Billy Vaughn	11
Chordettes	10
Coasters	10
Impressions	10
Dion & the Belmonts	9
Fleetwoods	9

8
ARTISTS WITH TWO OR MORE #1 SONGS

Of all the oldies that made No. 1 nationally, only twenty artists had two or more.

9

HITS BY MORE THAN ONE ARTIST

Many oldies were recorded and became hits by more than one artist. This happened in two ways.

First, remakes of hit songs, a few years after the originals, were not uncommon. Here are some prime examples.

C. C. Rider	Chuck Willis	1957
	Lavern Baker	1962
Devil or Angel	Clovers	1956
	Bobby Vee	1960
Fever	Little Willie John	1956
	Peggy Lee	1958
Goodnight My Love	Jessie Belvin	1956
	Ray Peterson	1959
Mountain of Love	Harold Dorman	1960
	Johnny Rivers	1964
Tragedy	Thomas Wayne	1959
	Fleetwoods	1961
You Don't Know Me	Jerry Vale	1956
	Ray Charles	1962

Second, and more important, were those oldies which were hits by more than one artist *at the same time.* Following is a list of the most outstanding examples of a song by more than one artist reaching the Top 40. A number of songs that were hits by more than one artist do not appear here, because one version did not make the Top 40—for example, "You Cheated" was a hit by both the Shields and the Slades. The Shield's version reached #15, but the slades reached only #42; There were three versions of "The Yellow Rose of Texas," but only the two artists reaching the Top 40 appear.

			POSITION
SONG	ARTIST	YEAR	NUMBER
Ain't That (It) a Shame	Pat Boone	1955	2
	Fats Domino	1955	16

| | | | POSITION |
SONG	ARTIST	YEAR	NUMBER
Alley-Oop	Dante & the		
	Evergreens.	1960 . . .	15
	Hollywood Argyles . .	1960	1
Almost Paradise	Lou Stein	1957 . . .	31
	Roger Williams.	1957 . . .	26
Around the World . . .	Montovani	1957 . . .	25
	Victor Young	1957 . . .	26
At My Front Door . . .	Pat Boone.	1955	7
	El Dorados	1955 . . .	35
Autumn Leaves	Steve Allen	1955 . . .	35
	Roger Williams.	1955	1
Ballad of Davy			
Crockett	Ernie Ford	1955	6
	Bill Hayes.	1955	1
	Fes Parker	1955 . . .	15
Banana Boat Song . . .	Harry Belafonte	1956	5
	Fontane Sisters.	1956 . . .	22
	Steve Lawrence	1956 . . .	30
	Vince Martin & the		
	Tarriers.	1956	6
	Sarah Vaughn	1956 . . .	31
Band of Gold	Don Cherry.	1955	5
	Kit Carson	1955 . . .	17
Black Denim Trousers .	Cheers.	1955	6
	Vaughn Monroe	1955 . . .	38
Blue Suede Shoes	Carl Perkins	1956	4
	Elvis Presley	1956 . . .	24
Blueberry Hill	Louis Armstrong. . . .	1956 . . .	29
	Fats Domino	1956	4
Bo Weevil	Teresa Brewer	1956 . . .	17
	Fats Domino	1956 . . .	35
Butterfly	Charlie Gracie	1956	7
	Andy Williams	1957	1
Canadian Sunset	Andy Williams	1956	8
	Hugo Winterhalter . .	1956	2
Children's Marching			
Song	Mitch Miller	1959 . . .	16
	Cyril Stapleton.	1959 . . .	13
Cinco Robles.	Russell Arms	1957 . . .	23
	Les Paul & Mary		
	Ford.	1957 . . .	35

			POSITION
SONG	ARTIST	YEAR	NUMBER
Cindy Oh Cindy	Eddie Fisher	1956 . . .	10
	Vince Martin & the		
	Tarriers.	1956 . . .	12
Crying in the Chapel. .	Sonny Til & the		
	Orioles	1953 . . .	11
	June Valli	1953	6
Daddy-O	Bonnie Lou.	1955 . . .	28
	Fontane Sisters.	1955 . . .	11
Dance with Me			
Henry	Georgia Gibbs	1955	2
	Etta James	1955 . . .	12
Dark Moon.	Bonnie Guitar	1957	8
	Gale Storm	1957	5
Days of Wine & Roses .	Henry Mancini.	1963 . . .	33
	Andy Williams	1963 . . .	26
Dear Heart.	Jack Jones.	1964 . . .	30
	Andy Williams	1964 . . .	24
Early in the Morning. .	Buddy Holly	1958 . . .	32
	Rinky-Dinks	1958 . . .	24
Earth Angel	Crew Cuts	1955	8
	Penguins	1954	8
Eddie My Love	Chordettes	1956 . . .	18
	Fontane Sisters.	1956 . . .	12
	Teen Queens.	1956 . . .	22
11th Hour Melody . . .	Lou Busch	1956 . . .	35
	Al Hibbler	1956 . . .	21
Exodus	Ferrante & Teicher. .	1960	2
	Eddie Harris	1961 . . .	36
	Montovani	1960 . . .	31
Four Walls	Jim Lowe	1957 . . .	20
	Jim Reeves	1957 . . .	12
From the Vine Came			
the Grape	Gaylords.	1954	8
	Hilltoppers	1954 . . .	12
Gee Whiz	Innocents	1961 . . .	28
	Carla Thomas	1961 . . .	10
Go on with the			
Wedding.	Kitty Kallen	1955 . . .	39
	Patti Page.	1955 . . .	11
Goodnight Sweetheart .	McGuire Sisters	1954	8
	Spaniels	1954	5

			POSITION
SONG	ARTIST	YEAR	NUMBER
Graduation Day	Four Freshmen	1956	27
	Rover Boys	1956	20
Happiness Street	Tony Bennett	1956	38
	Georgia Gibbs	1956	25
He	Al Hibbler	1955	7
	McGuire Sisters	1955	12
Heart & Soul	Cleftones	1961	18
	Jan & Dean	1961	25
Hot Rod Lincoln	Johnny Bond	1960	26
	Charlie Ryan	1960	33
Hula Hoop Song	Teresa Brewer	1958	38
	Georgia Gibbs	1958	32
Hummingbird	Chordettes	1955	8
	Les Paul & Mary Ford	1955	10
I Hear You Knockin'	Smiley Lewis	1955	2
	Gale Storm	1955	2
I'll Be Home	Pat Boone	1956	5
	Flamingos	1956	10
I'm in Love Again	Fats Domino	1956	5
	Fontane Sisters	1956	38
I'm Walkin'	Fats Domino	1957	5
	Ricky Nelson	1957	7
In the Middle of the House	Rusty Draper	1956	20
	Vaughn Monroe	1956	21
Innamorata	Dean Martin	1956	27
	Jerry Vale	1956	30
It's Almost Tomorrow	David Carroll	1955	34
	Dream Weavers	1955	8
	Snooky Lanson	1955	20
	Jo Stafford	1955	19
Ivory Tower	Cathy Carr	1956	6
	Gale Storm	1956	6
	Otis Williams & the Charms	1956	12
Joker, The	Hilltoppers	1957	37
	Billy Myles	1957	30
Ka-Ding-Dong	Diamonds	1956	35
	Hilltoppers	1956	38
Ko Ko Mo	Perry Como	1955	4
	Crew Cuts	1955	10
	Gene & Eunice	1955	7

158

SONG	ARTIST	YEAR	POSITION NUMBER
Last Date	Floyd Cramer	1960	2
	Lawrence Welk	1960	21
Let Me Go Lover	Teresa Brewer	1954	8
	Joan Weber	1954	1
Limbo Rock	Champs	1962	40
	Chubby Checker	1962	2
Ling Ting Tong	Charms	1955	26
	Five Keys	1954	28
Lisbon Antigua	Mitch Miller	1956	30
	Nelson Riddle	1955	2
Lollipop	Chordettes	1958	2
	Ronald & Ruby	1958	39
Long Tall Sally	Pat Boone	1956	18
	Little Richard	1956	13
Look for a Star	Dean Hawley	1960	29
	Garry Miles	1960	16
	Gary Mills	1960	26
	Billy Vaughn	1960	19
Love is a Many Splendored Thing	Don Cornell	1955	7
	Four Aces	1955	1
Love Love Love	Clovers	1956	30
	Diamonds	1956	30
Mack the Knife	Bobby Darin	1959	1
	Ella Fitzgerald	1960	27
Mama Sang a Song	Walter Brennan	1962	38
	Stan Kenton	1962	32
Marianne	Terry Gilkyson & the Easy Riders	1957	5
	Hilltoppers	1957	8
Melody of Love	David Carroll	1954	2
	Four Aces	1955	1
	Billy Vaughn	1954	2
Memories Are Made of This	Dean Martin	1955	1
	Gale Storm	1955	16
Mr. Wonderful	Teddi King	1956	32
	Peggy Lee	1956	23
	Sarah Vaughn	1956	38
Mona Lisa	Carl Mann	1959	25
	Conway Twitty	1959	29

SONG	ARTIST	YEAR	POSITION NUMBER
Moon River	Jerry Butler	1961	11
	Henry Mancini	1961	11
Moonglow & Theme from Picnic	George Cates	1956	4
	McGuire Sisters	1956	13
	Morris Stoloff	1956	2
My Boy Flat Top	Boyd Bennett & the Rockets	1955	39
	Dorothy Collins	1955	22
My Coloring Book	Kitty Kallen	1962	18
	Sandy Stewart	1962	20
No More	DeJohn Sisters	1954	8
	McGuire Sisters	1955	23
Nuttin' for Christmas	Barry Gordon	1955	7
	Fontane Sisters	1955	36
	Joe Ward	1955	22
	Ricky Zhand	1955	40
On the Street Where You Live	Vic Damone	1956	8
	Eddie Fisher	1956	28
Only You	Hilltoppers	1955	9
	Platters	1955	1
Party Doll	Buddy Knox	1957	2
	Steve Lawrence	1957	10
Pledge of Love	Ken Copeland	1957	17
	Mitchell Torok	1957	26
Poor People of Paris	Les Baxter	1956	1
	Russ Morgan	1956	26
Raunchy	Ernie Freeman	1957	12
	Bill Justis	1957	3
	Billy Vaughn	1957	33
Rip It Up	Bill Haley & the Comets	1956	30
	Little Richard	1956	27
Seven Days	Dorothy Collins	1955	22
	Crew Cuts	1956	20
Seventeen	Boyd Bennett & the Rockets	1955	5
	Fontane Sisters	1955	6
Sh-Boom	Chords	1954	9
	Crew Cuts	1954	1

SONG	ARTIST	YEAR	POSITION NUMBER
Shake, Rattle & Roll . .	Bill Haley & the Comets	1954	7
	Joe Turner	1954	2
Shangri-La	Vic Dana	1964	27
	Robert Maxwell	1964	15
Shifting Whispering Sands	Rusty Draper.	1955	7
	Billy Vaughn	1955	5
Sincerely	McGuire Sisters	1954	1
	Harvey & the Moonglows.	1954	2
Singing the Blues	Guy Mitchell	1956	1
	Marty Robbins	1956	26
Sittin' in the Balcony. .	Eddie Cochran.	1957	18
	Johnny Dee.	1957	38
Slow Walk	Sil Austin	1956	19
	Bill Doggett	1956	26
Song from Moulin Rouge	Percy Faith (with Felicia Sanders) . . .	1953	1
	Mantovani.	1953	13
Standing on the Corner	Four Lads.	1956	3
	Dean Martin	1956	29
Story Untold	Crew Cuts	1956	16
	Nutmegs.	1955	2
Stranded in the Jungle	Cadets.	1956	18
	Gadabouts.	1956	39
	Jayhawks	1956	29
Stranger on the Shore .	Mr. Acker Bilk.	1962	1
	Andy Williams	1962	38
Tammy	Ames Brothers	1957	29
	Debbie Reynolds . . .	1957	1
Teenage Prayer	Gloria Mann	1956	21
	Gale Storm	1955	9
Tequila	Champs	1958	1
	Eddie Platt	1958	35
The Day the Rains Came.	Jane Morgan	1958	21
	Raymond LeFevre . .	1958	30

SONG	ARTIST	YEAR	POSITION NUMBER
The Three Bells.	Browns	1959	 1
	Dick Flood	1959	. . . 23
Theme from the Man with the Golden Arm.	Elmer Bernstein. . . .	1956	. . . 32
	Richard Maltby	1956	. . . 14
Theme from the Three Penny Opera (Moritat)	Louis Armstrong. . . .	1956	. . . 20
	Richard Hayman. . . .	1956	. . . 12
	Dick Hyman Trio . . .	1956	 9
	Billy Vaughn	1956	. . . 37
	Lawrence Welk	1956	. . . 31
Tonight You Belong to Me.	Lennon Sisters	1956	. . . 15
	Patience & Prudence.	1956	 6
True Love	Bing Crosby & Grace Kelly	1956	 4
	Jane Powell.	1956	. . . 24
Tutti Fruitti	Pat Boone.	1956	. . . 12
	Little Richard	1955	. . . 21
Tweedle Dee	Lavern Baker.	1955	. . . 22
	Georgia Gibbs	1955	 3
Twist, The	Hank Ballard & the Midnighters	1960	. . . 28
	Chubby Checker. . . .	1960	 1
Unchained Melody . . .	Roy Hamilton	1955	 9
	Al Hibbler	1955	. . . 19
Volare[1]	Dean Martin	1958	. . . 15
	Dominico Modugno. .	1958	 1
Wake the Town & Tell the People.	Les Baxter	1955	. . . 10
	Mindy Carson	1955	. . . 20
Wayward Wind	Gogi Grant	1956	 1
	Tex Ritter.	1956	. . . 28
Wheels	String-a-Longs	1961	 3
	Billy Vaughn	1961	. . . 28
When the White Lilacs Bloom Again	Billy Vaughn	1956	. . . 22
	Helmut Zacharias . . .	1956	. . . 16

[1]Modugno's version was known as "Nel Blu Di Pinto Di Blu."

162

			POSITION
SONG	ARTIST	YEAR	NUMBER
White Silver Sands . . .	Dave Gardner	1957 . . .	28
	Don Rondo	1957 . . .	10
Why Do Fools Fall in			
Love	Diamonds	1956 . . .	16
	Frankie Lymon & the		
	Teenagers	1956	7
	Gale Storm	1956 . . .	15
Wonderland by Night .	Anita Bryant	1960 . . .	18
	Bert Kaempfert	1960	1
	Louis Prima	1960 . . .	15
Wringle Wrangle	Bill Hayes	1957 . . .	33
	Fes Parker	1957 . . .	21
Yellow Rose of Texas . .	Johnny Desmond . . .	1955	6
	Mitch Miller	1955	1
You Send Me	Teresa Brewer	1957 . . .	31
	Sam Cooke	1957	1
Young Love	Crew Cuts	1957 . . .	24
	Tab Hunter	1957	1
	Sonny James	1956	2

10
COMBINED ARTISTS

A number of oldie hits were the result of two or more successful artists combining their talents on a single record.

Paul Anka—George Hamilton IV—Johnny Nash
    (The Teen Commandments, 1958)

Brook Benton & Dinah Washington
    (Baby (You've Got What It Takes), A Rockin' Good Way, 1960)

Betty Everett & Jerry Butler
    (Let It Be Me, 1964)

Marvin Gaye & Mary Wells
    (Once Upon a Time, What's the Matter with You Baby, 1964)

Steve Lawrence & Eydie Gorme
    (I Want to Stay Here, 1963)

Jane Morgan & Roger Williams
    (Two Different Worlds, 1956)

Bobby Rydell & Chubby Checker
    (Jingle Bell Rock, 1961/1962)

167

Kalin Twins *(courtesy Lee's Music Center, Miami, Fla.)*

Poni-Tails *(courtesy Lee's Music Center, Miami, Fla.)*

11

"ONE-HIT" ARTISTS

Throughout the rock 'n roll years, there were more than one hundred "one-hit" artists, each of whom had a record that made the Top 10, but never had another reach the Top 40. Included in these were 16 songs that reached #1 in the country (indicated below by *); of those, four were recorded by artists who never had another song reach the charts at all (indicated below by **). Listed below are a hundred of the best known.

The Boy From New York City . . . . Ad Libs
The Birds and the Bees . . . . Jewel Akens
Midnight in Moscow . . . . Kenny Ball
I've Had It . . . . Bell Notes
*Stranger On the Shore . . . . Mr. Acker Bilk
Percolator . . . . Billy Joe & the
                                              Checkmates
He'll Have to Stay . . . . Jeannie Black
Let the Little Girl Dance . . . . Billy Bland
Bobby's Girl . . . . Marcie Blane
Mr. Lee . . . . Bobbettes
There's a Moon Out Tonight . . . . Capris
Ivory Tower . . . . Cathy Carr
Rhythm of the Rain . . . . Cascades
*Hey! Baby . . . . Bruce Channel
Pipeline . . . . Chantays
A Million To One . . . . Jimmy Charles
Black Denim Trousers . . . . Cheers
Party Lights . . . . Claudine Clark
The Fool . . . . Sanford Clark
Baby Sittin' Boogie . . . . Buzz Clifford
Do You Love Me . . . . Contours
Oh Julie . . . . Crescendos
*Teen Angel . . . . Mark Dinning
My Heart is an Open Book . . . . Carl Dobkins, Jr.
What's Your Name . . . . Don & Juan
**Little Star . . . . Elegants

171

Mule Skinner Blues	Fendermen
Mockingbird	Inez Foxx
Keep On Dancing	Gentrys
I Know	Barbara George
*Ringo	Lorne Greene
Dark Moon	Bonnie Guitar
Rainbow	Russ Hamilton
Tie Me Kangaroo Down, Sport	Rolf Harris
Little Bitty Pretty One	Thurston Harris
Love You So	Ron Holden
**Alley-Oop	Hollywood Argyles
Little Honda	Hondells
Sorry (I Ran All the Way Home)	Impalas
Apache	Jorgen Ingmann
Waterloo	Stonewall Jackson
Jennie Lee	Jan & Arnie
Sally Go 'Round the Roses	Jaynetts
Over the Mountain; Across the Sea	Johnnie & Joe
You Talk Too Much	Joe Jones
Mother-In-Law	Ernie K-Doe
I Like It Like That	Chris Kenner
Wolverton Mountain	Claude King
Pretty Little Angel Eyes	Curtis Lee
Those Oldies But Goodies	Little Caesar & the Romans
Please Help Me I'm Falling	Hank Locklin
Sailor	Lolita
Susie Darlin'	Robin Luke
Let's Think About Living	Bob Luman
Who Put the Bomp	Barry Mann
Shout! Shout! (Knock Yourself Out)	Ernie Maresca
Last Night	Mar-Keys
Deck of Cards	Wink Martindale
From a Jack to a King	Ned Miller
*Nel Blu Dipinto Di Blu	Domenico Modugno
Book of Love	Monotones
Popsicles & Icicles	Murmaids
Willie and the Hand Jive	Johnny Otis
Manhatten Spiritual	Reg Owen
All American Boy	Bill Parsons
Blue Suede Shoes	Carl Perkins
Sea of Love	Phil Phillips

172

*Monster Mash	Bobby (Boris) Pickett
Born Too Late	Poni-Tails
Midnight Mary	Joey Powers
Denise	Randy & the Rainbows
Silhouettes	Rays
(Just Like) Romeo and Juliet	Reflections
Endless Sleep	Jody Reynolds
Angel Baby	Rosie & the Originals
Short Shorts	Royal Teens
Image of a Girl	Safaris
*Sukiyaki	Kyu Sakamoto
Let Me In	Sensations
Daddy's Home	Shep & the Limelites
This Time	Troy Shondell
**Get a Job	Silhouettes
**Dominique	Singing Nun
16 Reasons	Connie Stevens
Pink Shoe Laces	Dodie Stevens
What Kind of Fool (Do You Think I Am)	Tams
*To Know Him is to Love Him	Teddy Bears
Loop De Loop	Johnny Thunder
*Telstar	Tornadoes
Tell Him No	Travis & Bob
Happy Happy Birthday Baby	Tune Weavers
*Mr. Custer	Larry Verne
Washington Square	Village Stompers
Guitar Boogie Shuffle	Virtues
Tragedy	Thomas Wayne
White on White	Danny Williams
*Stay	Maurice Williams & the Zodiacs
Last Kiss	J. Frank Wilson & the Cavaliers
*Purple People Eater	Sheb Wooley
Dinner With Drac	John Zacherle

"The King" *(R.C.A.)*

12
THE MOST

ARTISTS WITH THE MOST #1 SONGS

ARTISTS WITH THE MOST
SONGS REACHING THE TOP 40

Mighty Good. 1959
Young Emotions. 1960
I'm Not Afraid. 1960
Yes Sir, That's My Baby 1960
You Are the Only One. 1961
Travelin' Man 1961
Hello Mary Lou. 1961
A Wonder Like You 1961
Everlovin' 1961
Young World. 1962
Teen Age Idol. 1962
It's Up to You 1962
String Along 1963
Fools Rush In 1963
For You. 1963
The Very Thought of You. 1964

ARTISTS WITH THE MOST SONGS IN AUTHORS' TOP 100

Elvis Presley. 10
  Don't Be Cruel/Hound Dog . . . . #2
  Heartbreak Hotel. . . . . #6
  All Shook Up. #9
  Love Me Tender . . . . #15
  I Want You, I Need You, I Love You . . . . #24
  (Let Me Be Your) Teddy Bear . . . . #32
  Jailhouse Rock. . . . . #52
  Don't . . . . #60
  Are You Lonesome Tonight. . . . . #70

Everly Brothers. 3
  Wake Up Little Susie. . . . . #14
  All I Have to Do Is Dream . . . . #38
  Bye Bye Love . . . . #44

Platters 3
  The Great Pretender. . . . . #3
  My Prayer . . . . #23
  Only You. . . . . #30

183

ARTISTS WITH THE MOST SONGS IN STATISTICAL TOP 100

ARTISTS WITH THE MOST SONGS IN TOP 100 INSTRUMENTALS

Duane Eddy. **4**
 Because They're Young . . . . #43
 Rebel Rouser . . . . #63
 Forty Miles of Bad Road. . . . . #68
 Cannonball. . . . . #94

Herb Alpert & the Tijuana Brass **3**
 A Taste of Honey. . . . . #51
 The Lonely Bull. . . . . #56
 Zorba The Greek . . . . #80

Bill Black's Combo. **3**
 White Silver Sands . . . . #73
 Don't Be Cruel . . . . #78
 Smokie—Pt. 2. #97

Floyd Cramer **3**
 Last Date. . . . . #16
 On the Rebound . . . . #53
 San Antonio Rose. . . . . #75

Ferrante & Teicher **3**
 Exodus . . . . #13
 Theme from the Apartment . . . . #50
 Tonight. . . . . #71

Billy Vaughn. **3**
 Sail Along Silvery Moon . . . . #9
 The Shifting Whispering Sands. . . . . #22
 A Swingin' Safari . . . . #89

Roger Williams **3**
 Autumn Leaves. #5
 Near You. . . . . #66
 Almost Paradise. . . . . #98

ARTISTS MOST
OFTEN SELECTED
"ARTIST OF THE YEAR"

Elvis Presley. 5
  1956
  1957
  1958
  1960
  1962

Beach Boys. 3
  1963
  1964
  1965

Four Seasons. 2
  1962
  1964

Connie Francis 2
  1959
  1960

Bill Haley & the Comets 2
  1954
  1955

Platters 2
  1955
  1956

Bobby Vinton 2
  1963
  1964

186

ARTISTS WITH THE MOST "SONGS OF THE YEAR"

Elvis Presley. 9
 Don't Be Cruel/Hound Dog 1956
 Heartbreak Hotel. 1956
 I Want You, I Need You, I Love You 1956
 Love Me Tender 1956
 All Shook Up. 1957
 Jailhouse Rock. 1957
 (Let Me Be Your) Teddy Bear 1957
 Don't 1958
 It's Now Or Never 1960

Beach Boys. 3
 Surfin' U.S.A.. 1963
 I Get Around 1964
 Help Me Rhonda 1965

Everly Brothers. 3
 Bye Bye Love 1957
 Wake Up Little Susie. 1957
 All I Have to Do Is Dream 1958

Platters 3
 Only You. 1955
 The Great Pretender. 1955
 My Prayer 1956

ARTISTS WITH THE MOST SONGS ON THE CHARTS 6 MONTHS OR MORE

Elvis Presley. 5
    Heartbreak Hotel. . . . . 27 Weeks
    Hound Dog . . . . 28 Weeks
    Don't Be Cruel . . . . 27 Weeks
    All Shook Up. . . . . 30 Weeks
    Jailhouse Rock. . . . . 27 Weeks

Pat Boone 3
    Love Letters in the Sand . . . . 34 Weeks
    Bernardine. . . . . 26 Weeks
    April Love . . . . 26 Weeks

Johnny Mathis. 3
    Wonderful, Wonderful. . . . . 39 Weeks
    It's Not for Me to Say . . . . 34 Weeks
    Chances Are. . . . . 28 Weeks

ARTISTS WITH THE MOST 2-SIDED HITS (BOTH MAKING THE TOP 40)

Elvis Presley. 25
    Heartbreak Hotel/I Was the One
    I Want You, I Need You, I Love You/My Baby Left Me
    Hound Dog/Don't Be Cruel
    Love Me Tender/Anyway You Want Me
    Too Much/Playing for Keeps
    (Let Me Be Your) Teddy Bear/Loving You
    Jailhouse Rock/Treat Me Nice
    Don't/I Beg of You

Wear My Ring Around Your Neck/Doncha' Think It's Time
Hard Headed Woman/Don't Ask Me Why
I Got Stung/One Night
A Fool Such As I/I Need Your Love Tonight
A Big Hunk o' Love/My Wish Came True
Stuck on You/Fame and Fortune
It's Now Or Never/A Mess of Blues
Are You Lonesome Tonight/I Gotta Know
Surrender/Lonely Man
I Feel So Bad/Wild in the Country
Little Sister/Marie's the Name of His Latest Flame
Can't Help Falling in Love/Rock-a-Hula Baby
Good Luck Charm/Anything That's Part of You
Bossa Nova Baby/Witchcraft
Kissin' Cousins/It Hurts Me
Viva Las Vegas/What'd I Say
Ain't That Loving You Baby/Ask Me

I'm Walking/A Teenager's Romance
Be-Bop Baby/Have I Told You Lately That I Love You
Stood Up/Waitin' in School
My Bucket Gots' a Hole in It/Believe What You Say
I Got a Feeling/Lonesome Town
Never Be Anyone Else But You/It's Late
Just a Little Too Much/Sweeter Than You
I Wanna Be Loved/Mighty Good
I'm Not Afraid/Yes Sir, That's My Baby
Travelin' Man/Hello Mary Lou
A Wonder Like You/Everlovin'

At My Front Door/No Other Arms
Tutti Fruitti/I'll Be Home
Chains of Love/Friendly Persuasion
Don't Forbid Me/Anastasia
Why Baby Why/I'm Waiting Just for You
Love Letters in the Sand/Bernardine
Remember You're Mine/There's a Gold Mine in the Sky
A Wonderful Time Up There/It's Too Soon to Know
If Dreams Came True/That's How Much I Love You
For My Good Fortune/Gee, But It's Lonely

13
MOVIE AND T.V. OLDIES

Andy Williams *(Columbia)*

Many movie and T.V. themes became oldie hits. Here is the authors' choice of the top 20.

1. Rock Around the Clock (Blackboard Jungle)
2. Love Me Tender
3. Jailhouse Rock
4. Tammy
5. Theme from a Summer Place
6. April Love
7. Moonglow & Theme from Picnic
8. Town Without Pity
9. The Yellow Rose of Texas
10. Exodus
11. The Ballad of Davy Crockett
12. High School Confidential
13. Moon River (Breakfast at Tiffanys)
14. Where the Boys Are
15. More (Mondo Cane)
16. Never On Sunday
17. The Song From Moulin Rouge
18. Sink the Bismarck
19. Viva Las Vegas
20. The Girl Can't Help It

14
SPECIAL INTEREST OLDIES

The arts have always served as a mirror of the times. Rock 'n' roll music was certainly no exception. During the oldie years, many of the songs related directly to subjects of special interest to the record-buying public, the teen-agers. A number of these "subjects of song" follow, along with some of the oldie hits that related to the particular subject.

SCHOOL

Back to School Again	(Timmie Rogers)
Be True to Your School	(Beach Boys)
Graduation Day	(Four Freshmen, Rover Boys)
Graduation's Here	(Fleetwoods)
Hey School Girl	(Tom & Jerry)
High School Confidential	(Jerry Lee Lewis)
High School U.S.A.	(Tommy Facenda)
Queen of the Senior Prom	(Mills Brothers)
School Day	(Chuck Berry)
School Is In	(Gary "U.S." Bonds)
School Is Out	(Gary "U.S." Bonds)
Stayin' In	(Bobby Vee)

CLOTHES

Black Slacks	(Joe Bennett & the Sparkletones)
Black Denim Trousers	(Cheers)
Blue Suede Shoes	(Carl Perkins, Elvis Presley)
Bobby Sox to Stockings	(Frankie Avalon)
Hi-Heel Sneakers	(Tommy Tucker)
Itsy Bitsy Teeny Weenie Yellow Polka Dot Bikini	(Brian Hyland)
No Chemise, Please	(Gerry Granahan)
Short Shorts	(Royal Teens)
A White Sport Coat	(Marty Robbins)

197

SOCIAL LIFE

At the Hop	(Danny & the Juniors)
Having a Party	(Sam Cooke)
Let's Have a Party	(Wanda Jackson)
Lonely Weekends	(Charlie Rich)
Queen of the Hop	(Bobby Darin)
Saturday Night at the Movies	(Drifters)
Sittin' in the Balcony	(Eddie Cochran, Johnny Dee)

GOING STEADY

Born Too Late	(Poni-Tails)
Breaking Up Is Hard to Do	(Jivin' Gene, Neil Sedaka)
The Diary	(Neil Sedaka)
First Date, First Kiss, First Love	(Sonny James)
First Quarrel	(Paul & Paula)
Goin' Steady	(Tommy Sands)
Teenage Crush	(Tommy Sands)
A Teenager's Romance	(Ricky Nelson)
Too Young to Go Steady	(Nat "King" Cole)
Wear My Ring Around Your Neck	(Elvis Presley)

MUSIC

Hit Record	(Brook Benton
Rock & Roll Is Here to Stay	(Danny & the Juniors)
Rock & Roll Music	(Chuck Berry)
Those Oldies But Goodies	(Little Caesar & the Romans)

FADS

First Name Initial	(Annette)
The Hula Hoop Song	(Teresa Brewer, Georgia Gibbs)
My Boy Flat Top	(Boyd Bennett & the Rockets, Dorothy Collins)
See You Later, Alligator	(Bill Haley & the Comets)
Sidewalk Surfin'	(Jan & Dean)
Surfin' U.S.A.	(Beach Boys)

CARS

Dead Man's Curve	(Jan & Dean)
Drag City	(Jan & Dean)
409	(Beach Boys)
G.T.O.	(Ronny & the Daytonas)
Hey Little Cobra	(Rip Chords)

Hot Rod Lincoln	(Charlie Ryan, Johnny Bond)
Little Deuce Coupe	(Beach Boys)
Little Old Lady (from Pasadena)	(Jan & Dean)
Stick Shift	(Duals)
Three Window Coupe	(Rip Chords)

VACATION

Here Comes Summer	(Jerry Keller)
See You in September	(Tempos)
Summer's Gone	(Paul Anka)
Summertime Blues	(Eddie Cochran)
Summertime; Summertime	(Jamies)
Those Lazy-Hazy-Crazy Days of Summer	(Nat "King" Cole)
Vacation	(Connie Francis)
Wonderful Summer	(Robin Ward)

15

NOVELTY SONGS

Following is a sample of some of the best "oldie" novelty songs.

SONG	ARTIST	YEAR
The Flying Saucer	Buchanan & Goodman	1956
The Old Philosopher	Eddie Lawrence	1956
Ape Call	Nervous Norvis	1956
Transfusion	Nervous Norvis	1956
Flying Saucer the 2nd	Buchanan & Goodman	1957
Santa & the Satellite	Buchanan & Goodman	1957
The Banana Boat Song	Stan Freberg	1957
Wun'erful Wun'erful	Stan Freberg	1957
The Chipmunk Song	Chipmunks	1958
The Blob	Five Blobs	1958
The Little Blue Man	Betty Johnson	1958
Witch Doctor	David Seville	1958
The Purple People Eater	Sheb Wooley	1958
Dinner with Drac	John Zacherle	1958
Kookie Kookie (Lend Me Your Comb)	Edward Byrnes	1959
Alvin's Harmonica	Chipmunks	1959
Alvin Twist	Chipmunks	1959
Along Came Jones	Coasters	1959
The Battle of Kookamonga	Homer & Jethro	1959
Ambrose (Part 5)	Linda Laurie	1959
The Mummy	Bob McFadden	1959
The Clouds	Spacemen	1959
The Little Space Girl	Jesse Lee Turner	1959
Alvin's Orchestra	Chipmunks	1960
Alley-Oop	Hollywood Argyles	1960
Itsy Bitsy Teeny Weeny Yellow Polka Dot Bikini	Brian Hyland	1960
Mr. Custer	Larry Verne	1960
More Money for You and Me	Four Preps	1961

203

SONG	ARTIST	YEAR
The Astronaut	Jose Jimenez	1961
Small Sad Sam	Phil McLean	1961
Jeremiah Peabody's Poly Unsaturated Quick Dissolving Fast Acting Pleasant Tasting Green and Purple Pills	Ray Stevens	1961
Monster Mash	Bobby (Boris) Pickett	1962
Monster's Holiday	Bobby (Boris) Pickett	1962
Ahab the Arab	Ray Stevens	1962
Martian Hop	Ran-Dells	1963
Hello Muddah, Hello Faddah	Allan Sherman	1963
Harry the Hairy Ape	Ray Stevens	1963
Leader of the Laundromat	Detergents	1964
The Name Game	Shirley Ellis	1964
Haunted House	Jumpin' Gene Simmons	1964

16

ANSWER SONGS

Answer songs were a big fad of the rock years. They were recorded as an "answer" to a previous hit. Here are a half-dozen of the best known.

He'll Have to Stay . . . . Jeannie Black
  (He'll Have to Go . . . . Jim Reeves)
I'm the Girl from Wolverton Mountain. . . . . Jo-Ann Campbell
  (Wolverton Mountain . . . . Claude King)
(I Can't Help You) I'm Falling Too . . . . . . Skeeter Davis
  (Please Help Me I'm Falling. . . . . Hank Locklin)
Don't Let Him Shop Around . . . . Debbie Dean
  (Shop Around. . . . . Smokey Robinson
                                          & the Miracles)
I'll Save the Last Dance For You . . . . Damita Jo
  (Save the Last Dance For Me . . . . Drifters)
He Walks Like a Man . . . . Jody Miller
  (Walk Like a Man . . . . Four Seasons)

Chubby Checker *(James J. Kriegsmann)*

17
DANCE SONGS

Dancing was a vital part of the rock 'n' roll generation. In fact, a number of oldie hits were also the names of dances. The following oldies named some of the most popular dances of the fifties and sixties. This is not intended to show *all* the songs naming dances, but rather to show the dances themselves.

Alley Cat (Bent Fabric, 1962)
Birdland (Chubby Checker, 1963)
Do the Bird (Dee Dee Sharpe, 1963)
Blame It on the Bossa Nova (Eydie Gorme, 1963)
Boo-Ga-Loo (Tom & Jerrio, 1965)
Dance to the Bop (Gene Vincent, 1957)
The Bounce (Olympics, 1963)
Bristol Stomp (Dovells, 1961)
Bunny Hop (Applejacks, 1959)
Tea for Two Cha-Cha (Tommy Dorsey, 1958)
The Cinnamon Cinder (Pastel Six, 1962)
Do the Clam (Elvis Presley, 1965)
Do the New Continental (Dovells, 1962)
The Dog (Rufus Thomas, 1963)
The Fish (Bobby Rydell, 1961)
The Fly (Chubby Checker, 1961)
Foot Stompin'—Part I (Flares, 1961)
The Freeze (Tony & Joe, 1958)
Do the Freddie (Chubby Checker, 1965)
Harlem Shuffle (Bob & Earl, 1963)
Hitch Hike (Marvin Gaye, 1963)
The Hoochi Coochi Coo (Hank Ballard & the Midnighters, 1960)
Hucklebuck (Chubby Checker, 1961)
Hully Gully (Olympics, 1960)
The Jam (Bobby Gregg & His Friends, 1962)
The Jerk (Larks, 1964)
Limbo Rock (Chubby Checker, 1962)
The Loco-Motion (Little Eva, 1962)
The Madison (Al Brown's Tunetoppers, 1960)

Mashed Potato Time (Dee Dee Sharpe, 1962)
The Matador (Major Lance, 1964)
Dance the Mess Around (Chubby Checker, 1961)
The Monkey Time (Major Lance, 1963)
Peppermint Twist (Joey Dee & the Starliters, 1961)
Pony Time (Chubby Checker, 1961)
Popeye the Hitch Hiker (Chubby Checker, 1962)
The Push & The Kick (Mark Valentino, 1962)
The Shag (Billy Graves, 1959)
Shake (Sam Cooke, 1965)
(I Do the) Shimmy Shimmy (Bobby Freeman, 1960)
Hard Times (The Slop) (Noble Watts, 1957)
The Stroll (The Diamonds, 1957)
C'mon and Swim (Bobby Freeman, 1964)
The Switch-a-Roo (Hank Ballard & the Midnighters, 1961)
Blue Tango (Bill Black's Combo, 1960)
Let's Turkey Trot (Little Eva, 1963)
The Twist (Chubby Checker, 1960)
Wah-Wahtusi (Orlons, 1962)
The Walk (Jimmy McCracklin, 1958)
Rock & Roll Waltz (Kay Starr, 1955)

18

TRAGEDY SONGS

Jimmy Dean *(Columbia)*

Marty Robbins *(Columbia)*

Tragedy, death in particular, was the topic of a number of oldie hits. Subjects ranged from gang leaders to girl friends. There was even a true-to-life tragedy song (Three Stars), a tribute to three rock artists (Buddy Holly, the Big Bopper and Ritchie Valens) who died in a plane crash. Here are some of the biggest "tragedies" of the rock 'n' roll era.

SONG	ARTIST	YEAR
Artificial Flowers	Bobby Darin	1960
Big Bad John	Jimmy Dean	1961
Black Denim Trousers	Cheers	1955
Ebony Eyes	Everly Brothers	1961
El Paso	Marty Robbins	1959
Endless Sleep	Jody Reynolds	1958
Last Kiss	J. Frank Wilson & the Cavaliers	1964
Laurie	Dickey Lee	1965
Leader of the Pack	Shangri-Las	1964
Moody River	Pat Boone	1961
One of Us	Patti Page	1960
Patches	Dickey Lee	1962
Teen Angel	Mark Dinning	1959
Tell Laura I Love Her	Ray Peterson	1960
Three Stars	Tommy Dee	1959

19
NAME SONGS

Does your name appear in any oldie title? Following is a list, alphabetically by name, of all the oldie titles containing a person's first name.

Ray Peterson *(R.C.A.)*

Coasters *(Columbia)*

Abigail
Abigail Beecher (Freddy Cannon)

Adam
Adam & Eve (Paul Anka)

Ahab
Ahab the Arab (Ray Stevens)

Alice
Alice in Wonderland (Neil Sedaka)

Alvin
Alvin's Harmonica (Chipmunks)
Alvin's Orchestra (Chipmunks)
The Alvin Twist (Chipmunks)

Ambrose
Ambrose (Part 5) (Linda Laurie)

Anastasia
Anastasia (Pat Boone)

Angela
Angela Jones (Johnny Ferguson)

Anna
Anna (Arthur Alexander)

Ann, Annie
Annie Had a Baby (Midnighters)
Bristol Twistin' Annie (Dovells)
Patti Ann (Johnny Crawford)
Work With Me, Annie (Midnighters)

Armen
Armen's Theme (Joe Reisman, David Seville)

Barbara
Barbara (Temptations)
Barbara-Ann (Regents)
Please Don't Ask About Barbara (Bobby Vee)

219

Ben
Theme from Ben Casey   (Valjean)

Bernadette
The Village of St. Bernadette   (Andy Williams)

Bernardine
Bernardine   (Pat Boone)

Betty
Betty & Dupree   (Chuck Willis)

Betty-Lou
Betty-Lou Got a New Pair of
  Shoes   (Bobby Freeman)

Bill, Billy
Billy   (Kathy Linden)
Won't You Come Home Bill Baily (Bobby Darin)

Bobby
Bobby's Girl   (Marcie Blaine)
Wait 'Til My Bobby Gets Home   (Darlene Love)

Bonnie
Bonnie Came Back   (Duane Eddy)
I've Got Bonnie   (Bobby Rydell)

Candy
Candy Girl   (Four Seasons)

Cara
Cara Mia   (Jay & the Americans)

Carol
Carol   (Chuck Berry)
Oh! Carol   (Neil Sedaka)

Caterina
Caterina   (Perry Como)

Cathy
Cathy's Clown   (Everly Brothers)
Close to Cathy   (Mike Clifford)

Charlie
Charlie Brown   (Coasters)

Cinderella
Cinderella   (Jack Ross)

220

Cindy

Cindy Oh Cindy   (Eddie Fisher, Vince Martin & the Tarriers)

Cindy's Birthday   (Johnnie Crawford)

Claudette

Claudette   (Everly Brothers)

Clementine

Clementine   (Bobby Darin)

Corina

Corina Corina   (Joe Turner, Ray Peterson)

Danny

Danny Boy   (Conway Twitty)

Davy

The Ballad of Davy Crockett   (Fess Parker, Bill Hayes)

Dawn

Dawn   (Four Seasons)

Dean

Hey Jean Hey Dean   (Dean & Jean)

Deliah

Deliah Jones   (McGuire Sisters)

Denise

Denise   (Randy & the Rainbows)

Diana

Diana   (Paul Anka)

Remember Diana   (Paul Anka)

Diane

Diane   (Bachelors)

Little Diane   (Dion)

Dinah

De De Dinah   (Frankie Avalon)

Dominique

Dominique   (Singing Nun)

Donna

Donna   (Ritchie Valens)

Don't Believe Him Donna   (Lenny Miles)

Donna the Prima Donna   (Dion)

221

Eddie
Eddie My Love
(Chordettes, Fontane Sisters, Teen Queens)

Elena
Maria Elena
(Los Indios Trabajaras)

Eloise
Eloise
(Kay Thompson)

Elsie
Lazy Elsie Molly
(Chubby Checker)

Eve
Adam & Eve
(Paul Anka)

Fannie
Fannie Mae
(Buster Brown)
Short Fat Fannie
(Larry Williams)

Frankie
Frankie
(Connie Francis)
Frankie & Johnny
(Sam Cooke)

Georgia
Georgia on My Mind
(Ray Charles)

Gidget
Gidget
(James Darren)

Gina
Gina
(Johnny Mathis)

Ginnie, Ginny
Ginnie Bell
(Paul Dino)
Ginny Come Lately
(Brian Hyland)

Glendora
Glendora
(Perry Como)

Gloria
Gloria
(Passions)

Henrietta
Henrietta
(Jimmy Dee)

Henry
Dance with Me Henry
(Georgia Gibbs, Etta James)

Ivan
Dear Ivan   (Jimmy Dean)

Jack
Hit the Road, Jack   (Ray Charles)

James
James (Hold the Ladder
   Steady)   (Sue Thompson)

Jamie
Jamie   (Eddie Holland)

Jane
Plain Jane   (Bobby Darin)

Jean
Hey Jean Hey Dean   (Dean & Jean)

Jed
The Ballad of Jed Clampett   (Flatt & Scruggs)

Jennie, Jenny
Jennie Lee   (Jan & Arnie)
Jenny Jenny   (Little Richard)
Poor Jenny   (Everly Brothers)

Jeremiah
Jeremiah Peabody's Poly
   Unsaturated Quick
   Dissolving Fast Acting
   Pleasant Tasting Green and
   Purple Pills   (Ray Stevens)

Jim, Jimmy
Go Jimmy Go   (Jimmy Clanton)
Goodbye Jimmy, Goodbye   (Kathy Linden)
Jimmy's Girl   (Johnny Tillotson)
Just Tell Her Jim Said Hello   (Elvis Presley)

Jo-Ann
Jo-Ann   (Playmates)

Joe
Down at Papa Joe's   (Dixiebelles)
Killer Joe   (Rocky Fellers)
Ragtime Cowboy Joe   (Chipmunks)
Surfer Joe   (Surfaris)

John, Johnny

Big John	(Shirelles)
Big Bad John	(Jimmy Dean)
Frankie & Johnny	(Sam Cooke)
Johnny Angel	(Shelly Fabares)
Johnny B. Goode	(Chuck Berry)
Johnny Get Angry	(Joanie Sommers)
Johnny Jingo	(Hayley Mills)
Johnny Loves Me	(Shelly Fabares)
Johnny Will	(Pat Boone)

Jo-Jo

Jo-Jo the Dog Faced Boy	(Annette)

Josephine

Josephine	(Bill Black's Combo)
My Girl, Josephine	(Fats Domino)
Yes Tonight, Josephine	(Johnny Ray)

Judy

Judy's Turn to Cry	(Lesley Gore)

Julie

Oh Julie	(Crescendos)

Juliette

(Just Like) Romeo & Juliette	(Reflections)

Kate

Shimmy Like Kate	(Olympics)

Larry

Hats Off to Larry	(Del Shannon)

Laura

Tell Laura I Love Her	(Ray Peterson)

Laurie

Laurie	(Dickey Lee)

Leroy

Leroy	(Jack Scott)

Liberty

(The Man Who Shot) Liberty Valance	(Gene Pitney)

Linda
Linda   (Jan & Dean)
Linda Lu   (Ray Sharpe)
I Saw Linda Yesterday   (Dickey Lee)

Lisa
Mona Lisa   (Carl Mann, Conway Twitty)

Lorraine
Darling Lorraine   (Knockouts)

Louie
Louie, Louie   (Kingsmen)

Lucille
Lucille   (Little Richard, Everly
      Brothers)

Lulu
Honolulu Lulu   (Jan & Dean)

Mack
Mack the Knife   (Bobby Darin)

Maria
Maria   (Johnny Mathis)
Maria Elena   (Los Indios Trabajaras)

Marianne
Marianne   (Terry Gilkyson & the Easy
      Riders, Hilltoppers)

Marie
Marie   (Bachelors)
Marie's the Name of His Latest
   Flame   (Elvis Presley)
Tina Marie   (Perry Como)

Marina
Marina   (Rocco Granata)

Marlena
Marlena   (Four Seasons)

Martha
Mostly Martha   (Crew Cuts)

Mary

Hello Mary Lou	(Ricky Nelson)
Lazy Mary	(Lou Monte)
Mary Lee	(Rainbows)
Mary's Little Lamb	(James Darren)
Mary Lou	(Ronnie Hawkins)
Midnight Mary	(Joey Powers)
Take a Message to Mary	(Everly Brothers)
What Will Mary Say	(Johnny Mathis)

Mary Ann

Mary Ann Regrets	(Burl Ives)

Matilda

Twistin' Matilda	(Jimmy Soul)
Waltzing Matilda	(Jimmy Rodgers)

Maybelline

Maybelline	(Chuck Berry)

Michael

Michael	(Highwaymen)

Mickey

Mickey's Monkey	(Smokey Robinson & the Miracles)

Minnie

Skinny Minnie	(Bill Haley & the Comets)

Molly

Good Golly Miss Molly	(Little Richard)
Lazy Elsie Molly	(Chubby Checker)
Main Title and Molly O	(Dick Jacobs)

Mona

Mona Lisa	(Conway Twitty)

Nadine

Nadine	(Chuck Berry)

Nola

Nola	(Billy Williams)

Norman

Norman	(Sue Thompson)

Otto
Crazy Otto   (Johnny Maddox)

Patricia
Patricia   (Prez Prado)

Patti
Patti Ann   (Johnny Crawford)

Paul
Tall Paul   (Annette)

Paula
Hey Paula   (Paul & Paula)

Peggy
Peggy Sue   (Buddy Holly)

Pepe
Pepe   (Duane Eddy)

Pete, Peter
Big Boy Pete   (Olympics)
Peter Gunn   (Ray Anthony, Duane Eddy)

Priscilla
Priscilla   (Eddie Cooley & the Dimples)

Rhonda
Help Me Rhonda   (Beach Boys)

Ringo
Ringo   (Lorne Greene)

Romeo
(Just Like) Romeo & Juliet   (Reflections)

Ronnie
Ronnie   (Four Seasons)

Ruby
Ruby   (Ray Charles)
Ruby Ann   (Marty Robbins)
Ruby Baby   (Dion)
Ruby Duby Du   (Tobin Matthews)

Rudolph
Rudolph the Red Nosed
    Reindeer   (Chipmunks)

Rudy
Rudy's Rock   (Bill Haley & the Comets)

Sally
Long Tall Sally   (Little Richard, Pat Boone)
Sally Go 'Round the Roses   (Jaynettes)

Sam
Mohair Sam   (Charlie Rich)
Small Sad Sam   (Phil McLean)

Samson
Run Samson Run   (Neil Sedaka)

Sandy
Sandy   (Larry Hall, Dion, Ronny &
                                  the Daytonas)

Sheila
Sheila   (Tommy Roe)

Sherry
A Letter from Sherry   (Dale Ward)
Sherry   (Four Seasons)

Sue, Susie, Suzie, Suzy
Peggy Sue   (Buddy Holly)
Run Around Sue   (Dion)
Susie Darlin'   (Robin Luke, Tommy Roe)
Susie Q   (Dale Hawkins)
That's My Little Susie   (Ritchie Valens)
Tra La La La Suzy   (Dean & Jean)
Wake Up Little Susie   (Everly Brothers)

Stevie
Workout Stevie, Workout   (Little Stevie Wonder)

Tammy
Tammy   (Ames Brothers, Debbie
                                  Reynolds)

Teddy
Ready Teddy   (Little Richard)
Teddy   (Connie Francis)

Therese
St. Therese of the Roses   (Billy Ward & the Dominos)

Tina
Tina Marie   (Perry Como)

Tom
Tom Dooley   (Kingston Trio)

Venus
Venus   (Frankie Avalon)
Venus in Blue Jeans   (Jimmy Clanton)

Wendy
Wendy   (Beach Boys)

Willie
Willie and the Hand Jive   (Johnny Otis)

Yogi
Yogi   (Ivy Three)

Zorba
Zorba the Greek   (Herb Alpert & the Tijuana
                                    Brass)

Zorro
Zorro   (Chordettes)

20
LONGEST AND SHORTEST TITLES

Do you know what oldies have the longest and shortest titles?

LONGEST

Jeremiah Peabody's Poly Unsaturated Quick Dissolving Fast Acting Pleasant Tasting Green and Purple Pills
(Ray Stevens, 1961: 90 letters)

Itsy Bitsy Teenie Weenie Yellow Polka Dot Bikini
(Brian Hyland, 1960: 41 letters)

I'm Gonna Sit Right Down and Write Myself a Letter
(Billy Williams, 1957: 40 letters)

Your Ma Said You Cried in Your Sleep Last Night
(Kenny Dino, 1961: 38 letters)

Rockin' Pneumonia and the Boogie Woogie Flu
(Huey "Piano" Smith, 1957: 36 letters)

Seven Little Girls Sitting in the Back Seat
(Paul Evans, 1959: 36 letters)

SHORTEST

He (Al Hibbler, 1955; McGuire Sisters, 1956: 2 letters)

409 (Beach Boys, 1962: 3 letters)

Gee (Crows, 1955: 3 letters)

G.T.O. (Ronny & the Daytonas, 1964: 3 letters)

Nag (Halos, 1961: 3 letters)

7–11 (Gone All-Stars, 1958: 3 letters)

Til (Angels, 1961; Roger Williams, 1957: 3 letters)

Why (Frankie Avalon, 1959: 3 letters)

Yep (Duane Eddy, 1959: 3 letters)

You (Aquatones, 1958: 3 letters)

TRIVIA QUIZ

1. What label did Elvis record for before R.C.A.?

2. Charlie Rich, a Country & Western star of the seventies, had two oldie hits in the sixties. Name them.

3. What superstar of the seventies sang with the Mitchell Trio (formerly Chad Mitchell Trio) in the mid-sixties?

4. In 1959, Hank Ballard wrote, and later recorded, a song which introduced a new dance. Though it was a hit, it was recorded in 1960 by another artist and went on to become one of the greatest dance crazes of all time. What is the song and who is the artist?

5. At least a dozen artists or groups have "Little" in their names. How many can you name?

6. What late artist started as the lead singer of the Dominos, left to form his own group, the Drifters, with whom he also sang lead, and later enjoyed a very successful career as a solo?

7. What two other former lead singers of the Drifters also had big hits as solo artists?

8. One of his early efforts as a song writer was "The Blob." He went on to become one of the truly great composers. Who is he?

9. What two oldie artists, known primarily as movie stars, had #1 oldie hits?

10. Four songs made #1 nationally and were the *only* songs by those artists to ever reach the top 100 charts. Name the songs and the artists.

11. Tom & Jerry sang "Hey! School Girl" in 1957. Who did they become in the sixties?

12. Nick Todd recorded "Plaything" in 1957 and was moderately successful. His older brother became one of the biggest names in music during the oldie era. Who is this famous brother?

13. What oldie artist wrote the theme song for the "Tonight" show?

14. Elvis is credited by many to have had the original hit of "Blue Suede Shoes." Who actually had it?

15. What novelty song was #1 in the country in 1962 and re-leased again in 1973 to become a hit again by the same artist?

16. In 1958, Gerry Granahan recorded "No Chemise Please." At the same time, he was recording as the lead singer of another group. Name the group.

17. Richard Penniman was one of the biggest stars of rock 'n' roll when he quit performing to join the ministry. He came back to re-establish his stardom. Who is he?

18. His record, "Ain't Got No Home," earned him the nickname "Frogman." Who is he?

19. She was first a member of the Blossoms; while with the Blossoms she sang the lead for the Crystal's hit, "He's a Rebel"; she then became a member of the Bob B. Soxx & the Blue Jeans; she then left to establish a solo career, scoring with "Wait Til My Bobby Gets Home" and "Today I Met the Boy I'm Gonna Marry." Who is she?

20. Tommy Dee recorded "Three Stars" in tribute to three giants of the rock 'n' roll era who were all killed in the same plane crash. Name these artists.

21. What movie theme song, recorded by Percy Faith, reached #1 in the country?

22. What two oldie artists were former Mousketeers?

23. Who coined the term "rock 'n' roll"?

24. His career is bigger today than it was in 1961, when he recorded "Bless You" and "Halfway to Paradise." Who is he?

25. What oldie has the longest title? The shortest title?

26. "Theme from the Three Penny Opera," also called "Moritat," was an instrumental hit by a number of artists in 1956. In 1959 it came out as a vocal, reached #1 in the country, and became an all-time hit. What is the song?

27. Over 40 different versions of the *same song* were recorded by the *same artist*. What is the song?

28. There are two *different* songs with the same title. The Five Satins did one and Dion & the Belmonts did the other. What is the name of these two songs?

29. What song was the theme song of the movie "Blackboard Jungle" and considered by most to be the theme song of rock 'n' roll?

30. Six novelty songs became #1 in the country. How many can you name?

31. What two title songs of Elvis Presley movies became #1?

32. There are six songs whose *title* contained the make or model of a car. How many can you name?

33. More than twenty oldies have the word "angel" in the title. How many can you name?

34. Buddy Knox ("Party Doll") and Jimmy Bowen ("I'm Stickin' with You") belonged to the same group. They each sang lead on their respective hits. What was the name of the group?

35. What well-known solo singer also recorded under the group name the Rinky Dinks?

36. They had some success as an instrumental group with "Torquay" and "Bulldog." They later teamed up with a vocalist and produced a #1 song. Name the group, the vocalist and the song.

37. What female recording star helped Edward Byrnes have a big hit with the words, "Kookie, Kookie Lend Me Your Comb"?

38. This background group had a hit of their own called "I'm Blue." What is the name of the group and who did they back?

39. There are nine oldies with a day of the week in the title. How many can you name?

40. See how many of the twenty oldies you can name whose titles contain the name of a U.S. city.

41. Jimmy Dean had a top ten song in 1962, praising the wartime deeds of John F. Kennedy. What is the song?

42. The Kingston Trio, a folk group, had a #1 hit on the pop charts in 1958. Name the song.

43. Elvis Presley had the most #1 songs of the oldie era, the most Top 40 songs and the most songs in the statistical Top 100. The same artist was second to Elvis in all three categories. Who is the artist?

44. Name the female and group artists having the most oldies in the Top 40 for their careers.

45. Name the song in which the four preps imitated a number of oldie artists singing their hits.

46. Who was the man behind "The Chipmunks"?

47. His real career was acting, with appearances in such films as "Rebel Without a Cause" and "Exodus." As a singer, he had one big hit, "Start Movin'." Who was he?

48. What oldie was a hit by Dean Martin, later by Bobby Rydell, and finally, in Italian, by Dominico Modugno?

49. In 1964, the Shangri-Las had a #1 hit, "Leader of the Pack." Shortly thereafter, another group recorded a "parody" of the song. What is the song, and who is the group?

50. What two songs naming dances reached #1 in the country?

TRIVIA QUIZ ANSWERS

1. Sun

2. Lonely Weekends (1960)
   Mohair Sam (1965)

3. John Denver

4. The Twist—Chubby Checker

5. Little Anthony & the Imperials
   Little Caesar & the Romans
   Little Dippers
   Little Esther Phillips
   Little Eva
   Little Joe & the Thrillers
   Little Joey & the Flips
   Little Peggy March
   Little Richard
   Little Johnnie Taylor
   Little Stevie Wonder
   Little Willie John

6. Clyde McPhatter

7. Ben E. King (Spanish Harlem; Stand By Me)
   Bobby Hendricks (Itchy Twitchy Feeling)

8. Burt Bacharach

9. Tab Hunter (Young Love)
   Debbie Reynolds (Tammy)

10. The Elegants (Little Star)
    The Hollywood Argyles (Alley-Oop)
    The Silhouettes (Get a Job)
    The Singing Nun (Dominique)

11. Simon & Garfunkel

12. Pat Boone

13. Paul Anka

14. Carl Perkins, February, 1956: #4
    (Elvis Presley, March, 1956: #24)

15. Monster Mash—Bobby (Boris) Pickett

16. Dickey Doo & the Don'ts
    (Click Clack, Nee Nee Na Na Na Na Nu Nu)

17. Little Richard

18. Clarence "Frogman" Henry

19. Darlene Love

20. The Big Bopper, Buddy Holly, Ritchie Valens

21. Theme from a Summer Place

22. Annette Funicello and Johnny Crawford

23. Disc Jockey Alan Freed

24. Tony Orlando (and Dawn)

25. Jeremiah Peabody's Poly Unsaturated Quick Dissolving Fast
    Acting Pleasant Tasting Green and Purple Pills—Ray Stevens,
    1961: 90 letters.
    He—Al Hibbler; McGuire Sisters, 1955: 2 letters

26. Mack the Knife (Bobby Darin)

27. High School U.S.A. (Tommy Facenda)

28. In the Still of the Nite (Five Satins)
    In the Still of the Night (Dion & the Belmonts)

29. Rock Around the Clock

30. The Chipmunk Song (1958)
    Witch Doctor (1958)
    The Purple People Eater (1958)
    Alley-Oop (1960)
    Mr. Custer (1960)
    Monster Mash (1962)

31. Love Me Tender, Jailhouse Rock

32. 409 (Beach Boys)
    Hot Rod Lincoln (Charlie Ryan, Johnny Bond)
    Little Deuce Coupe (Beach Boys)
    Hey Little Cobra (Rip-Chords)
    Three Window Coupe (Rip-Chords)
    G.T.O. (Ronny & the Daytonas)

242

33. A Letter to an Angel (Jimmy Clanton)
Angel Baby (Dean Martin)
Angel Baby (Rosie & the Originals)
Angel on My Shoulder (Shelby Flint)
Angel Smile (Nat "King" Cole)
Angels in the Sky (Crew Cuts)
Blue Angel (Roy Orbison)
City of Angels (Highlights)
Come on Little Angel (Belmonts)
Devil or Angel (Clovers, Bobby Vee)
Earth Angel (Penguins)
Johnny Angel (Shelly Fabares)
Look Homeward Angel (Johnnie Ray)
My Little Angel (Four Lads)
My Special Angel (Bobby Helms)
Next Door to an Angel (Neil Sedaka)
Pretty Little Angel Eyes (Curtis Lee)
Rockin' Little Angel (Ray Smith)
Teen Angel (Mark Dinning)
Tears from an Angel (Troy Shondell)
The Angels Listened In (Crests)
Walkin' with My Angel (Bobby Vee)

34. Rhythm Orchids

35. Bobby Darin

36. Jimmy Gilmer & the Fireballs: Sugar Shack

37. Connie Stevens

38. Ikettes—they backed Ike & Tina Turner

39. Another Saturday Night
Blue Monday
Fell in Love on Monday
I Met Him on a Sunday
Never on Sunday
That Sunday That Summer
Saturday Night at the Movies
Sunday and Me
A Sunday Kind of Love

40. Abilene
    The Battle of New Orleans
    The Boy from New York City
    Chattanooga Choo Choo
    Chattanooga Shoe Shine Boy
    Detroit City
    El Paso
    Honolulu Lulu
    Kansas City
    The Little Old Lady (from Pasadena)
    Memphis
    Miami
    New Orleans
    Philadelphia, U.S.A.
    Talahassee Lassie
    Tucumcari
    Twenty-four Hours from Tulsa
    Viva Las Vegas
    Walking to New Orleans
    Way Down Yonder in New Orleans

41. P.T. 109

42. Tom Dooley

43. Pat Boone

44. Female—Connie Francis
    Group—Everly Brothers

45. More Money For You and Me

46. David Seville

47. Sal Mineo

48. Volare (Nel Blu Di Pinto Di Blu)

49. Leader of the Laundromat (Detergents)

50. The Twist
    The Loco-Motion

244

TITLE INDEX

Eddie Fisher *(R.C.A.)*

The following oldie titles appear together with the month and year in which the songs can be found. "Non-oldie" titles that made the top 40, but are not considered "oldies" by the authors, are listed alphabetically at the end of this index.

A

ABC Boogie	Bill Haley & the Comets	11/55
A.B.C.'s of Love	Frankie Lymon & the Teenagers	10/56
Abigail Beecher	Freddy Cannon	2/64
Abilene	George Hamilton IV	6/63
About This Thing Called Love	Fabian	3/60
Action	Freddy Cannon	8/65
Adam & Eve	Paul Anka	4/60
After School	Randy Starr	3/57
After the Lights Go Down Low	Al Hibbler	7/56
Ahab the Arab	Ray Stevens	6/62
Ain't Got No Home	Clarence "Frogman" Henry	12/56
Ain't That a Shame	Pat Boone	6/55
Ain't (That) It a Shame	Fats Domino	7/55
Ain't That a Shame	Four Seasons	4/63
Ain't That Just Like a Woman	Fats Domino	1/61
Ain't That Loving You Baby	Elvis Presley	10/64
Al Di La	Emelio Pericoli	5/62
Alice in Wonderland	Neil Sedaka	3/62
All Alone Am I	Brenda Lee	9/62
All American Boy	Bill Parsons	12/58
All at Once You Love Her	Perry Como	11/55
All I Could Do Was Cry	Etta James	5/60
All I Have to Do Is Dream	Everly Brothers	4/58
All I Have to Do Is Dream	Richard Chamberlain	2/63
All in My Mind	Maxine Brown	1/61
All My Love	Jackie Wilson	7/60
(All of a Sudden) My Heart Sings	Paul Anka	2/58
(All of a Sudden) My Heart Sings	Mel Carter	10/65
All Shook Up	Elvis Presley	3/57
All the Time	Johnny Mathis	4/58
All the Way	Frank Sinatra	10/57

Allegheny Moon	Patti Page	6/56
Alley Cat	Bent Fabric	7/62
Alley-Oop	Dante & the Evergreens	6/60
Alley-Oop	Hollywood Argyles	6/60
Alligator Wine	Screamin' Jay Hawkins	4/58
Almost Grown	Chuck Berry	4/59
Almost Paradise	Lou Stein	2/57
Almost Paradise	Roger Williams	2/57
Alone	Shepherd Sisters	9/57
Alone	Four Seasons	6/64
Alone at Last	Jackie Wilson	10/60
Along Came Jones	Coasters	4/59
Alvin Twist	Chipmunks	3/62
Alvin's Harmonica	Chipmunks	2/59
Alvin's Orchestra	Chipmunks	2/60
Always	Sammy Turner	11/59
Am I Losing You	Jim Reeves	10/60
Am I That Easy to Forget	Debbie Reynolds	1/60
Am I the Man	Jackie Wilson	10/60
Ambrose (Part 5)	Linda Laurie	2/59
Amen	Impressions	11/64
✓ Among My Souvenirs	Connie Francis	11/59
Amor	Ben E. King	8/61
Anastasia	Pat Boone	12/56
And That Reminds Me	Della Reese	8/57
Angel Baby	Dean Martin	7/58
Angel Baby	Rosie & the Originals	12/60
Angel on My Shoulder	Shelby Flint	1/61
Angel Smile	Nat "King" Cole	1/58
Angels in the Sky	Crew Cuts	11/55
Angels Listened In	Crests	8/59
Angela Jones	Johnny Ferguson	2/60
Anna	Arthur Alexander	10/62
Annie Had a Baby	Midnighters	8/54
Another Saturday Night	Sam Cooke	4/63
Another Sleepless Night	Jimmy Clanton	5/60
Anybody But Me	Brenda Lee	10/61
Any Day Now	Chuck Jackson	4/62
Any More	Teresa Brewer	8/60
Anything That's Part of You	Elvis Presley	3/62
Anyway You Want Me	Elvis Presley	10/56
Apache	Jorgen Ingmann	1/6
Ape Call	Nervous Norvus	7/56
Apple Green	June Valli	3/60
April Love	Pat Boone	10/57
Are You Lonesome Tonight	Elvis Presley	11/60
Are You Really Mine	Jimmie Rodgers	8/58
* Are You Satisfied	Rusty Draper	11/55
Are You Sincere	Andy Williams	2/58
Armen's Theme	Joe Reisman	11/56
Armen's Theme	David Seville	12/56
Around the World	Victor Young	5/57

248

Around the World	Montovani	6/57
Artificial Flowers	Bobby Darin	10/60
As If I Didn't Know	Adam Wade	7/61
✓ As Usual	Brenda Lee	12/63
Asia Minor	Kokomo	2/61
Ask Me	Elvis Presley	10/64
Astronaut, The	Jose Jiminez	7/61
At My Front Door	El Dorados	9/55
At My Front Door	Pat Boone	11/55
At the Hop	Danny & the Juniors	11/57
Auctioneer	Leroy Van Dyke	11/56
Autumn Leaves	Steve Allen	10/55
Autumn Leaves	Roger Williams	10/55
Autumn Leaves	Victor Young	10/55

B

Baby Blue	Echoes	3/61
Baby Doll	Andy Williams	11/56
Baby Don't You Cry	Ray Charles	2/64
Baby Don't You Weep	Garnett Mimms & the Enchanters	11/63
Baby Elephant Walk	Lawrence Welk	6/62
Baby I Love You	Ronettes	12/63
Baby I Need Your Loving	Four Tops	8/64
Baby I'm Yours	Barbara Lewis	6/65
Baby It's You	Shirelles	12/61
Baby Oh Baby	Shells	12/60
Baby Sittin' Boogie	Buzz Clifford	1/61
Baby Talk	Jan & Dean	8/59
Baby What You Want Me To Do	Jimmy Reed	2/60
Baby Workout	Jackie Wilson	3/63
Baby (You've Got What It Takes)	Brook Benton & Dinah Washington	1/60
Back in the USA	Chuck Berry	6/59
Back to School Again	Timmie Rogers	9/57
Bad Boy	Jive Bombers	1/57
Bad Boy	Marty Wilde	2/60
Bad Girl	Neil Sedaka	11/63
Bad Motorcycle	Storey Sisters	2/58
Ballad of a Teenage Queen	Johnny Cash	1/58
Ballad of Davy Crockett	Fess Parker	2/55
Ballad of Davy Crockett	Bill Hayes	2/55
Ballad of Jed Clampett	Flatt & Scruggs	12/62
Ballad of Paladin	Duane Eddy	7/62
Ballad of the Alamo	Marty Robbins	10/60
Ballad of Thunder Road	Robert Mitchum	9/58
Ballerina	Nat "King" Cole	1/57
Banana Boat Song	Fontane Sisters	12/56
Banana Boat Song	Vince Martin & the Tarriers	12/56
Banana Boat Song	Sarah Vaughn	12/56

249

Banana Boat Song	Harry Belafonte	1/57
Banana Boat Song	Steve Lawrence	1/57
Banana Boat Song	Stan Freberg	4/57
Band of Gold	Kit Carson	11/55
Band of Gold	Don Cherry	11/55
Barbara	Temptations	2/60
Barbara Ann	Regents	5/61
Battle of Kookamonga	Homer & Jethro	9/59
Battle of New Orleans	Johnny Horton	5/59
✓ Be Anything (But Be Mine)	Connie Francis	5/64
Be-Bop-A-Lula	Gene Vincent	6/56
Be-Bop-Baby	Ricky Nelson	9/57
Be My Baby	Ronettes	8/63
Be My Boy	Paris Sisters	4/61
Be My Guest	Fats Domino	11/59
Be True to Your School	Beach Boys	11/63
Be True to Yourself	Bobby Vee	6/63
Beat, The	Rockin' R's	3/59
Beatnik Fly	Johnny & the Hurricanes	2/60
Because They're Young	Duane Eddy	5/60
Beechwood 4–5789	Marvelettes	8/62
Been So Long	Pastels	2/58
Beep Beep	Playmates	11/58
Believe Me	Royal Teens	11/58
Believe What You Say	Ricky Nelson	3/58
Belonging to Someone	Patti Page	1/58
Bernardine	Pat Boone	5/57
Best Part of Breakin' Up	Ronettes	4/64
Better Tell Him No	Starlets	4/61
Betty and Dupree	Chuck Willis	1/58
Betty Lou Got a New Pair of Shoes	Bobby Freeman	8/58
Bewildered	James Brown	3/61
Beyond the Sea	Roger Williams	2/56
Beyond the Sea	Bobby Darin	1/60
Big Bad John	Jimmy Dean	10/61
Big Beat	Fats Domino	12/57
Big Bopper's Wedding	Big Bopper	12/58
Big Boy Pete	Olympics	5/60
Big Cold Wind	Pat Boone	8/61
Big Girls Don't Cry	Four Seasons	10/62
Big Hunk O'Love	Elvis Presley	7/59
Big Hurt, The	Miss Toni Fisher	11/59
Big Iron	Marty Robbins	3/60
Big John	Shirelles	10/61
Big Man	Four Preps	4/58
Big Man in Town	Four Seasons	11/64
Bilbao Song	Andy Williams	4/61
Billy	Kathy Linden	3/58
Bimbombey	Jimmie Rodgers	11/58
Bird Dance Beat	Trashmen	2/64
Bird Dog	Everly Brothers	8/58

250

Bird on My Head	David Seville	6/58
Birdland	Chubby Checker	5/63
Birds & the Bees	Jewel Akens	1/65
Bird's the Word	Rivingtons	3/63
Birth of the Boogie	Bill Haley & the Comets	3/55
Birthday Party	Pixies Three	8/63
Black Denim Trousers	Cheers	10/55
Black Denim Trousers	Vaughn Monroe	10/55
Black Slacks	Joe Bennett & the Sparkletones	8/57
Blame It on the Bossa Nova	Eydie Gorme	1/63
Bless Our Love	Gene Chandler	9/64
Bless You	Tony Orlando	8/61
Blob, The	Five Blobs	10/58
Blue Angel	Roy Orbison	9/60
Blue Bayou	Roy Orbison	9/63
Blue Blue Day	Don Gibson	6/58
Blue Hawaii	Billy Vaughn	1/59
Blue Monday	Fats Domino	12/56
Blue Moon	Elvis Presley	9/56
Blue Moon	Marcels	3/61
Blue Moon of Kentucky	Elvis Presley	8/54
Blue on Blue	Bobby Vinton	5/63
Blue Suede Shoes	Carl Perkins	2/56
Blue Suede Shoes	Elvis Presley	3/56
Blue Tango	Bill Black's Combo	12/60
Blue Velvet	Bobby Vinton	8/63
Blue Winter	Connie Francis	2/64
Blues Stay Away From Me	Ace Cannon	4/62
Blueberry Hill	Fats Domino	9/56
Blueberry Hill	Louis Armstrong	10/56
Bluebird, the Buzzard & the Oriole	Bobby Day	1/59
Bo Diddley	Bo Diddley	5/55
Bo Weevil	Teresa Brewer	2/56
Bo Weevil	Fats Domino	2/56
Bobby's Girl	Marcie Blaine	10/62
Bobby Sox to Stockings	Frankie Avalon	5/59
Boll Weevil Song	Brook Benton	5/61
Bon Voyage	Janice Harper	8/57
Bonanza	Al Caiola	4/61
Bongo Rock	Preston Epps	5/59
Bongo Stomp	Little Joey & the Flips	6/62
Bonnie Came Back	Duane Eddy	1/60
Bony Moronie	Larry Williams	11/57
Boo-Ga-Loo	Tom & Jerrio	5/65
Book of Love	Monotones	3/58
Born to Be Together	Ronettes	2/65
Born to Be With You	Chordettes	5/56
Born to Lose	Ray Charles	5/62
Born Too Late	Poni-Tails	7/58
Boss Guitar	Duane Eddy	2/63

Bossa Nova Baby	Elvis Presley	10/63
Bounce, The	Olympics	4/63
Boy from New York City	Ad Libs	1/65
Boy Next Door	Secrets	11/63
Boy Without a Girl	Frankie Avalon	5/59
Boys Do Cry	Joe Bennett & the Sparkletones	10/57
Brass Buttons	String-a-Longs	4/61
Bread & Butter	Newbeats	8/64
Break Away	Newbeats	1/65
Break It to Me Gently	Brenda Lee	1/62
Breakin' in a Brand New Broken Heart	Connie Francis	4/61
Breaking Up is Hard to Do	Jivin' Gene	9/59
Breaking Up is Hard to Do	Neil Sedaka	6/62
Breathless	Jerry Lee Lewis	2/58
Bring It on Home to Me	Sam Cooke	6/62
Bristol Stomp	Dovells	9/61
Bristol Twistin' Annie	Dovells	5/62
Broken-Hearted Melody	Sarah Vaughn	7/59
Bulldog	Fireballs	1/60
Bumble Bee	Lavern Baker	11/60
Bumble Boogie	B. Bumble & the Stingers	4/61
Bunny Hop	Applejacks	3/59
Burn That Candle	Bill Haley & the Comets	11/55
Burning Bridges	Jack Scott	4/60
Bus Stop Song	Four Lads	8/56
Bust Out	Busters	9/63
Busted	Ray Charles	9/63
But I Do	Clarence "Frogman" Henry	2/61
Butterfly	Charlie Gracie	2/57
Butterfly	Andy Williams	2/57
Butterfly Baby	Bobby Rydell	2/63
Buzz Buzz Buzz	Hollywood Flames	11/57
Bye Bye Baby	Mary Wells	2/61
Bye Bye Baby	Four Seasons	1/65
Bye Bye Love	Everly Brothers	5/57

C

Cajun Queen	Jimmy Dean	1/62
Calcutta	Lawrence Welk	12/60
Calendar Girl	Neil Sedaka	12/60
California Girls	Beach Boys	7/65
California Sun	Rivieras	1/64
Call Me	Johnny Mathis	10/58
Call Me Mr. In-Between	Burl Ives	5/62
Call On Me	Bobby Bland	1/63
Can I Get a Witness	Marvin Gaye	10/63
Can't Get Used to Losing You	Andy Williams	3/63
Can't Help Falling in Love	Elvis Presley	12/61
Canadian Sunset	Hugo Winterhalter	6/56
Canadian Sunset	Andy Williams	8/56

252

Candy Girl	Four Seasons	7/63
Candy Man	Roy Orbison	8/61
Cannonball	Duane Eddy	11/58
Cara Mia	David Whitfield	7/54
Cara Mia	Jay & the Americans	6/65
Caravan	Santo & Johnny	3/60
Caribbean	Mitchell Torok	8/59
Carol	Chuck Berry	8/58
Cast Your Fate to the Wind	Vince Guaraldi Trio	12/62
Cast Your Fate to the Wind	Sounds Orchestral	3/65
Casual Look	Six Teens	7/56
Catch a Falling Star	Perry Como	1/58
Caterina	Perry Como	3/62
Cathy's Clown	Everly Brothers	4/60
C.C. Rider	Chuck Willis	4/57
Certain Smile	Johnny Mathis	6/58
C'est Si Bon	Conway Twitty	1/61
Cha Cha Cha, The	Bobby Rydell	10/62
Chain Gang	Bobby Scott	2/55
Chain Gang	Sam Cooke	8/60
Chains	Cookies	11/62
Chains of Love	Pat Boone	9/56
Chances Are	Johnny Mathis	9/57
Change Is Gonna Come	Sam Cooke	1/65
Chanson D'Amour	Art & Dotty Todd	4/58
Chantilly Lace	Big Bopper	8/58
Chapel in the Moonlight	Kitty Kallen	7/54
Chapel in the Moonlight	Bachelors	10/65
Chapel of Love	Dixie Cups	5/64
Charlie Brown	Coasters	2/59
Charms	Bobby Vee	3/63
Chattanooga Choo Choo	Floyd Cramer	1/62
Chattanooga Shoe Shine Boy	Freddy Cannon	2/60
Cherry Pie	Marvin & Johnny	4/54
Cherry Pie	Skip & Flip	4/60
Cherry Pink & Apple Blossom White	Prez Prado	2/55
Children's Marching Song	Mitch Miller	1/59
Children's Marching Song	Cyril Stapleton	1/59
China Doll	Ames Brothers	2/60
Chip Chip	Gene McDaniels	1/62
Chipmunk Song	Chipmunks	12/58
Church Bells May Ring	Willows	3/56
Church Bells May Ring	Diamonds	4/56
Cinco Robles	Russell Arms	1/57
Cinco Robles	Les Paul & Mary Ford	1/57
Cinderella	Jack Ross	3/62
Cindy's Birthday	Johnny Crawford	5/62
Cindy, Oh Cindy	Eddie Fisher	10/56
Cindy, Oh Cindy	Vince Martin & the Tarriers	10/56
Cinnamon Cinder	Pastel Six	12/62
City of Angels	Highlights	10/56

Clap Your Hands	Beau Marks	5/60
Clapping Song	Shirley Ellis	3/65
Class, The	Chubby Checker	4/59
Claudette	Everly Brothers	4/58
Clementine	Bobby Darin	3/60
Click-Clack	Dickey Doo & the Don'ts	2/58
Clinging Vine	Bobby Vinton	8/64
Close to Cathy	Mike Clifford	9/62
Close Your Eyes	Five Keys	3/55
Closer You Are	Channels	12/58
Clouds, The	Spacemen	10/59
C'Mon Everybody	Eddie Cochran	11/58
C'Mon and Swim	Bobby Freeman	7/64
Come a Little Bit Closer	Jay and the Americans	9/64
Come and Get These Memories	Martha & the Vandellas	4/61
Come Back Silly Girl	Lettermen	2/62
Come Go With Me	Del Vikings	2/57
Come Home	Bubber Johnson	7/55
Come Into My Heart	Lloyd Price	1/59
Come On	Tommy Roe	1/64
Come On & Get Me	Fabian	9/59
Come On, Let's Go	Ritchie Valens	9/58
Come On Little Angel	Belmonts	7/62
Come Softly To Me	Fleetwoods	3/59
Come To Me	Johnny Mathis	2/58
Come To Me	Marv Johnson	3/59
Come What May	Clyde McPhatter	5/58
Coney Island Baby	Excellents	11/62
Confidential	Sonny Knight	11/56
Conscience	James Darren	4/62
Continental Walk	Hank Ballard & the Midnighters	4/61
Convicted	Oscar McLollie	12/55
Cool Shake	Del Vikings	7/57
Corina Corina	Joe Turner	5/56
Corina Corina	Ray Peterson	11/60
Cotton Candy	Al Hirt	4/64
Cotton Fields	Highwaymen	12/61
Could This Be Magic	Dubs	10/57
Count Every Star	Donnie & the Dreamers	5/61
Count Every Star	Linda Scott	4/62
Country Boy	Fats Domino	2/60
Cousin of Mine	Sam Cooke	9/64
Cradle of Love	Johnny Preston	4/60
Crazy	Patsy Cline	10/61
Crazy Arms	Bob Becham	1/60
Crazy Eyes for You	Bobby Hamilton	8/58
Crazy Love	Paul Anka	4/58
Crazy Man Crazy	Bill Haley & the Comets	5/53
Crazy Otto	Johnny Maddox	1/55
Croce Di Oro	Patti Page	9/55

254

Crossfire	Johnny & the Hurricanes	4/59
Crossfire	Orlons	9/63
Crowd, The	Roy Orbison	6/62
Cry Baby	Bonnie Sisters	2/56
Cry Baby	Garnet Mimms & the	
	Enchanters	8/63
Cry Baby Cry	Angels	3/62
Cry To Me	Betty Harris	9/63
Crying	Roy Orbison	8/61
Crying in the Chapel	Sonny Til & the Orioles	7/53
Crying in the Chapel	June Valli	7/53
Crying in the Chapel	Elvis Presley	4/65
Crying in the Rain	Everly Brothers	1/62
Crying Time	Ray Charles	12/65
Cupid	Sam Cooke	6/61

D

Da Doo Ron Ron	Crystals	4/63
Daddy Cool	Rays	10/57
Daddy's Home	Shep & the Limelites	4/61
Daddy-O	Bonnie Lou	8/55
Daddy-O	Fontane Sisters	10/55
Daisy Petal Pickin'	Jimmy Gilmer & the Fireballs	12/63
Dance by the Light of the		
Moon	Olympics	12/60
Dance Dance Dance	Beach Boys	11/64
Dance Everyone Dance	Betty Madigan	8/58
Dance on Little Girl	Paul Anka	6/61
Dance the Mess Around	Chubby Checker	4/61
Dance to the Bop	Gene Vincent	11/57
Dance with Me	Drifters	10/59
Dance with Me Henry	Etta James	2/55
Dance with Me Henry	Georgia Gibbs	3/55
Dance with the Guitar Man	Duane Eddy	10/62
Dancin' Party	Chubby Checker	6/62
Dancing in the Street	Martha & the Vandellas	8/64
Danke Schoen	Wayne Newton	7/63
Danny Boy	Conway Twitty	10/59
Dark Moon	Gale Storm	4/57
Dark Moon	Bonnie Guitar	4/57
Darling Lorraine	Knockouts	1/60
Dawn	Four Seasons	2/64
Day the Rains Came	Jane Morgan	9/58
Day the Rains Came	Raymond LeFevre	11/58
Days of Wine & Roses	Henry Mancini	1/63
Days of Wine & Roses	Andy Williams	3/63
Dean Man's Curve	Jan & Dean	3/64
Dear Heart	Jack Jones	11/64
Dear Heart	Andy Williams	11/64
Dear Ivan	Jimmy Dean	1/62
Dear Lady Twist	Gary "U.S." Bonds	12/61
Dear Lonely Hearts	Nat "King" Cole	11/62

Dear One	Larry Finnegan	2/62
Deck of Cards	Wink Martindale	9/59
De De Dinah	Frankie Avalon	1/58
Dedicated to the One I Love	Shirelles	1/61
Deep Purple	Billy Ward & the Dominoes	9/57
Deep Purple	Nino Tempo & April Stevens	9/63
Delicious	Jim Backus & Friend	7/58
Deliah Jones	McGuire Sisters	4/56
Denise	Randy & the Rainbows	6/63
Deserie	Charts	7/64
Detroit City	Bobby Bare	6/63
Devil or Angel	Clovers	1/56
Devil or Angel	Bobby Vee	8/60
Devil Woman	Marty Robbins	7/62
Devoted to You	Everly Brothers	8/58
Diamonds & Pearls	Paradons	8/60
Diana	Paul Anka	7/57
Diane	Bachelors	4/64
Diary, The	Neil Sedaka	12/58
Dim Dim the Lights	Bill Haley & the Comets	11/54
Ding-A-Ling	Bobby Rydell	5/60
Dinner with Drac	John Zacherle	3/58
Do I Love You	Ronettes	6/64
Do the Bird	Dee Dee Sharp	3/63
Do the Clam	Elvis Presley	2/65
Do the Freddie	Chubby Checker	4/65
Do the New Continental	Dovells	1/62
Do Wah Diddy Diddy	Manfred Mann	9/64
Do You Love Me	Contours	8/62
Do You Want to Dance	Bobby Freeman	5/58
Do You Wanna Dance	Beach Boys	2/65
Does Your Chewing Gum Lose It's Flavor	Lonnie Donegan	8/61
Doncha' Think It's Time	Elvis Presley	4/58
Don't	Elvis Presley	1/58
Don't Ask Me Why	Elvis Presley	6/58
Don't Be Afraid, Little Darlin'	Steve Lawrence	3/63
Don't Be Angry	Nappy Brown	4/55
Don't Be Cruel	Elvis Presley	8/56
Don't Be Cruel	Bill Black's Combo	8/60
Don't Believe Him Donna	Lenny Miles	1/61
Don't Bet Money Honey	Linda Scott	7/61
Don't Blame Me	Everly Brothers	10/61
Don't Break the Heart That Loves You	Connie Francis	2/62
Don't Come Knockin'	Fats Domino	7/60
Don't Cry Baby	Etta James	8/61
Don't Forbid Me	Pat Boone	12/56
Don't Go Home	Playmates	6/58
Don't Go Near the Indians	Rex Allen	9/62
Don't Go to Strangers	Vaughn Monroe	1/56
Don't Go to Strangers	Etta Jones	11/60

Don't Hang Up	Orlons	10/62
Don't Just Stand There	Patty Duke	6/65
Don't Let Go	Roy Hamilton	1/58
Don't Let Him Shop Around	Debbie Dean	2/61
Don't Pity Me	Dion & the Belmonts	12/58
Don't Play That Song	Ben E. King	4/62
Don't Say Goodnight & Mean Goodbye	Shirelles	6/63
Don't Say Nothin' Bad	Cookies	3/63
Don't Set Me Free	Ray Charles	2/63
Don't Take Your Guns to Town	Johnny Cash	1/59
Don't Throw Away All Those Teardrops	Frankie Avalon	3/60
Don't Worry	Marty Robbins	2/61
Don't Worry Baby	Beach Boys	5/64
Don't You Believe It	Andy Williams	9/62
Don't You Just Know It	Huey "Piano" Smith	3/58
Don't You Know	Della Reese	9/59
Dog, The	Rufus Thomas	2/62
Dogface Soldier	Russ Morgan	9/55
Doggin' Around	Jackie Wilson	4/60
Doll House	Donnie Brooks	12/60
Dominique	Singing Nun	11/63
Donde Esta Santa Claus	Augie Rios	12/58
Donna	Richie Valens	11/58
Donna the Prima Donna	Dion	9/63
Door Is Still Open to My Heart	Dean Martin	9/64
Do-Re-Mi	Lee Dorsey	12/61
Down at Papa Joe's	Dixiebelles	9/63
Down by the Station	Four Preps	1/60
Down in the Boondocks	Billy Joe Royal	7/65
Down the Aisle	Patti LaBelle & the Blue Belles	9/63
Down the Aisle of Love	Quin-Tones	8/58
Drag City	Jan & Dean	12/63
Dragnet	Ray Anthony	8/53
Dream Baby	Roy Orbison	2/62
Dream Lover	Bobby Darin	4/59
Dream on Little Dreamer	Perry Como	4/65
Dreamer, The	Neil Sedaka	7/63
Dreamin'	Johnny Burnett	7/60
Dreamy Eyes	Four Preps	2/56
Dreamy Eyes	Johnny Tillotson	11/58
Drip Drop	Dion	11/63
Drownin' My Sorrows	Connie Francis	8/63
Drums Are My Beat	Sandy Nelson	2/62
Duke of Earl	Gene Chandler	1/62
Dutchman's Gold	Walter Brennan	5/60
Dungaree Doll	Eddie Fisher	11/55
Dum Dum	Brenda Lee	6/61

257

E

Early in the Morning	Rinky Dinks	7/58
Early in the Morning	Buddy Holly	8/58
Earth Angel	Penguins	12/54
Earth Angel	Crew Cuts	1/55
Easier Said Than Done	Essex	6/63
Ebb Tide	Lenny Welch	3/64
Ebb Tide	Righteous Brothers	12/65
Ebony Eyes	Everly Brothers	2/61
Eddie My Love	Chordettes	2/56
Eddie My Love	Fontane Sisters	2/56
Eddie My Love	Teen Queens	2/56
18 Yellow Roses	Bobby Darin	5/63
El Paso	Marty Robbins	11/59
El Rancho Rock	Champs	5/58
El Watusi	Ray Barreto	4/63
11th Hour Melody	Al Hibbler	1/56
11th Hour Melody	Lou Busch	2/56
Eloise	Kay Thompson	2/56
Emotions	Brenda Lee	1/61
Empty Arms	Teresa Brewer	3/57
Empty Arms	Ivory Joe Hunter	4/57
Enchanted	Platters	3/59
Enchanted Island	Four Lads	6/58
Enchanted Island	Islanders	10/59
Enchanted Sea	Martin Denny	11/59
End, The	Earl Grant	9/58
End of the World	Skeeter Davis	1/63
Endless Sleep	Jody Reynolds	5/58
Endlessly	Brook Benton	4/59
Eso Beso	Paul Anka	11/62
Eventually	Brenda Lee	7/61
Everlovin'	Ricky Nelson	10/61
Every Beat of My Heart	Pips	5/61
Every Breath I Take	Gene Pitney	8/61
Every Little Bit Hurts	Brenda Holloway	5/64
Every Night	Chantels	3/58
Every Step of the Way	Johnny Mathis	5/63
Everybody	Tommy Roe	10/63
Everybody Likes to Cha Cha Cha	Sam Cooke	3/59
Everybody Loves a Lover	Doris Day	7/58
Everybody Loves a Lover	Shirelles	12/62
Everybody Loves Me But You	Brenda Lee	4/62
Everybody's Somebody's Fool	Connie Francis	5/60
Everyday I Have to Cry	Steve Alaimo	1/63
Everyone's Laughing	Spaniels	6/57
Everything's All Right	Newbeats	10/64
Exodus	Ferrante & Teicher	11/60
Exodus	Mantovani	11/60
Exodus	Eddie Harris	4/61

F

Fabulous	Charlie Gracie	5/57
Fabulous Character	Sarah Vaughn	7/56
Fallen Star	Jimmy Newman	6/57
Fallin'	Connie Francis	10/58
Falling	Roy Orbison	6/63
Fame & Fortune	Elvis Presley	4/60
Fannie Mae	Buster Brown	2/60
Farther up the Road	Bobby Bland	7/57
Feel So Fine	Johnny Preston	6/60
Feel So Good	Shirley & Lee	7/55
Fell in Love on Monday	Fats Domino	3/61
Fever	Little Willie John	6/56
Fever	Peggy Lee	7/58
Find Another Girl	Jerry Butler	3/61
Finger Poppin' Time	Hank Ballard & the	
	Midnighters	5/60
Fingertips—Part 2	Little Stevie Wonder	6/63
Firefly	Tony Bennett	9/58
First Date, First Kiss, First		
Love	Sonny James	3/57
First Name Initial	Annette	11/59
First Quarrel	Paul & Paula	6/63
Fish, The	Bobby Rydell	7/61
500 Miles from Home	Bobby Bare	10/63
Flaming Star	Elvis Presley	4/61
Fly, The	Chubby Checker	10/61
Fly Me to the Moon Bossa		
Nova	Joe Harnell	12/62
Flying Circle	Frank Slay	12/61
Flying Saucer	Buchanan & Goodman	7/56
Flying Saucer the 2nd	Buchanan & Goodman	7/57
Follow That Dream	Elvis Presley	5/62
Follow the Boys	Connie Francis	3/62
Fool, The	Sanford Clark	7/56
Fool, The	Gallahads	8/56
Fool In Love	Ike & Tina Turner	9/60
Fool Never Learns	Andy Williams	1/64
Fool #1	Brenda Lee	10/61
Fool Such As I	Elvis Presley	3/59
Fools Fall in Love	Drifters	2/57
Fool's Hall of Fame	Pat Boone	9/59
Fools Rush In	Brook Benton	11/60
Fools Rush In	Ricky Nelson	9/63
Foolish Little Girl	Shirelles	3/63
Footsteps	Steve Lawrence	3/60
Foot Stompin'—Part I	Flares	9/61
For a Penny	Pat Boone	3/59
For Love	Lloyd Price	5/60
For My Baby	Brook Benton	2/61
For My Good Fortune	Pat Boone	9/58
For You	Ricky Nelson	12/63

For Your Love	Ed Townsend	4/58
For Your Precious Love	Jerry Butler	6/58
For Your Precious Love	Garnett Mimms & the Enchanters	11/63
Forever	Little Dippers	1/60
Forever	Pete Drake	3/64
Forever Darling	Ames Brothers	2/56
Forget Him	Bobby Rydell	11/64
Forget Me Not	Kalin Twins	10/58
Fortune Teller	Bobby Curtola	5/62
Forty Miles of Bad Road	Duane Eddy	6/58
409	Beach Boys	10/62
Four Walls	Jim Reeves	4/57
Four Walls	Jim Lowe	5/57
Frankie	Connie Francis	5/59
Frankie & Johnny	Brook Benton	8/61
Frankie & Johnny	Sam Cooke	7/63
Fraulein	Bobby Helms	7/57
Free	Tommy Leonetti	5/56
Freeze, The	Tony & Joe	7/58
Freight Train	Rusty Draper	5/67
Friendly Persuasion	Pat Boone	9/56
From a Jack to a King	Ned Miller	12/62
From the Vine Came the Grape	Gaylords	1/54
From the Vine Came the Grape	Hilltoppers	2/54
Fun Fun Fun	Beach Boys	2/64
Funny	Maxine Brown	4/61
Funny	Joe Hinton	8/64
Funny How Time Slips Away	Jimmy Elledge	11/61
Funny Way of Laughin'	Burl Ives	4/62

G

Garden of Eden	Joe Valino	10/56
Gee	Crows	4/54
Gee, But It's Lonely	Pat Boone	9/58
Gee Whittakers	Pat Boone	11/55
Gee Whiz	Carla Thomas	2/61
Gee Whiz	Innocents	11/61
Georgia on My Mind	Ray Charles	10/60
Get a Job	Silhouettes	1/58
(Ghost Riders) in the Sky	Ramrods	1/61
Ghost Town	Don Cherry	7/56
Gidget	James Darren	5/59
Gina	Johnny Mathis	9/62
Gingerbread	Frankie Avalon	7/58
Ginnie Bell	Paul Dino	1/61
Ginny Come Lately	Brian Hyland	3/62
Girl Can't Help It	Little Richard	1/57
Girl Come Running	Four Seasons	6/65
Girl in My Dreams	Cliques	5/56

260

Girl of My Best Friend	Ral Donner	4/61
Girl with the Golden Braids	Perry Como	5/57
(Girls, Girls, Girls) Made to Love	Eddie Hodges	6/62
Girls Grow Up Faster Than Boys	Cookies	11/63
Give Him a Great Big Kiss	Shangri-Las	12/64
Give Myself a Party	Don Gibson	10/58
Give Us This Day	Joni James	7/56
Give Us Your Blessings	Shangri-Las	5/65
Glendora	Perry Como	5/56
Gloria	Passions	2/60
Glory of Love	Roomates	4/61
Go Away Little Girl	Steve Lawrence	11/62
Go, Jimmy, Go	Jimmy Clanton	12/59
Go on with the Wedding	Kitty Kallen	12/55
Go on with the Wedding	Patti Page	12/55
God, Country and My Baby	Johnny Burnette	10/61
Goin' Out of My Head	Little Anthony & the Imperials	11/64
Goin' Steady	Tommy Sands	5/57
Going, Going, Gone	Brook Benton	1/64
Gone	Ferlin Husky	2/57
Gone Gone Gone	Everly Brothers	10/64
Gonna Find Me a Bluebird	Marvin Rainwater	5/57
Gonna Get Along Without Ya Now	Patience & Prudence	11/56
Good Golly, Miss Molly	Little Richard	2/58
Good Luck Charm	Elvis Presley	3/62
Good News	Sam Cooke	1/64
Good Rockin' Tonight	Elvis Presley	8/54
Good Time Baby	Bobby Rydell	1/61
Good Times	Sam Cooke	5/64
Good Timin'	Jimmy Jones	4/60
Goodbye Baby	Jack Scott	12/58
Goodbye Baby, Goodbye	Solomon Burke	4/64
Goodbye Cruel World	James Darren	10/61
Goodbye Jimmy, Goodbye	Kathy Linden	4/59
Goodnight	Roy Orbison	2/65
Goodnight My Love	Jessie Belvin	11/56
Goodnight My Love	McGuire Sisters	11/56
Goodnight My Love	Ray Peterson	11/59
Goodnight My Love	Fleetwoods	6/63
Goodnight Sweetheart	McGuire Sisters	6/54
Goodnite Sweetheart Goodnite	Spaniels	4/54
Goody Goody	Frankie Lymon & the Teenagers	7/57
Got a Girl	Four Preps	4/60
Got a Match	Daddy-O's	6/58
Got a Match	Frank Gallop	6/58
Gotta Travel On	Billy Grammer	11/58
Got To Get You Off My Mind	Solomon Burke	3/65

Graduation Day	Four Freshmen	5/56
Graduation Day	Rover Boys	5/56
Graduation's Here	Fleetwoods	5/59
Grass Is Greener	Brenda Lee	9/63
Gravy	Dee Dee Sharp	6/62
Great Balls of Fire	Jerry Lee Lewis	11/57
Great Pretender	Platters	11/55
Greatest Hurt	Jackie Wilson	1/62
Green Door, The	Jim Lowe	9/56
Green Fields	Brothers Four	2/60
Green Green	New Christy Minstrels	6/63
Green Mosquito, The	Tune Rockers	8/58
Green Onions	Booker T. & the M.G.'s	8/62
G. T. O.	Ronny & the Daytonas	8/64
Guess Things Happen That Way	Johnny Cash	5/58
Guess Who	Jessie Belvin	4/59
Guitar Boogie Shuffle	Virtues	3/59
Gum Drop	Crew Cuts	8/55
Gypsy Cried	Lou Christie	1/63
Gypsy Rover	Highwaymen	11/61
Gypsy Woman	Impressions	10/61

H

Half Heaven-Half Heartache	Gene Pitney	12/62
Halfway to Paradise	Tony Orlando	5/61
Handy Man	Jimmy Jones	1/60
Handy Man	Del Shannon	7/64
Hang Up My Rock & Roll Shoes	Chuck Willis	4/58
Hanging Tree	Marty Robbins	2/59
Happiness Street	Tony Bennett	8/56
Happiness Street	Georgia Gibbs	8/56
Happy Birthday Blues	Kathy Young & the Innocents	2/61
Happy Birthday, Sweet Sixteen	Neil Sedaka	11/61
Happy-Go-Lucky Me	Paul Evans	5/60
Happy Happy Birthday Baby	Tune Weavers	9/57
Happy Organ	Dave "Baby" Cortez	3/59
Happy Reindeer	Dancer, Prancer & Nervous	12/59
Happy Whistler	Don Robertson	4/56
Harbor Lights	Platters	1/60
Hard Headed Woman	Elvis Presley	6/58
Hard Times (The Slop)	Noble Watts	12/57
Harlem Nocturne	Viscounts	1/60
Harlem Shuffle	Bob & Earl	12/63
Harry the Hairy Ape	Ray Stevens	6/63
Hats Off to Larry	Del Shannon	6/61
Haunted House	Jumpin' Gene Simmons	8/64
Have a Good Time	Sue Thompson	6/62
Have I Told You Lately That I Love You	Ricky Nelson	9/57
Have You Heard	Duprees	11/63

Having a Party	Sam Cooke	5/62
Hawaiian Wedding Song	Andy Williams	1/59
He	Al Hibbler	10/55
He	McGuire Sisters	10/55
He Knows I Love Him Too Much	Paris Sisters	1/62
He Will Break Your Heart	Jerry Butler	11/60
He Walks Like a Man	Jody Miller	2/64
He'll Have to Go	Jim Reeves	1/60
He'll Have to Stay	Jeannie Black	5/60
He's a Rebel	Crystals	9/62
He's Got the Whole World (In His Hands)	Laurie London	3/58
He's Mine	Platters	3/57
He's My Dreamboat	Connie Francis	10/61
He's So Fine	Chiffons	2/62
He's Sure The Boy I Love	Crystals	12/62
He's the Great Imposter	Fleetwoods	9/62
Heart and Soul	Cleftones	5/61
Heart and Soul	Jan & Dean	7/61
Heart in Hand	Brenda Lee	7/62
Hearts of Stone	Jewels	8/54
Hearts of Stone	Charms	11/54
Hearts of Stone	Fontane Sisters	11/54
Hearts of Stone	Bill Black's Combo	2/61
Heartaches	Marcels	10/61
Heartaches by the Number	Guy Mitchell	10/59
Heartaches by the Number	Johnny Tillotson	8/65
Heartbeat	Buddy Holly	1/59
Heartbreak	Little Willie John	6/60
Heartbreak Hotel	Elvis Presley	2/56
Heartbreak Hotel	Stan Freberg	7/56
Heartbreak (It's Hurtin' Me)	Jon Thomas	6/60
Heat Wave	Martha & the Vandellas	8/63
Heaven and Paradise	Don Julian & the Meadowlarks	6/55
Heaven on Earth	Platters	7/56
Heavenly Lover	Teresa Brewer	3/59
Hello Heartache, Goodbye Love	Little Peggy March	9/63
Hello Mary Lou	Ricky Nelson	5/61
Hello Mudduh, Hello Faddah	Allan Sherman	8/63
Hello Stranger	Barbara Lewis	5/63
Hello Walls	Faron Young	4/61
Hello Young Lovers	Paul Anka	8/60
Help Me Rhonda	Beach Boys	4/65
Henrietta	Jimmy Dee	12/57
Her Royal Majesty	James Darren	2/62
Here Comes Summer	Jerry Keller	7/59
Hey! Baby	Bruce Channel	1/62
Hey Bobba Needle	Chubby Checker	3/64
Hey Girl	Freddy Scott	7/63
Hey, Let's Twist	Joey Dee & the Starliters	2/62

Hey Jean Hey Dean	Dean & Jean	2/64
Hey Little Cobra	Rip Chords	12/63
Hey Little Girl	Dee Clark	8/59
Hey! Little Girl	Del Shannon	12/61
Hey! Little Girl	Major Lance	10/63
Hey! Little Girl	Techniques	12/63
Hey Little One	Dorsey Burnett	6/60
Hey Paula	Paul & Paula	12/62
Hey! Schoolgirl	Tom & Jerry	12/57
Hey There Lonely Boy	Ruby & the Romantics	8/63
Hi-Heel Sneakers	Tommy Tucker	2/64
Hide and Go Seek	Bunker Hill	8/62
Hideaway	Four Esquires	9/58
Hide Away	Freddy King	3/61
Hide 'Nor Hair	Ray Charles	4/62
High Hopes	Frank Sinatra	6/59
High School Confidential	Jerry Lee Lewis	5/58
High School U.S.A.	Tommy Facenda	10/59
High Sign	Diamonds	4/58
Hippy Hippy Shake	Swinging Blue Jeans	3/64
Hit Record	Brook Benton	5/62
Hit the Road, Jack	Ray Charles	9/61
Hitch Hike	Marvin Gaye	1/63
Hold Me, Thrill Me, Kiss Me	Mel Carter	6/65
Honest I Do	Jimmy Reed	9/57
Honest I Do	Innocents	8/60
Honeycomb	Jimmie Rodgers	8/57
Honey Love	Drifters	5/54
Honky Tonk	Bill Doggett	8/56
Honky Tonk (Part 2)	Bill Doggett	2/61
Honolulu Lulu	Jan & Dean	9/63
Hoochi Coochi Coo	Hank Ballard & the Midnighters	12/60
Hooka Tooka	Chubby Checker	12/63
Hootenanny	Glencoves	6/63
Hopeless	Andy Williams	6/63
Hot Diggity	Perry Como	2/56
Hot Pastrami	Dartels	4/63
Hot Pastrami with Mashed Potatoes	Joey Dee & the Starliters	3/63
Hot Rod Lincoln	Charlie Ryan	5/60
Hot Rod Lincoln	Johnny Bond	8/60
Hotel Happiness	Brook Benton	11/62
Hound Dog	Elvis Presley	7/56
Hound Dog Man	Fabian	11/59
House of Blue Lights	Chuck Miller	5/55
House With Love In It	Four Lads	8/56
How About That	Dee Clark	12/59
How Do You Think I Feel	Elvis Presley	2/56
How Important Can It Be	Joni James	2/55
How Many Tears	Bobby Vee	6/61
How Sweet It Is	Marvin Gaye	12/64

264

How the Time Flies	Jerry Wallace	8/58
How's the World Treating You	Elvis Presley	2/56
Hucklebuck, The	Chubby Checker	10/60
Hula Hoop Song	Teresa Brewer	10/58
Hula Hoop Song	Georgia Gibbs	10/58
Hula Love	Buddy Knox	8/57
Hully Gully	Olympics	2/60
Hully Gully Baby	Dovells	8/62
Human	Tommy Hunt	9/61
Hummingbird	Les Paul & Mary Ford	7/55
Hummingbird	Chordettes	8/55
Hundred Pounds of Clay	Gene McDaniels	3/61
Hurt	Timi Yuro	7/61
Hurt So Bad	Little Anthony & the Imperials	2/65
Hushabye	Mystics	5/59

I

I Adore Him	Angels	10/63
I Ain't Never	Webb Pierce	8/59
I Almost Lost My Mind	Pat Boone	5/56
I Beg of You	Elvis Presley	1/58
I Believe	Bachelors	6/64
I Can Never Go Home Anymore	Shangri-Las	11/65
I Can't Help It	Johnny Tillotson	10/62
I Can't Help Myself	Four Tops	4/65
(I Can't Help You) I'm Falling Too	Skeeter Davis	8/60
I Can't Stay Mad at You	Skeeter Davis	9/63
I Can't Stop Loving You	Ray Charles	5/62
I Count the Tears	Drifters	12/60
I Cried a Tear	Laverne Baker	12/58
I Dig Girls	Bobby Rydell	10/59
(I Do the) Shimmy Shimmy	Bobby Freeman	6/60
I Don't Care if the Sun Don't Shine	Elvis Presley	10/56
I Don't Know Why	Linda Scott	11/61
I Don't Love You No More	Jimmy Norman	6/62
I Don't Want to be a Loser	Lesley Gore	5/64
I Don't Want to Cry	Chuck Jackson	2/61
I Don't Want to Take a Chance	Mary Wells	7/61
I Dreamed	Betty Johnson	11/56
I Dreamed of a Hill-Billy Heaven	Tex Ritter	7/61
I Fall to Pieces	Patsy Cline	5/61
I Feel Good	Shirley & Lee	2/56
I Feel So Bad	Elvis Presley	5/61
I Forgot to Remember to Forget	Elvis Presley	8/54
I Found a Girl	Jan & Dean	10/65

I Get Around	Beach Boys	5/64
I Go Ape	Neil Sedaka	3/59
I Got a Feeling	Ricky Nelson	10/58
I Got a Wife	Mark IV	2/59
I Got a Woman	Ricky Nelson	3/63
I Got a Woman	Freddy Scott	11/63
I Got Stripes	Johnny Cash	8/59
I Got Stung	Elvis Presley	11/58
I Got What I Wanted	Brook Benton	3/63
I Gotta Dance to Keep from Crying	Smokey Robinson & the Miracles	11/63
I Gotta Know	Elvis Presley	11/60
I Gotta Woman	Ray Charles	4/65
I Have a Boy Friend	Chiffons	11/63
I Hear You Knockin'	Smiley Lewis	8/55
I Hear You Knockin'	Gale Storm	10/55
I Hear You Knocking	Fats Domino	12/61
I Just Don't Know	Four Lads	5/57
I Just Don't Understand	Ann-Margaret	7/61
I Knew You When	Billy Joe Royal	9/65
I Know	Barbara George	11/61
I Like It Like That	Chris Kenner	6/61
I Like It Like That	Smokey Robinson & the Miracles	6/64
I Like Your Kind of Love	Andy Williams	5/57
I Love How You Love Me	Paris Sisters	9/61
I Love My Baby	Jill Corey	12/56
I Love the Way You Love	Marv Johnson	3/60
I Love You	Volumes	4/62
I Love You and Don't You Forget It	Perry Como	6/63
I Love You Baby	Paul Anka	12/57
I Love You Because	Al Martino	4/63
(I Love You) For Sentimental Reasons	Sam Cooke	12/57
I Love You in the Same Old Way	Paul Anka	8/60
I Love You More and More Every Day	Al Martino	2/64
I Love You So	Chantels	6/58
I Love You the Way You Are	Bobby Vinton	8/62
I Met Him on a Sunday	Shirelles	4/58
I Miss You So	Chris Conner	10/56
I Miss You So	Paul Anka	4/59
I Miss You So	Little Anthony & the Imperials	10/65
I Must Be Seeing Things	Gene Pitney	2/65
I Need Your Love Tonight	Elvis Presley	4/59
I Need Your Loving	Don Gardner & Dee Dee Ford	6/62
I Only Have Eyes For You	Flamingos	6/59

I Only Want To Be With You	Dusty Springfield	1/64
I Promise to Remember	Frankie Lymon & the	
	Teenagers	7/56
I Put a Spell on You	Screamin' Jay Hawkins	11/56
I Really Don't Want to Know	Tommy Edwards	5/60
I Really Love You	Stereos	10/61
I Remember You	Frank Ifield	9/62
I Rise, I Fall	Johnny Tillotson	5/64
I Saw Linda Yesterday	Dickey Lee	12/62
I Shot Mr. Lee	Bobbettes	7/60
I Sold My Heart to the Junk		
Man	Blue Belles	4/62
I Understand (Just How You		
Feel)	G-Clefs	9/61
I Waited Too Long	Laverne Baker	4/59
I Walk the Line	Johnny Cash	9/56
I Wanna Be Loved	Ricky Nelson	12/59
(I Wanna) Love My Life Away	Gene Pitney	2/61
I Wanna Thank You	Bobby Rydell	10/61
I Want to be Wanted	Brenda Lee	9/60
I Want to Stay Here	Steve Lawrence & Eydie	
	Gorme	7/63
I Want to Walk You Home	Fats Domino	8/59
I Want You, I Need You, I		
Love You	Elvis Presley	5/56
I Want You to be My Girl	Frankie Lymon & the	
	Teenagers	4/56
I Was Such a Fool	Connie Francis	10/62
I Was the One	Elvis Presley	2/56
I Will Follow Him	Little Peggy March	3/63
I Wish I Was a Princess	Little Peggy March	6/63
I Wish That We Were Married	Ronnie & the Hi-Lites	3/62
I (Who Have Nothing)	Ben E. King	6/63
I Wonder	Brenda Lee	7/63
I Wonder What She's Doing		
Tonight	Barry & the Tamerlanes	10/63
I Wonder Why	Dion & the Belmonts	5/58
I Wouldn't Trade You for the		
World	Bachelors	9/64
I'll Be Home	Pat Boone	1/56
I'll Be Home	Flamingos	1/56
I'll Be in Trouble	Temptations	5/64
I'll Be Satisfied	Jackie Wilson	6/59
I'll Be There	Bobby Darin	7/60
I'll Be There	Damita Jo	7/61
I'll Come Running Back to		
You	Sam Cooke	12/57
I'll Keep Holding On	Marvelettes	4/65
I'll Make All Your Dreams		
Come True	Ronnie Dove	8/65
I'll Never Dance Again	Bobby Rydell	6/62
I'll Never Smile Again	Platters	8/61

I'll Remember Today	Patti Page	10/57
I'll Remember Tonight	Pat Boone	11/58
I'll Save the Last Dance For You	Damita Jo	10/60
I'll See You in My Dreams	Pat Boone	1/62
I'll Take You Home	Drifters	9/63
I'll Touch a Star	Terry Stafford	5/64
I'll Try Something New	Smokey Robinson & the Miracles	5/62
I'll Wait For You	Frankie Avalon	10/58
I'm a Fool to Care	Joe Barry	4/61
I'm a Hog For You	Coasters	9/59
I'm a Man	Fabian	1/59
I'm a Telling You	Jerry Butler	7/61
I'm Blue	Ikettes	1/62
I'm Comin' On Back to You	Jackie Wilson	6/61
I'm Gettin' Better	Jim Reeves	6/60
I'm Gonna be a Wheel Someday	Fats Domino	8/59
I'm Gonna Be Strong	Gene Pitney	10/64
I'm Gonna Be Warm this Winter	Connie Francis	12/62
I'm Gonna Get Married	Lloyd Price	8/59
I'm Gonna Knock on Your Door	Eddie Hodges	6/61
I'm Gonna Sit Right Down and Write Myself a Letter	Billy Williams	5/57
I'm Hurtin'	Roy Orbison	12/60
I'm in Love Again	Fats Domino	4/56
I'm in Love Again	Fontane Sisters	5/56
I'm in Love with You	Pat Boone	5/56
I'm in the Mood for Love	Chimes	4/61
I'm Just a Dancing Partner	Platters	2/56
I'm Learning About Love	Brenda Lee	2/61
I'm Leaving It Up to You	Dale & Grace	10/63
I'm Movin' On	Ray Charles	11/59
I'm Movin' On	Matt Lucas	5/63
I'm Never Gonna Tell	Jimmie Rodgers	3/59
I'm Not Afraid	Ricky Nelson	9/60
I'm on the Outside (Looking In)	Little Anthony & the Imperials	8/64
I'm Ready	Fats Domino	5/59
I'm So Proud	Impressions	4/64
I'm Sorry	Platters	3/57
I'm Sorry	Brenda Lee	6/60
I'm Sorry I Made You Cry	Connie Francis	5/58
I'm Stickin' with You	Jimmy Bowen	2/57
I'm the Girl from Wolverton Mountain	Jo-Ann Campbell	8/62
I'm Waiting Just for You	Pat Boone	3/57
I'm Walkin'	Fats Domino	2/57

I'm Walking	Ricky Nelson	5/57
I'm Yours	Elvis Presley	8/65
I've Been Around	Fats Domino	11/59
I've Come of Age	Billy Storm	4/59
I've Got a Woman	Jimmy McGriff	10/62
I've Got Bonnie	Bobby Rydell	2/62
I've Got Sand in My Shoes	Drifters	9/64
I've Had It	Bell Notes	2/59
I've Told Every Little Star	Linda Scott	3/61
If a Man Answers	Bobby Darin	9/62
If a Woman Answers	Leroy Van Dyke	3/62
If Dreams Came True	Pat Boone	7/58
If I Didn't Care	Connie Francis	3/59
If I Didn't Care	Platters	1/61
If I Didn't Have a Dime	Gene Pitney	9/62
If I Give My Heart to You	Kitty Kallen	10/59
If I Had a Girl	Rod Lauren	12/59
If My Pillow Could Talk	Connie Francis	5/63
If You Don't Want My Love	Jaye P. Morgan	7/55
If You Gotta Make a Fool of Somebody	James Raye	11/61
If You Need Me	Solomon Burke	4/63
If You Wanna Be Happy	Jimmy Soul	3/63
Iko Iko	Dixie Cups	4/65
Image of a Girl	Safaris	6/60
In Dreams	Roy Orbison	2/63
In My Lonely Room	Martha & the Vandellas	4/64
In My Little Corner of the World	Anita Bryant	7/60
In My Room	Beach Boys	11/63
In the Middle of a Heartache	Wanda Jackson	10/61
In the Middle of an Island	Tony Bennett	7/57
In the Middle of the House	Vaughn Monroe	8/56
In the Middle of the House	Rusty Draper	9/56
In the Misty Moonlight	Jerry Wallace	7/64
In the Mood	Ernie Fields	9/59
In the Still of the Night	Dion & the Belmonts	7/60
In the Still of the Nite	Five Satins	8/56
Innamorata	Dean Martin	2/56
Innamorata	Jerry Vale	2/56
Irresistible You	Bobby Darin	12/61
Is a Blue Bird Blue	Conway Twitty	6/60
Is It True	Brenda Lee	10/64
Is There Any Chance	Marty Robbins	6/60
It Doesn't Matter Anymore	Buddy Holly	3/59
It Happened Today	Skyliners	10/59
It Hurts Me	Elvis Presley	2/64
It Hurts to be in Love	Gene Pitney	7/64
It Hurts to be Sixteen	Andrea Carroll	7/63
It Isn't Right	Platters	9/56
It Keeps on Rainin'	Fats Domino	5/61
It Keeps Right on A-Hurtin'	Johnny Tillotson	5/62

It Might as Well Rain Until September	Carole King	8/62
It Only Happened Yesterday	Jack Scott	8/60
It Only Hurts for a Little While	Ames Brothers	4/56
It Started All Over Again	Brenda Lee	6/62
It Was I	Skip & Flip	6/59
It's All in the Game	Tommy Edwards	8/58
It's All in the Game	Cliff Richard	12/63
It's All Right	Impressions	9/63
It's Almost Tomorrow	Snooky Lanson	7/55
It's Almost Tomorrow	David Carroll	11/55
It's Almost Tomorrow	Dream Weavers	11/55
It's Almost Tomorrow	Jo Stafford	11/55
(It's Been a Long Time) Pretty Baby	Gino & Gina	5/58
It's Gonna Work Out Fine	Ike & Tina Turner	8/61
It's Growing	Temptations	4/65
It's Just a Matter of Time	Brook Benton	2/59
It's Late	Ricky Nelson	3/59
It's My Party	Lesley Gore	5/63
It's Not For Me to Say	Johnny Mathis	4/57
It's Now or Never	Elvis Presley	7/60
It's Only Make Believe	Conway Twitty	9/58
It's Over	Roy Orbison	4/64
It's So Easy	Crickets	9/58
It's the Same Old Song	Four Tops	7/65
It's Time to Cry	Paul Anka	11/59
It's Too Soon to Know	Pat Boone	2/58
It's Up to You	Ricky Nelson	12/62
It's You I Love	Fats Domino	5/57
Italian Theme	Cyril Stapleton	8/56
Itchy Twitchy Feeling	Bobby Hendricks	8/58
Itsy Bitsy Teenie Weenie Yellow Polka Dot Bikini	Brian Hyland	7/60
Itty Bitty Pieces	James Ray	4/62
Ivory Tower	Cathy Carr	3/56
Ivory Tower	Otis Williams & the Charms	3/56
Ivory Tower	Gale Storm	4/56

J

Jailhouse Rock	Elvis Presley	10/57
Jam, The	Bobby Gregg & His Friends	3/62
Jamaica Farewell	Harry Belafonte	10/56
Jambalaya	Fats Domino	12/61
James (Hold the Ladder Steady)	Sue Thompson	9/62
Jamie	Eddie Holland	1/62
Java	Al Hirt	1/64
Jealous of You	Connie Francis	5/60
Jenny Jenny	Little Richard	6/57
Jennie Lee	Jan & Arnie	5/58

Jeremiah Peabody's Poly Unsaturated Quick Dissolving Fast Acting Pleasant Tasting Green and Purple Pills	Ray Stevens	8/61
Jerk, The	Larks	11/64
Jim Dandy	Lavern Baker	12/56
Jimmy's Girl	Johnny Tillotson	1/61
Jingle Bell Rock	Bobby Helms	12/57
Jingle Bell Rock	Bobby Rydell & Chubby Checker	12/61
Jo-Ann	Playmates	1/58
Jo-Jo the Dog Faced Boy	Annette	4/59
Johnny Angel	Shelly Fabares	3/62
Johnny B. Goode	Chuck Berry	4/58
Johnny Get Angry	Joanie Sommers	5/62
Johnny Jingo	Hayley Mills	3/62
Johnny Loves Me	Shelly Fabares	6/62
Johnny Will	Pat Boone	11/61
Joker, The	Hilltoppers	11/57
Joker, The	Billy Myles	11/57
Josephine	Bill Black's Combo	7/60
Judy's Turn to Cry	Lesley Gore	7/63
Juke Box Saturday Night	Nino & the Ebb Tides	9/61
Jump Over	Freddy Cannon	5/60
June Night	Jimmy Dorsey	8/57
Jura	Les Paul & Mary Ford	4/61
Just a Dream	Jimmy Clanton	7/58
Just a Little	Brenda Lee	10/60
Just a Little Too Much	Ricky Nelson	7/59
Just As Much As Ever	Bob Becham	8/59
Just Ask Your Heart	Frankie Avalon	9/59
Just Be True	Gene Chandler	7/64
Just Because	Lloyd Price	2/57
Just Between You and Me	Chordettes	8/57
Just Born	Perry Como	10/57
Just for Old Times Sake	McGuire Sisters	3/61
Just Keep It Up	Dee Clark	5/59
(Just Like) Romeo & Juliet	Reflections	4/64
Just Married	Marty Robbins	4/58
Just One Look	Doris Troy	6/63
Just One Time	Don Gibson	3/60
Just Once in My Life	Righteous Brothers	4/65
Just Out of Reach	Solomon Burke	9/61
Just Tell Her Jim Said Hello	Elvis Presley	8/62
Just to Be With You	Passions	10/59
Just to Hold My Hand	Clyde McPhatter	5/57
Just Walking in the Rain	Johnnie Ray	8/56

K

Ka-Ding-Dong	Diamonds	8/56
Ka-Ding-Dong	G-Clefs	7/56
Ka-Ding-Dong	Hilltoppers	9/56
Kansas City	Wilbert Harrison	4/59
Keep a Knockin'	Little Richard	9/57
Keep on Dancing	Gentrys	9/65
Keep on Pushing	Impressions	6/64
Keep Searchin'	Del Shannon	11/64
Keep Your Hands Off My Baby	Little Eva	11/62
Kewpie Doll	Perry Como	4/58
Kiddio	Brook Benton	8/60
Killer Joe	Rocky Fellers	3/63
Kind of Boy You Can't Forget	Raindrops	8/63
King of Clowns	Neil Sedaka	3/62
King of the Whole Wide World	Elvis Presley	9/62
Kiss Away	Ronnie Dove	11/65
Kiss Me Another	Georgia Gibbs	5/56
Kiss Me Quick	Elvis Presley	5/64
Kiss Me Sailor	Diane Renay	4/62
Kisses Sweeter Than Wine	Jimmie Rodgers	11/57
Kissin' Cousins	Elvis Presley	2/64
Kissin' on the Phone	Paul Anka	9/61
Kissin' Time	Bobby Rydell	7/59
Knee Deep in the Blues	Guy Mitchell	1/57
Ko Ko Mo	Perry Como	1/55
Ko Ko Mo	Crew Cuts	1/55
Ko Ko Mo	Gene and Eunice	7/55
Kookie, Kookie (Lend Me Your Comb)	Edward Byrnes	4/59
Kookie Little Paradise	Jo-Ann Campbell	8/60

L

La Bamba	Ritchie Valens	1/59
La Dee Dah	Billy & Lillie	12/57
La-Do-Dada	Dale Hawkins	8/58
La Paloma	Billy Vaughn	8/58
Lady Luck	Lloyd Price	2/60
Language of Love	John D. Loudermilk	11/61
Last Chance to Turn Around	Gene Pitney	5/65
Last Date	Floyd Cramer	10/60
Last Date	Lawrence Welk	10/60
Last Kiss	J. Frank Wilson & the Cavaliers	9/64
Last Night	Mar-Keys	7/61
Lasting Love	Sal Mineo	8/57
Laughing Boy	Mary Wells	2/63
Laurie	Dickey Lee	5/65
Lavender Blue	Sammy Turner	6/59
Lawdy Miss Clawdy	Gary Stites	2/60

272

Lay Down Your Arms	Chordettes	9/56
Lazy Elsie Molly	Chubby Checker	6/64
Lazy Mary	Lou Monte	3/58
Lazy River	Bobby Darin	2/61
Lazy Summer Night	Four Preps	8/58
Leader of the Laundromat	Detergents	12/64
Leader of the Pack	Shangri-Las	10/64
Leah	Roy Orbitson	10/62
Left Right Out of Your Heart	Patti Page	6/58
Leroy	Jack Scott	5/58
Let It Be Me	Everly Brothers	1/60
Let It Be Me	Betty Everett & Jerry Butler	9/64
(Let Me Be Your) Teddy Bear	Elvis Presley	6/57
Let Me Belong to You	Brian Hyland	8/61
Let Me Go Lover	Joan Weber	1/54
Let Me Go Lover	Teresa Brewer	12/54
Let Me In	Sensations	1/62
Let the Bells Keep Ringing	Paul Anka	4/58
Let the Four Winds Blow	Roy Brown	6/57
Let the Four Winds Blow	Fats Domino	7/61
Let the Good Times Roll	Shirley & Lee	8/56
Let the Little Girl Dance	Billy Bland	2/60
Let There Be Drums	Sandy Nelson	11/61
Let's Dance	Chris Montez	8/62
Lets Get Together	Haley Mills	9/61
Let's Go	Routers	11/62
Let's Go Again	Hank Ballard & the Midnighters	2/61
Let's Go Let's Go Let's Go	Hank Ballard & the Midnighters	9/60
Let's Go Steady Again	Neil Sedaka	4/63
Let's Hang On	Four Seasons	10/65
Let's Have a Party	Wanda Jackson	9/60
Let's Kiss and Make Up	Bobby Vinton	12/62
Let's Limbo Some More	Chubby Checker	2/63
Let's Lock the Door	Jay & the Americans	12/64
Let's Love	Johnny Mathis	1/59
Let's Think About Living	Bob Luman	9/60
Let's Turkey Trot	Little Eva	2/63
Let's Twist Again	Chubby Checker	6/61
Letter, The	Medallions	5/54
Letter from Sherry	Dale Ward	12/63
Letter Full of Tears	Gladys Knight & the Pips	12/61
Letter to An Angel	Jimmy Clanton	10/58
Liar Liar	Castaways	8/65
Lie to Me	Brook Benton	8/62
Life Is But a Dream	Harptones	3/54
Lightning Strikes	Lou Christie	12/65
Like I Love You	Edward Byrnes	8/59
Like Strangers	Everly Brothers	11/60
Like Young	Andre Previn	6/59
Limbo Rock	Champs	5/62

Limbo Rock	Chubby Checker	9/62
Linda	Jan & Dean	2/62
Linda Lu	Ray Sharpe	7/59
Ling Ting Tong	Five Keys	12/54
Ling Ting Tong	Charms	1/55
Lion Sleeps Tonight	Tokens	11/61
Lips of Wine	Andy Williams	9/57
Lipstick and Candy and Rubber Sole Shoes	Julius La Rosa	2/56
Lipstick on Your Collar	Connie Francis	5/59
Lipstick Traces	Benny Spellman	5/62
Lisbon Antigua	Nelson Riddle	11/55
Lisbon Antigua	Mitch Miller	1/56
Little Band of Gold	James Gilreath	3/63
Little Bit of Heaven	Ronnie Dove	6/65
Little Bit of Soap	Jarmels	8/61
Little Bitty Girl	Bobby Rydell	2/60
Little Bitty Pretty One	Thurston Harris	10/57
Little Bitty Pretty One	Bobby Day	11/57
Little Bitty Pretty One	Clyde McPhatter	6/62
Little Bitty Tear	Burl Ives	12/61
Little Black Book	Jimmy Dean	9/62
Little Blue Man	Betty Johnson	2/58
Little Boy Sad	Johnny Burnett	2/61
Little By Little	Micki Marlo	2/57
Little Coco Palm	Jenny Wallace	1/60
Little Darlin'	Diamonds	3/57
Little Darlin'	Gladiolas	3/57
Little Diane	Dion	7/62
Little Deuce Coupe	Beach Boys	8/63
Little Devil	Neil Sedaka	5/61
Little Dipper	Mickey Mozart Quintet	5/59
Little Egypt	Coasters	4/61
Little Girl I Once Knew	Beach Boys	11/65
Little Girl of Mine	Cleftones	4/56
Little Honda	Hondells	9/64
Little Latin Lupe Lu	Righteous Brothers	5/63
Little Love Can Go a Long, Long Way	Dream Weavers	4/56
Little Miss Blue	Dion	12/60
Little Old Lady (From Pasadena)	Jan & Dean	6/64
Little Red Rented Row Boat	Joe Dowell	6/62
Little Red Rooster	Sam Cooke	10/63
Little Sandy Sleighfoot	Jimmy Dean	12/57
Little Sister	Elvis Presley	8/61
Little Space Girl	Jessie Lee Turner	1/59
Little Star	Elegants	7/58
Little Things Mean a Lot	Kitty Kallen	3/54
Little Things Mean a Lot	Joni James	1/60
Little Town Flirt	Del Shannon	12/62
Little White Lies	Betty Johnson	4/57

Live Wire	Martha & the Vandellas	2/64
Living a Lie	Al Martino	10/63
Living Doll	Cliff Richard	10/59
Lizzie Borden	Mitchell Trio	1/62
Loco-Motion, The	Little Eva	6/62
Loddy Lo	Chubby Checker	11/63
Lollipop	Chordettes	3/58
Lollipop	Ronald & Ruby	3/58
Lollipops and Roses	Jack Jones	3/62
L-O-N-E-L-Y	Bobby Vinton	5/65
Lonely Blue Boy	Conway Twitty	1/60
Lonely Boy	Paul Anka	6/59
Lonely Bull	Herb Alpert & the Tijuana Brass	10/62
Lonely For You	Gary Stites	4/59
Lonely Guitar	Annette	7/59
Lonely Island	Sam Cooke	3/58
Lonely Man	Elvis Presley	3/61
Lonely Nights	Hearts	3/55
Lonely One	Duane Eddy	1/59
Lonely Street	Andy Williams	9/59
Lonely Surfer	Jack Nitzsche	8/63
Lonely Teardrops	Jackie Wilson	11/58
Lonely Teenager	Dion	10/60
Lonely Weekends	Charlie Rich	3/60
Lonesome Town	Ricky Nelson	10/58
Long Lonely Nights	Lee Andrews & the Hearts	8/57
Long Lonely Nights	Bobby Vinton	3/65
Long Tall Sally	Little Richard	3/56
Long Tall Sally	Pat Boone	4/56
Long Tall Texan	Murry Kellum	11/63
Longest Walk	Jaye P. Morgan	8/55
Look for a Star	Dean Hawley	6/60
Look for a Star	Garry Miles	6/60
Look for a Star	Gary Mills	6/60
Look for a Star	Billy Vaughn	6/60
Look Homeward Angel	Johnny Ray	1/57
Look in My Eyes	Chantels	9/61
Looking Back	Nat "King" Cole	4/58
Looking Through the Eyes of Love	Gene Pitney	7/65
Loop De Loop	Johnny Thunder	12/62
Losing You	Brenda Lee	4/63
Lost Love	H. B. Barnum	1/61
Lotta Lovin'	Gene Vincent	8/57
Louie Louie	Kingsmen	11/63
Love Came to Me	Dion	11/62
Love Is a Golden Ring	Frankie Laine	3/57
Love Is a Many Splendored Thing	Don Cornell	8/55
Love Is a Many Splendored Thing	Four Aces	8/55

Love Is All We Need	Tommy Edwards	11/58
Love Is Strange	Mickey & Sylvia	12/56
Love Letters	Ketty Lester	2/62
Love Letters in the Sand	Pat Boone	5/57
Love Love Love	Clovers	6/56
Love Love Love	Diamonds	6/56
Love Makes the World Go Round	Perry Como	10/58
Love Makes the World Go Round	Paul Anka	1/63
Love Me	Elvis Presley	11/56
Love Me to Pieces	Jill Corey	7/57
Love Me Tender	Elvis Presley	10/56
Love Me Tender	Henri Rene	11/56
Love Me Tender	Richard Chamberlain	10/62
Love Me Warm and Tender	Paul Anka	2/62
Love Me With All Your Heart	Ray Charles Singers	4/64
Love of My Life	Everly Brothers	1/58
Love of My Man	Theola Kilgore	4/63
Love Potion No. 9	Clovers	9/59
Love She Can Count On	Smokey Robinson & the Miracles	3/63
Love So Fine	Chiffons	9/63
Love Walked In	Dinah Washington	10/60
Love You Most of All	Sam Cooke	11/58
Love You So	Ron Holden	4/60
Lovely One	Four Voices	2/56
Lovely Lies	Manhattan Brothers	2/56
Lover Please	Clyde McPhatter	3/62
Lovers by Night, Strangers by Day	Fleetwoods	10/62
Lover's Concerto	Toys	9/65
Lover's Island	Blue Jays	8/61
Lovers Never Say Goodbye	Flamingos	1/59
Lover's Question	Clyde McPhatter	10/58
Lovers Who Wander	Dion	4/62
Lovesick Blues	Frank Ifield	12/62
Lovey-Dovey	Clovers	3/54
Lovey-Dovey	Buddy Knox	12/60
Loving You	Elvis Presley	6/57
Lucille	Little Richard	3/57
Lucille	Everly Brothers	9/60
Lucky Devil	Carl Dobkins, Jr.	12/59
Lucky Ladybug	Billy & Lillie	12/58
Lucky Lips	Ruth Brown	2/57
Lullaby of Birdland	Blue Stars	11/55
Lullabye of Love	Frank Gari	4/61

M

Mack the Knife	Bobby Darin	8/59
Mack the Knife	Ella Fitzgerald	5/60
Madison, The	Al Brown's Tunetoppers	4/60

276

Madison Time	Ray Bryant	4/60
Magic Moments	Perry Como	1/58
Magic Touch	Platters	3/56
Magnificent Seven	Al Caiola	12/60
Main Title & Molly-O	Dick Jacobs	3/56
Main Title from the Man with the Golden Arm	Elmer Bernstein	3/56
Majestic, The	Dion	12/61
Make It Easy on Yourself	Jerry Butler	7/62
Make Me a Miracle	Jimmie Rodgers	5/58
Make Me Your Baby	Barbara Lewis	9/65
Make the World Go Away	Timi Yuro	7/63
Make the World Go Away	Eddy Arnold	10/65
Makin' Love	Floyd Robinson	7/59
Mama	Connie Francis	2/60
Mama Didn't Lie	Jan Bradley	1/63
Mama From the Train	Patti Page	10/56
Mama Said	Shirelles	4/61
Mama Sang a Song	Bill Anderson	10/62
Mama Sang a Song	Walter Brennan	10/62
Mama Sang a Song	Stan Kenton	10/62
Mambo Rock	Bill Haley & the Comets	2/55
(Man Who Shot) Liberty Valance	Gene Pitney	4/62
Manhattan Spiritual	Reg Owen	12/58
Many Tears Ago	Connie Francis	11/60
March from the River Kwai	Mitch Miller	1/58
Maria	Johnny Mathis	6/60
Maria Elena	Los Indios Trabajaras	9/63
Marianne	Terry Gilkyson & the Easy Riders	1/57
Marianne	Hilltoppers	1/57
Marie	Bachelors	6/65
Marie's the Name of His Latest Flame	Elvis Presley	9/61
Marina	Rocco Granata	11/59
Marlena	Four Seasons	7/63
Martian Hop	Ran-Dells	8/63
Marvelous Toy	Mitchell Trio	11/63
Mary Ann Regrets	Burl Ives	11/62
Mary Lee	Rainbows	6/55
Mary Lou	Ronnie Hawkins	8/59
Mary's Little Lamb	James Darren	6/62
Mashed Potato Time	Dee Dee Sharp	3/62
Matador, The	Major Lance	3/64
May You Always	McGuire Sisters	1/59
Maybe	Chantels	1/58
Maybe Baby	Crickets	2/58
Maybe I Know	Lesley Gore	7/64
Maybelline	Chuck Berry	8/55
Maybelline	Johnny Rivers	8/64
Mean Woman Blues	Roy Orbison	9/63

Mecca	Gene Pitney	3/63
Melodie D'Amour	Ames Brothers	9/57
Melody of Love	David Carrol	12/54
Melody of Love	Billy Vaughn	12/54
Melody of Love	Four Aces	1/55
Memories Are Made of This	Dean Martin	11/55
Memories Are Made of This	Gale Storm	12/55
Memories of You	Four Coins	11/55
Memphis	Lonnie Mack	6/63
Memphis	Johnny Rivers	5/64
Mercy Mercy	Don Covay	9/64
Mess of Blues	Elvis Presley	7/60
Mexican Hat Rock	Apple Jacks	9/58
Mexico	Bob Moore	8/61
Miami	Eugene Church	8/59
Michael	Highwaymen	7/61
Mickey's Monkey	Smokey Robinson & the	
	Miracles	8/63
Midnight	Paul Anka	7/58
Midnight in Moscow	Kenny Ball	2/62
Midnight Mary	Joey Powers	11/63
Midnight Stroll	Revels	10/59
Midnite Special	Paul Evans	1/60
Mighty Good	Ricky Nelson	12/59
Miller's Cave	Bobby Bare	2/64
Million to One	Jimmy Charles	8/60
Miracle of Love	Eileen Rodgers	8/56
Misery	Dynamics	11/63
Missing You	Ray Peterson	8/61
Mission Bell	Donnie Brooks	6/60
Mr. Bass Man	Johnny Cymbal	2/63
Mr. Blue	Fleetwoods	9/59
Mr. Custer	Larry Verne	9/60
Mr. Lee	Bobbettes	7/57
Mr. Lonely	Bobby Vinton	10/64
Mr. Lucky	Henry Mancini	4/60
Mr. Sandman	Chordettes	10/64
Mr. Songwriter	Connie Stevens	8/62
Mr. Wonderful	Teddi King	2/56
Mr. Wonderful	Peggy Lee	2/56
Mr. Wonderful	Sarah Vaughn	2/56
Misty	Johnny Mathis	10/59
Misty	Lloyd Price	10/63
Mockingbird	Inez Foxx	6/63
Mockingbird, The	Four Lads	11/58
Model Girl	Johnny Maestro	2/61
Mohair Sam	Charlie Rich	8/65
Moments to Remember	Four Lads	9/54
Mona Lisa	Carl Mann	6/59
Mona Lisa	Conway Twitty	7/59
Money	Barret Strong	2/60
Money Honey	Drifters	10/53

Money Honey	Elvis Presley	5/56
Money Tree, The	Patience & Prudence	11/56
Money Tree, The	Margaret Whiting	11/56
Monkey Time	Major Lance	7/63
Monster Mash	Bobby (Boris) Pickett	9/62
Monster's Holiday	Bobby (Boris) Pickett	12/62
Moody River	Pat Boone	5/61
Moonglow and Theme from Picnic	George Cates	4/56
Moonglow and Theme from Picnic	Morris Stoloff	4/56
Moon River	Jerry Butler	10/61
Moon River	Henry Mancini	10/61
Moon Talk	Perry Como	7/58
Moonlight Gambler	Frankie Laine	11/56
Moonlight Serenade	Rivieras	2/59
Moonlight Swim	Nick Noble	8/57
Moonlight Swim	Tony Perkins	10/57
More	Perry Como	6/56
More	Kai Winding	7/63
More Money for You and Me	Four Preps	8/61
Morgen	Ivo Robic	8/59
Morning Side of the Mountain	Tommy Edwards	3/59
Most People Get Married	Patti Page	4/62
Mostly Martha	Crewcuts	12/55
Mother-In-Law	Ernie K-Doe	4/61
Mountain of Love	Harold Dorman	3/60
Mountain of Love	Johnny Rivers	10/64
Mountain's High	Dick & Dee Dee	8/61
Move Two Mountains	Marv Johnson	9/60
Mule Skinner Blues	Fendermen	5/60
Multiplication	Bobby Darin	12/61
Mummy, The	Bob McFadden	8/59
Mutual Admiration Society	Teresa Brewer	10/56
My Babe	Righteous Brothers	9/63
My Baby Left Me	Elvis Presley	5/56
My Blue Heaven	Fats Domino	4/56
My Bonnie Lassie	Ames Brothers	9/55
My Boy Flat Top	Boyd Bennett & the Rockets	11/55
My Boy Flat Top	Dorothy Collins	12/55
My Boy Lollypop	Millie Small	5/64
My Boyfriend's Back	Angels	8/63
My Boomerang Won't Come Back	Charlie Drake	1/62
My Bucket's Got a Hole in It	Ricky Nelson	3/58
My Coloring Book	Kitty Kallen	12/62
My Coloring Book	Sandy Stewart	12/62
My Dad	Paul Peters	11/62
My Dearest Darling	Etta James	9/60
My Dream	Platters	5/57
My Empty Arms	Jackie Wilson	1/61
My Girl	Temptations	1/65

My Girl Has Gone	Smokey Robinson & the Miracles	10/65
My Girl Josephine	Fats Domino	11/60
My Girl Sloopy	Vibrations	3/64
My Guy	Mary Wells	4/64
My Happiness	Connie Francis	12/58
My Heart Belongs to Only You	Bobby Vinton	2/64
My Heart Cries for You	Ray Charles	2/64
My Heart Has a Mind of It's Own	Connie Francis	8/60
My Heart is an Open Book	Carl Dobkins, Jr.	4/59
My Hero	Blue Notes	10/60
My Home Town	Paul Anka	5/60
My Kind of Girl	Matt Munro	6/61
My Last Date	Joni James	12/60
My Last Date With You	Skeeter Davis	12/60
My Little Angel	Four Lads	4/56
My Melancholy Baby	Tommy Edwards	5/59
My One Sin	Four Coins	9/57
My Own True Love	Jimmy Clanton	8/59
My Own True Love	Duprees	10/62
My Prayer	Platters	6/56
My Real Name	Fats Domino	5/62
My Special Angel	Bobby Helms	10/57
My Summer Love	Ruby & the Romantics	5/63
My Treasure	Hilltoppers	12/55
My True Confession	Brook Benton	6/63
My True Love	Jack Scott	6/58
My True Story	Jive Five	7/61
My Whole World Is Falling Down	Brenda Lee	7/63
My Wish Came True	Elvis Presley	7/59
Mystery Train	Elvis Presley	8/54
N		
Nadine	Chuck Berry	3/64
Nag	Halos	7/61
Name Game	Shirley Ellis	12/64
Nature Boy	Bobby Darin	6/61
Natural Born Lover	Fats Domino	11/60
Navy Blue	Diane Renay	1/64
Ne Ne Na Na Na Na Nu Nu	Dickey Doo & the Don'ts	4/58
Near You	Roger Williams	8/58
Need to Belong	Jerry Butler	11/63
Need You	Donnie Owens	10/58
Needles & Pins	Jackie Deshannon	5/63
Nel Blu Dipinto Di Blu	Domenico Modugno	8/58
New Girl in School	Jan & Dean	3/64
New Lovers	Pat Boone	2/60
New Mexico Rose	Four Seasons	10/63
New Orleans	Gary "U.S." Bonds	10/60

Never Be Anyone Else But You	Ricky Nelson	3/59
Never on Sunday	Don Costa	8/60
Never on Sunday	Chordettes	6/61
Next Door to an Angel	Neil Sedaka	10/62
Night	Jackie Wilson	3/60
Night Has a Thousand Eyes	Bobby Vee	12/62
Night Lights	Nat "King" Cole	10/56
Night Train	James Brown	4/62
Ninety-Nine Ways	Tab Hunter	3/57
Ninety Nine Years	Guy Mitchell	1/56
Nitty Gritty	Shirley Ellis	11/63
No Arms Can Ever Hold You	Gaylords	8/55
No Arms Can Ever Hold You	Georgie Shaw	10/55
No Arms Can Ever Hold You	Bachelors	12/64
No Chemise, Please	Gerry Granahan	5/58
No If's—No And's	Lloyd Price	5/60
No Love	Johnny Mathis	12/57
No More	De John Sisters	12/64
No More	McGuire Sisters	1/55
No No No	Chanters	6/61
No Not Much	Four Lads	1/56
No One	Connie Francis	1/61
No One	Ray Charles	6/63
No One Knows	Dion & the Belmonts	8/58
No One Will Ever Know	Jimmie Rodgers	9/62
No Other Arms	Pat Boone	9/55
No Other Arms, No Other Lips	Chordettes	3/59
No Particular Place to Go	Chuck Berry	5/64
Nobody But You	Dee Clark	12/58
Nobody Loves Me Like You	Flamingos	4/60
Nola	Billy Williams	1/59
Norman	Sue Thompson	12/61
North to Alaska	Johnny Horton	9/60
Not Me	Orlons	6/63
Not One Minute More	Della Reese	12/59
Not Too Young To Get Married	Bob B. Soxx & the Blue Jeans	6/63
Nothing Can Change This Love	Sam Cooke	9/62
Nothing Can Stop Me	Gene Chandler	4/65
Now and For Always	George Hamilton IV	3/58
Nowhere to Run	Martha & the Vandellas	2/65
Nut Rocker	B. Bumble & the Stingers	3/62
Nuttin' for Christmas	Fontane Sisters	11/55
Nuttin' for Christmas	Barry Gordon	11/55
Nuttin' for Christmas	Joe Ward	11/55
Nuttin' for Christmas	Ricky Zahnd	11/55
Nuttin' for Christmas	Stan Freberg	12/55

O

O Dio Mio	Annette	2/60
Oh Boy!	Crickets	11/57
Oh! Carol	Neil Sedaka	10/59
Oh Julie	Crescendos	12/57
Oh, Little One	Jack Scott	5/60
Oh Lonesome Me	Don Gibson	3/58
Oh No Not My Baby	Maxine Brown	10/64
Oh-Oh I'm Falling in Love Again	Jimmie Rodgers	2/58
Oh What a Night	Dells	7/56
Old Cape Cod	Patti Page	5/57
Old Lamplighter, The	Browns	3/60
Old Philosopher, The	Eddie Lawrence	8/56
Old Rivers	Walter Brennan	4/62
Old Shep	Elvis Presley	12/56
Ole Buttermilk Sky	Bill Black's Combo	6/61
On Broadway	Drifters	3/63
On My Word of Honor	Platters	12/56
On the Street Where You Live	Vic Damone	4/56
On the Street Where You Live	Eddie Fisher	5/56
On the Street Where You Live	Andy Williams	9/64
On the Rebound	Floyd Cramer	3/61
On Top of Spaghetti	Tom Glazer & the Children's Chorus	6/63
Once in a While	Chimes	11/60
Once Upon a Time	Rochell & the Candles	2/61
Once Upon a Time	Marvin Gaye & Mary Wells	6/64
One Boy	Joanie Sommers	7/60
One Broken Heart for Sale	Elvis Presley	2/63
One Fine Day	Chiffons	6/63
One in a Million	Platters	12/56
One Kiss for Old Time's Sake	Ronnie Dove	3/65
One Mint Julep	Ray Charles	3/61
One More Time	Ray Charles Singers	11/64
One Night	Elvis Presley	11/58
One of Us	Patti Page	6/60
One Summer Night	Danleers	6/58
One Summer Night	Diamonds	7/61
One Track Mind	Bobby Lewis	9/61
One Who Really Loves You	Mary Wells	3/62
Only in America	Jay & the Americans	8/63
Only Love Can Break a Heart	Gene Pitney	9/62
Only One Love	George Hamilton IV	2/57
Only Sixteen	Sam Cooke	6/59
Only the Lonely	Roy Orbison	6/60
Only You	Hilltoppers	11/55
Only You	Platters	7/55
Only You	Frank Pourcel	4/59
Ooh! My Soul	Little Richard	5/58
Ooh Poo Pah Doo—Part II	Jessie Hill	4/60

Ooo Baby Baby	Smokey Robinson & the Miracles	3/65
Our Day Will Come	Ruby & the Romantics	2/63
Our Love Affair	Tommy Charles	2/56
Our Winter Love	Bill Pursell	2/63
Out of Limits	Marketts	12/63
Out of My Mind	Johnny Tillotson	3/63
Out of Sight	James Brown	8/64
Out of Sight, Out of Mind	Five Keys	9/56
Outside My Window	Fleetwoods	2/60
Over & Over	Bobby Day	8/58
Over the Mountain; Across the Sea	Johnnie & Joe	5/57
Over the Mountain; Across the Sea	Bobby Vinton	3/63
Over the Rainbow	Dimensions	7/60
P		
Padre	Toni Arden	5/58
Painted Tainted Rose	Al Martino	7/63
Palisades Park	Freddy Cannon	5/62
Papa Loves Mambo	Perry Como	9/54
Papa Oom-Mow-Mow	Rivingtons	8/62
Papa's Got a Brand New Bag	James Brown	7/65
Paper Roses	Anita Bryant	4/60
Paper Tiger	Sue Thompson	1/65
Paralyzed	Elvis Presley	12/56
Part of Me	Jimmy Clanton	11/58
Part Time Love	Little Johnnie Taylor	8/63
Party Doll	Buddy Knox	2/57
Party Doll	Steve Lawrence	2/57
Party Lights	Jeannie Black	6/62
Patches	Dickey Lee	8/62
Patricia	Prez Prado	6/58
Patti Ann	Johnny Crawford	3/62
Peace in the Valley	Elvis Presley	6/57
Peanut Butter	Marathons	4/61
Peanuts	Little Joe & the Thrillers	9/57
Peek-A-Boo	Cadillacs	12/58
Peggy Sue	Buddy Holly	11/57
Pennies from Heaven	Skyliners	5/60
People Get Ready	Impressions	2/65
People Say	Dixie Cups	7/64
Pepe	Duane Eddy	12/60
Pepino the Italian Mouse	Lou Monte	12/62
Pepper-Hot Baby	Jaye P. Morgan	7/55
Peppermint Twist	Joey Dee & the Starliters	11/61
Percolator	Billy Joe & the Checkmates	1/62
Perfida	Ventures	11/60
Personality	Lloyd Price	5/59
Peter Gunn	Ray Anthony	1/59
Peter Gunn	Duane Eddy	10/60

Petite Fleur	Chris Barber's Jazz Band	1/59
Petticoats of Portugal	Dick Jacobs	10/56
Philadelphia U.S.A.	Nu-Tornados	11/58
Picnic	McGuire Sisters	4/56
Pineapple Princess	Annette	8/60
Pink Shoe Laces	Dodie Stevens	2/59
Pipeline	Chantays	3/63
Plain Jane	Bobby Darin	2/59
Playboy	Marvelettes	5/62
Playing for Keeps	Elvis Presley	1/57
Plaything	Ted Newman	9/57
Plaything	Nick Todd	10/57
Please Don't Ask About Barbara	Bobby Vee	2/62
Please Don't Go	Ral Donner	10/61
Please Don't Talk to the Lifeguard	Diane Ray	8/63
Please Help Me, I'm Falling	Hank Locklin	5/60
Please Love Me Forever	Tommy Edwards	10/58
Please Love Me Forever	Cathy Jean & the Roomates	3/61
Please Mr. Postman	Marvelettes	9/61
Please Mr. Sun	Tommy Edwards	2/59
Please Stay	Drifters	6/61
Please Tell Me Why	Jackie Wilson	3/61
Pledge of Love	Ken Copeland	3/57
Pledge of Love	Mitchell Torok	4/57
Pledging My Love	Johnny Ace	2/55
Poco-Loco	Gene & Eunice	8/59
Poetry in Motion	Johnny Tillotson	10/60
Point of No Return	Gene McDaniels	8/62
Poison Ivy	Coasters	8/59
Pony Time	Chubby Checker	1/61
Poor Boy	Elvis Presley	12/56
Poor Boy	Royaltones	10/58
Poor Fool	Ike & Tina Turner	12/61
Poor Jenny	Everly Brothers	4/59
Poor Little Fool	Ricky Nelson	6/58
Poor Little Rich Girl	Steve Lawrence	5/63
Poor Man's Roses	Patti Page	2/57
Poor People of Paris	Les Baxter	2/56
Poor People of Paris	Russ Morgan	2/56
Pop Pop Pop-Pie	Sherrys	10/62
Popeye the Hitchhiker	Chubby Checker	9/62
Popsicles & Icicles	Murmaids	1/63
Port Au Prince	Nelson Riddle	3/56
Portrait of My Love	Steve Lawrence	3/61
Portugese Washerwomen	Joe "Fingers" Carr	5/56
Pretty Blue Eyes	Steve Lawrence	11/59
Pretty Girls Everywhere	Eugene Church	12/58
Pretty Little Angel Eyes	Curtis Lee	7/61
Pretty Little Girl	Monarchs	2/58
Pretty Paper	Roy Orbison	12/63
Pretty Woman	Roy Orbison	8/64

284

Pride & Joy	Marvin Gaye	5/63
Primrose Lane	Jerry Wallace	8/59
Princess	Frank Gari	7/61
Princess in Rags	Gene Pitney	11/65
Priscilla	Eddie Cooley & the Dimples	10/56
Prisoner of Love	James Brown	4/63
Problems	Everly Brothers	11/58
Promise Me Love	Andy Williams	8/58
Proud	Johnny Crawford	1/63
P.T. 109	Jimmy Dean	3/62
Puddin 'n Tain	Alley Cats	1/63
Punish Her	Bobby Vee	9/62
Puppet on a String	Elvis Presley	11/65
Puppy Love	Paul Anka	2/60
Puppy Love	Barbara Lewis	1/64
Purple People Eater	Sheb Wooley	5/58
Push & the Kick	Mary Valentino	11/62
Pushover	Etta James	4/63
Pussy Cat	Ames Brothers	8/58
Put a Light in the Window	Four Lads	11/57
Put a Ring on My Finger	Les Paul & Mary Ford	8/58
Put Your Head on My Shoulder	Paul Anka	9/59

Q

Quarter to Three	Gary "U.S." Bonds	5/61
Queen of the Hop	Bobby Darin	10/58
Queen of the Senior Prom	Mills Brothers	5/57
Question	Lloyd Price	7/60
Quicksand	Martha & the Vandellas	11/63
Quiet Three	Duane Eddy	7/59
Quiet Village	Martin Denny	4/59
Quite a Party	Fireballs	7/61

R

Rag Doll	Four Seasons	6/64
Ragtime Cowboy Joe	Chipmunks	7/59
Rain Rain Go Away	Bobby Vinton	8/62
Rainbow	Russ Hamilton	6/57
Raindrops	Dee Clark	5/61
Rainin' In My Heart	Slim Harpo	6/61
Raining In My Heart	Buddy Holly	4/59
Ram-Bunk-Shush	Ventures	1/61
Rama Lama Ding Dong	Edsels	5/61
Ramblin' Rose	Nat "King" Cole	8/62
Ramrod	Duane Eddy	8/58
Rang Tang Ding Dong	Cellos	5/57
Raunchy	Ernie Freeman	11/57
Raunchy	Bill Justis	11/57
Raunchy	Billy Vaughn	11/57
Rave On	Buddy Holly	5/58
Raw-Hide	Link Wray	2/59
Razzle Dazzle	Bill Haley & the Comets	7/55

Ready for Your Love	Shep & the Limelights	7/61
Ready Teddy	Little Richard	6/56
Rebel	Carol Jarvis	8/57
Rebel Rouser	Duane Eddy	6/58
Recovery	Fontella Bass	12/65
Red River Rock	Johnny & the Hurricanes	8/59
Red River Rose	Ames Brothers	1/59
Red Sails in the Sunset	Platters	8/60
Red Sails in the Sunset	Fats Domino	9/63
Reelin' and Rockin'	Chuck Berry	2/58
Reet Petite	Jackie Wilson	10/57
Release Me	Little Esther Phillips	10/62
Remember Diana	Paul Anka	4/62
(Remember Me) I'm the One		
Who Loves You	Dean Martin	5/65
Remember Then	Earls	12/62
Remember (Walkin' in the		
Sand)	Shangri-Las	8/64
Remember When	Platters	6/59
Remember You're Mine	Pat Boone	8/57
Rescue Me	Fontalla Bass	10/65
Return to Me	Dean Martin	3/58
Return to Sender	Elvis Presley	10/62
Revenge	Brook Benton	11/61
Reveille Rock	Johnny & the Hurricanes	11/59
Rhythm of the Rain	Cascades	1/63
Ricochet	Teresa Brewer	10/53
Ride	Dee Dee Sharp	10/62
Ride Away	Roy Orbison	8/65
Ride the Wild Surf	Jan & Dean	9/64
Ride Your Pony	Lee Dorsey	7/65
Right or Wrong	Wanda Jackson	6/61
Right or Wrong	Ronnie Dove	10/64
Ring-A-Ling-A-Lario	Jimmie Rodgers	6/59
Ring of Fire	Johnny Cash	6/63
Ringo	Lorne Greene	10/64
Rinky Dink	Dave "Baby" Cortez	7/62
Rip It Up	Little Richard	6/56
Rip It Up	Bill Haley & the Comets	8/56
Robbin' the Cradle	Tony Bellus	5/59
R-O-C-K	Bill Haley & the Comets	3/56
Rock Love	Fontane Sisters	2/55
Rock Right	Georgia Gibbs	3/56
Rock-A-Beatin' Boogie	Bill Haley & the Comets	11/55
Rock-A-Billy	Guy Mitchell	3/57
Rock-A-Bye Your Baby with a		
Dixie Melody	Jerry Lewis	11/56
Rocka-Conga	Apple Jacks	12/58
Rock and Roll Waltz	Kay Starr	12/55
Rock-A-Hula Baby	Elvis Presley	12/61
Rock & Roll Is Here To Stay	Danny & the Juniors	2/58
Rock & Roll Music	Chuck Berry	11/57

286

Rock Around the Clock	Bill Haley & the Comets	5/55
Rock-In Robin	Bobby Day	8/58
Rock Island Line	Lonnie Donegon	3/56
Rock Your Little Baby to Sleep	Buddy Knox	5/57
Rockin' Around the Christmas Tree	Brenda Lee	12/60
Rockin' Crickets	Hot-Toddys	4/59
Rockin' Good Way	Brook Benton & Dinah Washington	5/60
Rockin' Little Angel	Ray Smith	1/60
Rockin' Pneumonia & the Boogie Woogie Flu	Huey "Piano" Smith	8/57
Roll Over Beethoven	Chuck Berry	6/56
Ronnie	Four Seasons	4/64
Rose & a Baby Ruth	George Hamilton IV	10/56
Roses Are Red	Bobby Vinton	6/62
Round & Round	Perry Como	2/57
Route 66 Theme	Nelson Riddle	6/62
Rubber Ball	Bobby Vee	12/60
Ruby	Ray Charles	11/60
Ruby Ann	Marty Robbins	11/62
Ruby Baby	Dion	1/63
Ruby Duby Du	Tobin Matthews	11/60
Ruby Duby Du	Charles Wolcott	11/60
Rudolph the Red Nosed Reindeer	Chipmunks	12/60
Rudy's Rock	Bill Haley & the Comets	10/56
Rumble	Link Wray	4/58
Rumors	Johnny Crawford	11/62
Run, Baby Run	Newbeats	10/65
Run Red Run	Coasters	12/59
Run Samson Run	Neil Sedaka	8/60
Run to Him	Bobby Vee	11/61
Runaround	Fleetwoods	5/60
Runaround	Regents	7/61
Runaround Sue	Dion	10/61
Runaway	Del Shannon	3/61
Running Bear	Johnny Preston	10/59
Running Scared	Roy Orbison	4/61
Rusty Bells	Brenda Lee	10/65

S

Sacred	Castels	6/61
Sad Mood	Sam Cooke	12/60
Sad Movies (Make Me Cry)	Sue Thompson	9/61
Sad Movies	Lennon Sisters	10/61
Sad, Sad Girl	Barbara Mason	8/65
Sail Along Silvery Moon	Billy Vaughn	12/57
Sailor	Lolita	10/60
St. Therese of the Roses	Billy Ward & the Dominos	8/56
Saints Rock N' Roll	Bill Haley & the Comets	3/56
Sally Go 'Round the Roses	Jaynettes	8/63

Same One	Brook Benton	8/60
San Antonio Rose	Floyd Cramer	6/61
Sandy	Larry Hall	11/59
Sandy	Dion	3/63
Sandy	Ronny & the Daytonas	12/65
Santa & the Satellite	Buchanan & Goodman	12/57
Santa Claus is Coming to Town	Four Seasons	12/62
Satin Pillows	Bobby Vinton	12/65
Saturday Night at the Movies	Drifters	11/64
Save It For Me	Four Seasons	8/64
Save the Last Dance For Me	Drifters	9/60
Saved	Lavern Baker	4/61
Say Man	Bo Diddley	9/59
Say Something Funny	Patty Duke	10/65
Say You	Ronnie Dove	7/64
Scarlet Ribbons	Browns	11/59
School Day	Chuck Berry	3/57
School Is In	Gary "U.S." Bonds	10/61
School Is Out	Gary "U.S." Bonds	7/61
Sea Cruise	Frankie Ford	2/59
Sea of Heartbreak	Don Gibson	6/61
Sea of Love	Phil Phillips	7/59
Sealed With a Kiss	Brian Hyland	6/62
Searchin'	Coasters	5/57
Second Fiddle	Kay Starr	5/56
Secret, The	Gordon MacRae	9/58
Secret Love	Doris Day	1/54
Secretly	Jimmie Rodgers	4/58
See Saw	Harvey & the Moonglows	8/56
See See Rider	Lavern Baker	12/62
See You In September	Tempos	7/59
See You Later, Alligator	Bill Haley & the Comets	12/55
Send Me Some Lovin'	Sam Cooke	1/63
Send Me the Pillow That You Dream On	Johnny Tillotson	8/62
Send for Me	Nat "King" Cole	6/57
September in the Rain	Dinah Washington	10/61
Seven Day Weekend	Gary "U.S." Bonds	6/62
Seven Days	Dorothy Collins	1/56
Seven Days	Crewcuts	1/56
Seven Days	Clyde McPhatter	1/56
7–11	Gone All-Stars	2/58
Seven Little Girls Sitting in the Back Seat	Paul Evans	9/59
Seventeen	Boyd Bennett & the Rockets	8/55
Seventeen	Fontane Sisters	8/55
Sexy Ways	Midnighters	6/54
Sh-Boom	Chords	6/54
Sh-Boom	Crewcuts	6/54
Sha La La	Manfred Mann	11/64
Shadrack	Brook Benton	1/62

288

Shag, The	Billy Graves	2/59
Shake	Sam Cooke	1/65
Shake a Hand	Faye Adams	8/53
Shake a Tail Feather	Five Du-Tones	5/63
Shake Me I Rattle	Marion Worth	12/62
Shake Rattle & Roll	Joe Turner	4/54
Shake Rattle & Roll	Bill Haley & the Comets	8/54
Shake, Shake, Shake	Jackie Wilson	7/63
Shame on Me	Bobby Bare	7/62
Shangri-La	Four Coins	5/57
Shangri-La	Vic Dana	3/64
Shangri-La	Robert Maxwell	3/64
Sharing You	Bobby Vee	5/62
She Can't Find Her Keys	Paul Peterson	3/62
She Cried	Jay & the Americans	3/62
She Say (Oom Dooby Doom)	Diamonds	2/59
She Understands Me	Johnny Tillotson	10/64
She Was Only Seventeen	Marty Robbins	8/58
She's A Fool	Lesley Gore	9/63
She's About A Mover	Sir Douglas Quintet	4/65
She's Everything	Ral Donner	12/61
She's Got You	Patsy Cline	1/62
She's Neat	Dale Wright	1/58
She's Not You	Elvis Presley	8/62
She's The One	Chart Busters	7/64
Sheila	Tommy Roe	7/62
Sherry	Four Seasons	8/62
Shifting Whispering Sands	Rusty Draper	10/55
Shifting Whispering Sands	Billy Vaughn	10/55
Shimmy Like Kate	Olympics	9/60
Shimmy, Shimmy, Ko-Ko-Bop	Little Anthony & the Imperials	12/59
Shish-Kebab	Ralph Marterie	4/57
Shoop Shoop Song	Betty Everett	2/64
Shop Around	Smokey Robinson & the Miracles	12/60
Short Fat Fannie	Larry Williams	6/57
Short Shorts	Royal Teens	1/58
Shout	Isley Brothers	9/59
Shout	Joey Dee & the Starliters	3/62
Shout! Shout! (Knock Yourself Out)	Ernie Maresca	3/62
Shu Rah	Fats Domino	3/61
Shut Down	Beach Boys	4/63
Shutters & Boards	Jerry Wallace	11/62
Sick & Tired	Fats Domino	4/58
Sidewalk Surfin'	Jan & Dean	10/64
Silhouettes	Rays	10/57
Silver Thread & Golden Needles	Springfields	8/62
Since I Don't Have You	Skyliners	2/59
Since I Fell For You	Lenny Welch	10/63

Since I Met You Baby	Mindy Carson	11/56
Since I Met You Baby	Ivory Joe Hunter	11/56
Since You've Been Gone	Clyde McPhatter	6/59
Sincerely	Harvey & the Moonglows	11/54
Sincerely	McGuire Sisters	12/54
Sing Boy Sing	Tommy Sands	2/58
Singin' on a Rainbow	Frankie Avalon	12/59
Singing the Blues	Guy Mitchell	10/56
Singing the Blues	Marty Robbins	10/56
Sink the Bismarck	Johnny Horton	3/60
Sittin' in the Balcony	Eddie Cochran	3/57
Sittin' in the Balcony	Johnny Dee	3/57
Six Days on the Road	Dave Dudley	6/63
Six Nights a Week	Crests	3/59
16 Candles	Crests	11/58
Sixteen Reasons	Connie Stevens	2/60
Sixteen Tons	Ernie Ford	11/55
Skinny Minnie	Bill Haley & the Comets	4/58
Slaughter on Tenth Avenue	Ventures	10/64
Sleep	Little Willie John	9/60
Sleep Walk	Santo & Johnny	8/59
Slippin' & Slidin'	Little Richard	4/56
Slow Twistin'	Chubby Checker	3/62
Slow Walk	Sil Austin	10/56
Slow Walk	Bill Doggett	11/56
Small Sad Sam	Phil McLean	12/61
Small World	Johnny Mathis	6/59
Smoke Gets in Your Eyes	Platters	11/58
Smokie, Part 2	Bill Black's Combo	12/59
Smoky Places	Corsairs	12/61
Snap Your Fingers	Joe Henderson	5/62
So Close	Brook Benton	5/59
So Fine	Fiestas	4/59
So Long Baby	Del Shannon	9/61
So Many Ways	Brook Benton	10/59
So Much In Love	Tymes	6/63
So Rare	Jimmy Dorsey	2/57
So This Is Love	Castels	4/62
So Tough	Casuals	2/58
So Tough	Kuf-Linx	2/58
Soft	Bill Doggett	10/57
Soft Summer Breeze	Eddie Heywood	6/56
Soft Summer Breeze	Diamonds	9/56
Soldier Boy	Shirelles	3/62
Some Enchanted Evening	Jay & the Americans	9/65
Some Kind of Wonderful	Drifters	3/61
Some Kind-A Earthquake	Duane Eddy	11/59
Someone	Johnny Mathis	3/59
Somebody Touched Me	Buddy Knox	8/58
Somebody Up There Likes Me	Perry Como	4/56
Something's Got a Hold on Me	Etta James	2/62
Sometimes	Danny & the Juniors	11/57

Somewhere	Tymes	12/63
Song for a Summer Night	Mitch Miller	7/56
Song from Moulin Rouge	Percy Faith (with Felicia Sanders)	3/53
Song from Moulin Rouge	Montovani	6/53
Soothe Me	Sims Twins	10/61
Sorry (I Ran All the Way Home)	Impalas	3/59
Soul Twist	King Curtis	2/62
South Street	Orlons	2/62
Southtown U.S.A.	Dixie Belles	1/64
Spanish Eyes	Al Martino	12/65
Spanish Harlem	Ben E. King	1/61
Spanish Lace	Gene McDaniels	11/62
Speedo	Cadillacs	11/55
Speedy Gonzalez	Pat Boone	6/62
Splish Splash	Bobby Darin	6/58
Stagger Lee	Lloyd Price	12/58
Stairway to Heaven	Neil Sedaka	4/60
Stand By Me	Ben E. King	5/61
Standing on the Corner	Four Lads	4/56
Standing on the Corner	Dean Martin	5/56
Standing on the Corner	Mills Brothers	5/56
Stardust	Billy Ward & the Dominos	6/57
Stardust	Nino Tempo & April Stevens	2/64
Starbright	Johnny Mathis	3/60
Starlight Starbright	Linda Scott	7/61
Start Movin'	Sal Mineo	5/57
Stay	Maurice Williams & the Zodiacs	10/60
Stay	Four Seasons	2/64
Stay Awhile	Dusty Springfield	3/64
Stayin' In	Bobby Vee	2/61
Steel Guitar & a Glass of Wine	Paul Anka	5/62
Step by Step	Crests	3/60
Sticks and Stones	Ray Charles	7/60
Stick Shift	Duals	9/61
Still	Bill Anderson	4/63
Stood Up	Ricky Nelson	12/57
Stop and Think It Over	Dale & Grace	1/64
Stop the Music	Shirelles	9/62
Stop the Wedding	Etta James	7/62
Story of My Life	Marty Robbins	11/57
Story of My Love	Conway Twitty	2/59
Story of My Love	Paul Anka	1/61
Story Untold	Nutmegs	5/55
Story Untold	Crew Cuts	6/55
Stranded in the Jungle	Jayhawks	6/56
Stranded in the Jungle	Cadets	7/56
Stranded in the Jungle	Gadabouts	7/56
Stranger in Town	Del Shannon	2/65

Stranger on the Shore	Mr. Acker Bilk	3/62
Stranger on the Shore	Andy Williams	6/62
String Along	Fabian	2/60
String Along	Ricky Nelson	5/63
Stripper, The	David Rose	5/62
Stroll, The	Diamonds	12/57
Stuck on You	Elvis Presley	4/60
Stupid Cupid	Connie Francis	7/58
Such a Night	Elvis Presley	7/64
(Such an) Easy Question	Elvis Presley	6/65
Sugar Dumpling	Sam Cooke	7/65
Sugar Moon	Pat Boone	4/58
Sugar Shack	Jimmy Gilmer & the Fireballs	9/63
Sugartime	McGuire Sisters	12/57
Sukiyaki	Kyu Sakamoto	5/63
Summer Set	Monty Kelly	3/60
Summertime; Summertime	Jamies	8/58
Summertime Blues	Eddie Cochran	8/58
Summer's Gone	Paul Anka	10/60
Sunday and Me	Jay & the Americans	11/65
Sunday Kind of Love	Harptones	10/53
Sunshine, Lollypops & Rainbows	Lesley Gore	6/65
Surf City	Jan & Dean	6/63
Surfer Girl	Beach Boys	8/63
Surfer Joe	Surfaris	8/63
Surfer's Stomp	Markettes	1/62
Surfin' Bird	Trashmen	12/63
Surfin' Safari	Beach Boys	8/62
Surfin' U.S.A.	Beach Boys	3/63
Surrender	Elvis Presley	2/61
Susie Darlin'	Robin Luke	8/58
Susie Darlin'	Tommy Roe	10/62
Susie-Q	Dale Hawkins	6/57
Suspicion	Terry Stafford	2/64
Sway	Bobby Rydell	11/60
Sweet Little Sixteen	Chuck Berry	2/58
Sweet Nothin's	Brenda Lee	12/59
Sweet Old Fashioned Girl	Teresa Brewer	5/56
Sweet William	Millie Small	8/64
Sweeter Than You	Ricky Nelson	7/59
Sweets for My Sweet	Drifters	9/61
Swingin' Safari	Billy Vaughn	7/62
Swingin' School	Bobby Rydell	5/60
Swingin' Shepherd Blues	Moe Koffman Quartet	1/58
Swingin' Shepherd Blues	Johnny Pate Quintet	1/58
Switch-A-Roo	Hank Ballard & the Midnighters	7/61

T

Ta Ta	Clyde McPhatter	7/60
Take a Message to Mary	Everly Brothers	4/59
Take Good Care of Her	Adam Wade	3/61
Take Good Care of My Baby	Bobby Vee	8/61
Take Me Back	Little Anthony & the Imperials	6/65
Take These Chains from My Heart	Ray Charles	4/63
Talk Back Trembling Lips	Johnny Tillotson	11/63
Talk That Talk	Jackie Wilson	11/59
Talk to Me	Sunny & the Sunglows	9/63
Talk to Me, Talk to Me	Little Willie John	3/58
Talkin' to the Blues	Jim Lowe	5/57
Talking About My Baby	Impressions	1/64
Tall Cool One	Wailers	5/59
Tall Oak Tree	Dorsey Burnett	2/60
Tall Paul	Annette	1/59
Tallahassee Lassie	Freddy Cannon	5/59
Tammy	Ames Brothers	6/57
Tammy	Debbie Reynolds	7/57
Taste of Honey	Herb Alpert & the Tijuana Brass	9/65
Tea for Two Cha Cha	Tommy Dorsey	8/58
Teach Me Tonight	George Maharis	4/62
Teacher, Teacher	Johnny Mathis	4/58
Tear, A	Gene McDaniels	7/61
Tear Drop	Santo & Johnny	12/59
Tear Drops	Lee Andrews & the Hearts	11/57
Tear Fell	Teresa Brewer	2/56
Tear of the Year	Jackie Wilson	1/61
Tears and Roses	Al Martino	5/64
Tears from an Angel	Troy Shondell	12/61
Tears on My Pillow	Little Anthony & the Imperials	8/58
Teasin'	Quaker City Boys	12/58
Teddy	Connie Francis	3/60
Teen Angel	Mark Dinning	12/59
Teen Beat	Sandy Nelson	9/59
Teen Commandments	Paul Anka—George Hamilton 1V—Johnny Nash	12/58
Teen-Age Crush	Tommy Sands	2/57
Teenage Idol	Ricky Nelson	8/62
Teenager in Love	Dion & the Belmonts	4/59
Teenage Prayer	Gloria Mann	11/55
Teenage Prayer	Gale Storm	12/55
Teenager's Romance	Ricky Nelson	5/57
Tell Him	Exciters	12/62
Tell Him I'm Not Home	Chuck Jackson	2/62
Tell Him No	Travis & Bob	3/59
Tell Laura I Love Her	Ray Peterson	6/60
Tell Me	Dick & Dee Dee	3/62

293

Tell Me Why	Norman Fox & the Rob Roys	12/57
Tell Me Why	Belmonts	5/61
Tell Me Why	Bobby Vinton	5/64
Telstar	Tornadoes	11/62
Temptation	Everly Brothers	6/61
Ten Commandments of Love	Harvey & the Moonglows	9/58
Ten Thousand Drums	Carl Smith	7/59
Tennessee Waltz	Sam Cooke	6/64
Tequila	Champs	2/58
Tequila	Eddie Platt	2/58
Thank You Pretty Baby	Brook Benton	7/59
That Lucky Old Sun	Ray Charles	12/63
That Old Black Magic	Louis Prima & Keely Smith	11/58
That Old Black Magic	Bobby Rydell	5/61
That Stranger Used To Be My Girl	Trade Martin	10/62
That Sunday That Summer	Nat "King" Cole	8/63
That'll Be the Day	Crickets	8/57
That's All I Want From You	Jaye P. Morgan	11/54
That's All There Is To That	Nat "King" Cole	6/56
That's All Right	Elvis Presley	8/54
That's All You Gotta Do	Brenda Lee	6/60
That's Amore	Dean Martin	11/53
That's How Heartaches Are Made	Baby Washington	3/63
That's How Much I Love You	Pat Boone	7/58
That's It—I Quit—I'm Movin' On	Sam Cooke	3/61
That's Life	Gabriel & the Angels	11/62
That's My Little Susie	Ritchie Valens	4/59
That's Old Fashioned	Everly Brothers	5/62
That's the Way Boys Are	Lesley Gore	3/64
That's What Girls Are Made For	Spinners	7/61
That's What Love Is Made Of	Smokey Robinson & the Miracles	9/64
That's When Your Heartaches Begin	Elvis Presley	4/57
That's Why	Jackie Wilson	3/59
That's Your Mistake	Otis Williams & the Charms	1/56
Theme for Young Lovers	Percy Faith	5/60
Theme from a Summer Place	Percy Faith	1/60
Theme from a Summer Place	Lettermen	6/65
Theme from Ben Casey	Valjean	5/62
Theme from Dixie	Duane Eddy	3/61
Theme from Dr. Kildare	Richard Chamberlain	6/62
Theme from the Apartment	Ferrante & Teicher	7/60
Theme from the Man with the Golden Arm	Richard Maltby	3/56
Theme from the Man with the Golden Arm	Billy May	3/56
Theme from the Proud Ones	Nelson Riddle	7/56

Theme from the Three Penny Opera (Moritat)	Richard Hayman	1/56
Theme from the Three Penny Opera (Moritat)	Dick Hyman Trio	1/56
Theme from the Three Penny Opera (Moritat)	Billy Vaughn	1/56
Theme from the Three Penny Opera (Moritat)	Louis Armstrong	2/56
Theme from the Three Penny Opera (Moritat)	Les Paul & Mary Ford	2/56
Theme from the Three Penny Opera (Moritat)	Lawrence Welk	2/56
Theme from the Unforgiven	Don Costa	5/60
Then He Kissed Me	Crystals	8/63
There Goes My Heart	Joni James	9/58
There Goes My Baby	Drifters	6/59
There! I've Said It Again	Bobby Vinton	11/63
There Is Something On Your Mind	Big Jay McNeely	5/59
There Must Be a Way	Joni James	1/59
There She Goes	Jerry Wallace	1/61
There You Go	Johnny Cash	11/56
There's a Gold Mine in the Sky	Pat Boone	8/57
There's a Moon Out Tonight	Capris	1/61
There's No Other	Crystals	11/61
There's Only One of You	Four Lads	3/58
There's Something on Your Mind	Bobby Marchan	6/60
Thing of the Past	Shirelles	7/61
Things	Bobby Darin	7/62
Think	"5" Royales	7/57
Think	James Brown	5/60
Think	Brenda Lee	3/64
Think It Over	Crickets	7/58
Think Twice	Brook Benton	2/61
Thirteen Women	Bill Haley & the Comets	5/55
This Bitter Earth	Dinah Washington	6/60
This Friendly World	Fabian	11/59
This I Swear	Skyliners	6/59
This Is My Story	Gene & Eunice	5/55
This Little Girl	Dion	4/62
This Little Girl of Mine	Everly Brothers	2/58
This Little Girl's Gone Rockin'	Ruth Brown	9/58
This Magic Moment	Drifters	2/60
This Should Go On Forever	Rod Bernard	3/59
This Time	Troy Shondell	9/61
Those Lazy-Hazy-Crazy Days of Summer	Nat "King" Cole	5/63
Those Oldies But Goodies	Little Caesar & the Romans	5/61
Thou Shalt Not Steal	Dick & Dee Dee	11/64
Thousand Miles Away	Heartbeats	12/56

Thousand Stars	Kathy Young & the Innocents	10/60
Three Bells	Browns	8/59
Three Bells	Dick Flood	9/59
Three Hearts in a Tangle	Roy Drusky	4/61
Three Nights a Week	Fats Domino	9/60
Three Stars	Tommy Dee	4/59
Three Steps to the Altar	Shep & the Limelites	10/61
Three Window Coupe	Rip Chords	4/64
Tick Tock	Marvin & Johnny	8/54
Tie Me Kangaroo Down, Sport	Rolf Harris	6/63
Ties That Bind	Brook Benton	4/60
Tiger	Fabian	6/59
Tijuana Taxi	Herb Alpert & the Tijuana Brass	2/65
Til	Roger Williams	10/57
Til	Angels	10/61
'Til I Kissed You	Everly Brothers	8/59
Till Death Do Us Part	Bob Braun	7/62
Till Then	Classics	6/63
Till There Was You	Anita Bryant	7/59
Time and the River	Nat "King" Cole	2/60
Tina Marie	Perry Como	8/55
T. L. C. Tender Love & Care	Jimmie Rodgers	1/60
To a Sleeping Beauty	Jimmy Dean	1/62
To a Soldier Boy	Tassels	7/59
To Be Loved	Jackie Wilson	4/58
To Be Loved (Forever)	Pentagons	2/61
To Each His Own	Platters	10/60
To Know Him Is To Love Him	Teddy Bears	9/58
To the Aisle	Five Satins	7/57
To You My Love	Nick Noble	2/56
Today	New Christy Minstrels	4/64
Today I Met the Boy I'm Gonna Marry	Darlene Love	4/63
Together	Connie Francis	7/61
Togetherness	Frankie Avalon	9/60
Tom Dooley	Kingston Trio	10/58
Tomboy	Perry Como	3/59
Tonight	Ferrante & Teicher	10/61
Tonight (Could be the Night)	Velvets	6/61
Tonight I Fell in Love	Tokens	3/61
Tonight My Love Tonight	Paul Anka	3/61
Tonite Tonite	Mellow Kings	8/57
Tonight You Belong to Me	Patience & Prudence	7/56
Tonight You Belong to Me	Karen Chandler & Jimmy Wakely	9/56
Tonight You Belong to Me	Lennon Sisters	9/56
Tonight's the Night	Shirelles	9/60
Too Many Rivers	Brenda Lee	5/64
Too Many Fish in the Sea	Marvelettes	11/64
Too Much	Elvis Presley	1/57
Too Much Tequila	Champs	1/60

Too Young to go Steady	Nat "King" Cole	3/56
Topsy I	Cozy Cole	9/58
Topsy II	Cozy Cole	8/58
Torquay	Fireballs	10/59
Torero	Renato Carosone	4/58
Torture	Kris Jensen	9/62
Tossin' & Turnin'	Bobby Lewis	4/61
Tower of Strength	Gene McDaniels	10/61
Town Without Pity	Gene Pitney	11/61
Tra La La	Georgia Gibbs	11/56
Tra La La La Suzy	Dean & Jean	1/63
Tracks of My Tears	Smokey Robinson & the Miracles	7/65
Tracy's Theme	Spencer Ross	1/60
Tragedy	Thomas Wayne	2/59
Tragedy	Fleetwoods	4/61
Train of Love	Annette	6/60
Transfusion	Nervous Norvis	5/56
Transistor Sister	Freddy Cannon	8/61
Travelin' Man	Ricky Nelson	4/61
Treasure of Love	Clyde McPhatter	5/56
Treasure of Your Love	Eileen Rodgers	8/58
Treat Me Nice	Elvis Presley	10/57
Triangle	Janie Grant	4/61
Tricky	Ralph Marterie	2/57
Trouble in Paradise	Crests	6/60
Trouble Is My Middle Name	Bobby Vinton	12/62
True Love	Bing Crosby & Grace Kelly	8/56
True Love	Jane Powell	8/56
True Love Never Runs Smooth	Gene Pitney	7/63
True Love True Love	Drifters	11/59
True True Happiness	Johnny Tillotson	8/59
Trust In Me	Etta James	3/61
Try Me	James Brown	12/58
Try the Impossible	Lee Andrews & the Hearts	5/58
Tucumcari	Jimmie Rodgers	9/59
Tuff	Ace Cannon	12/61
Turn Around	Dick & Dee Dee	11/63
Tumbling Tumbleweeds	Billy Vaughn	3/58
Turn Me Loose	Fabian	4/59
Turn on Your Love Light	Bobby Bland	12/61
Turvy II	Cozy Cole	12/58
Tutti Fruitti	Little Richard	12/55
Tutti Fruitti	Pat Boone	1/56
Tweedle Dee	Laverne Baker	1/55
Tweedle Dee	Georgia Gibbs	1/55
Twelfth of Never	Johnny Mathis	10/57
Twenty-Four Hours from Tulsa	Gene Pitney	10/63
Twenty Miles	Chubby Checker	2/62
26 Miles	Four Preps	1/58
Twilight Time	Platters	3/58

Twist, The	Hank Ballard & the Midnighters	7/60
Twist, The	Chubby Checker	8/60
Twist & Shout	Isley Brothers	6/62
Twist-Her	Bill Black's Combo	12/61
Twist It Up	Chubby Checker	7/63
Twist Twist Senora	Gary "U.S." Bonds	3/62
Twistin' Matilda	Jimmy Soul	3/62
Twistin' Postman	Marvelettes	1/62
Twistin' the Night Away	Sam Cooke	2/62
Twistin' U.S.A.	Danny & the Juniors	9/60
Twixt Twelve & Twenty	Pat Boone	6/59
Two Different Worlds	Don Rondo	10/56
Two Different Worlds	Jane Morgan & Roger Williams	10/56
Two Faces Have I	Lou Christie	3/63
Two Hound Dogs	Bill Haley & the Comets	7/55
Two Fools	Frankie Avalon	9/59
Two Kinds of People in the World	Little Anthony & the Imperials	8/58
Two Lovers	Mary Wells	12/62
Two of a Kind	Sue Thompson	3/62
Two Tickets to Paradise	Brook Benton	9/63

U		
Uh! Oh! Part 2	Nutty Squirrels	11/59
Um Um Um Um Um Um	Major Lance	1/64
Unchain My Heart	Ray Charles	12/61
Unchained Melody	Al Hibbler	3/55
Unchained Melody	Roy Hamilton	4/55
Unchained Melody	Righteous Brothers	7/65
Under the Boardwalk	Drifters	6/64
Understand Your Man	Johnny Cash	2/64
Underwater	Frogmen	4/61
Unforgettable	Dinah Washington	10/59
Up a Lazy River	Si Zentner	11/61
Up on the Roof	Drifters	11/62
Uptown	Crystals	3/62
Use Your Head	Mary Wells	1/65
Utopia	Frank Gari	12/60

V		
Vacation	Connie Francis	7/62
Valley of Tears	Fats Domino	5/57
Venus	Frankie Avalon	2/59
Venus in Blue Jeans	Jimmy Clanton	8/62
Very Precious Love	Ames Brothers	4/58
Very Thought of You	Ricky Nelson	4/64
Village of Love	Nathaniel Mayer	4/62
Village of St. Bernadette	Andy Williams	12/59
Viva Las Vegas	Elvis Presley	5/64

Volare	Dean Martin	8/58
Volare	Bobby Rydell	7/60

W

W-P-L-J	Four Deuces	6/55
Wah Watusi, The	Orlons	6/62
Wait a Minute	Coasters	2/61
Wait and See	Fats Domino	10/57
Wait for Me	Playmates	10/60
Wait 'Til My Bobby Gets Home	Darlene Love	7/63
Waitin' in School	Ricky Nelson	12/57
Wake the Town and Tell the People	Les Baxter	8/55
Wake the Town and Tell the People	Mindy Carson	8/55
Wake Up Little Susie	Everly Brothers	9/57
Walk, The	Jimmy McCracklin	2/58
Walk Away	Matt Munro	11/64
Walk—Don't Run	Ventures	7/60
Walk—Don't Run '64	Ventures	7/64
Walk Hand in Hand	Tony Martin	4/56
Walk Like a Man	Four Seasons	1/63
Walk on By	Leroy Van Dyke	11/61
Walk on the Wild Side	Brook Benton	2/62
Walk on the Wild Side	Jimmy Smith	5/62
Walk Right Back	Everly Brothers	2/61
Walk Right In	Rooftop Singers	1/63
Walkin' After Midnight	Patsy Cline	2/57
Walkin' Miracle	Essex	8/62
Walkin' With Mr. Lee	Lee Allen	1/58
Walking Along	Diamonds	11/58
Walking in the Rain	Ronettes	10/64
Walking Proud	Major Lance	10/63
Walking the Dog	Rufus Thomas	10/63
Walking to New Orleans	Fats Domino	6/60
Waltzing Matilda	Jimmie Rodgers	1/60
Wanderer, The	Dion	12/61
Wanting You	Roger Williams	11/55
Warmed Over Kisses	Brian Hyland	9/62
Washington Square	Village Stompers	9/63
Water Boy	Don Shirley Trio	7/61
Waterloo	Stonewall Jackson	5/59
Watermelon Man	Mongo Santamaria	3/63
Watusi	Vibrations	2/61
Way Down Yonder in New Orleans	Freddie Cannon	11/59
Way I Walk	Jack Scott	7/59
Way You Do the Things You Do	Temptations	2/64
Way You Look Tonight	Lettermen	9/61
Ways of a Woman in Love	Johnny Cash	8/58

Wayward Wind	Gogi Grant	4/56
Wayward Wind	Tex Ritter	6/56
We Belong Together	Robert & Johnny	2/58
We Got Love	Bobby Rydell	10/59
Wear My Ring Around Your Neck	Elvis Presley	4/58
Wedding, The	June Valli	11/58
Wedding, The	Julie Rogers	11/64
Welcome Home Baby	Shirelles	6/62
Well I told You	Chantels	11/61
Wendy	Beach Boys	10/64
West of the Wall	Miss Toni Fisher	5/62
Western Movies	Olympics	7/58
What a Difference a Day Makes	Dinah Washington	5/59
What a Guy	Raindrops	4/63
What a Party	Fats Domino	10/61
What a Price	Fats Domino	1/61
What a Surprise	Johnny Maestro	4/61
What a Sweet Thing That Was	Shirelles	7/61
What Am I Living For	Chuck Willis	5/58
What Am I Living For	Conway Twitty	4/60
What Color is a Man	Bobby Vinton	9/65
What Does a Girl Do	Shirelles	9/63
What in the World's Come Over You	Jack Scott	1/60
What Is Love	Playmates	7/59
What Kind of Love is This	Joey Dee & the Starliters	8/62
What Kind of Fool (Do You Think I Am)	Tams	12/63
What Now	Gene Chandler	12/64
What Will Mary Say	Johnny Mathis	1/63
What'd I Say	Ray Charles	7/59
What'd I Say	Jerry Lee Lewis	4/61
What'd I Say	Bobby Darin	3/62
What'd I Say	Elvis Presley	5/64
What's a Matter Baby	Timi Yuro	7/62
What's Easy for Two Is So Hard for One	Mary Wells	10/63
What's So Good About Goodbye	Smokey Robinson & the Miracles	1/62
What's the Matter with You Baby	Marvin Gaye & Mary Wells	5/64
What's Your Name	Don & Juan	2/62
Whatever Will Be, Will Be	Doris Day	6/56
Wheels	String-A-Longs	1/61
Wheels	Billy Vaughn	2/61
When	Kalin Twins	6/58
When I Grow Up	Beach Boys	9/64
When I Fall in Love	Lettermen	11/61
When I See You	Fats Domino	8/57

When My Blue Moon Turns to Gold Again	Elvis Presley	11/56
When My Dreamboat Comes Home	Fats Domino	7/56
When My Little Girl Is Smiling	Drifters	2/62
When the Boy in Your Arms	Connie Francis	11/61
When the White Lilacs Bloom Again	Billy Vaughn	8/56
When the White Lilacs Bloom Again	Florian Zabach	8/56
When the White Lilacs Bloom Again	Helmut Zacharias	8/56
When We Get Married	Dreamlovers	8/61
When Will I Be Loved	Everly Brothers	6/60
When You Dance	Turbans	11/55
When You Wish Upon a Star	Dion & the Belmonts	5/60
Where Are You	Frankie Avalon	6/60
Where Are You	Dinah Washington	5/62
Where Have You Been	Arthur Alexander	5/62
Where or When	Dion & the Belmonts	1/60
Where the Boys Are	Connie Francis	1/61
Where Were You (On Our Wedding Day)	Lloyd Price	3/59
Whispering	Nino Tempo & April Stevens	2/63
Whispering Bells	Del Vikings	6/57
White on White	Danny Williams	3/64
White Silver Sands	Owen Bradley Quintet	7/57
White Silver Sands	Dave Gardner	7/57
White Silver Sands	Don Rondo	7/57
White Silver Sands	Bill Black's Combo	3/60
White Sport Coat	Marty Robbins	4/57
Who Do You Love	Sapphires	1/64
Who Needs You	Four Lads	1/57
Who Put the Bomp	Barry Mann	8/61
Who's Sorry Now	Connie Francis	2/58
Whole Lot of Shakin' Going On	Jerry Lee Lewis	6/57
Whole Lotta Lovin'	Fats Domino	11/58
Why	Frankie Avalon	11/59
Why Baby Why	Pat Boone	3/57
Why Do Fools Fall in Love	Diamonds	2/56
Why Do Fools Fall in Love	Frankie Lymon & the Teenagers	2/56
Why Do Fools Fall in Love	Gale Storm	2/56
Why Do I Love You So	Johnny Tillotson	1/60
Why Do Lovers Break Each Other's Hearts	Bob B. Soxx & the Blue Jeans	2/63
Why Don't They Understand	George Hamilton IV	11/57
Why Don't You Believe Me	Duprees	8/63
Why You Wanna Make Me Blue	Temptations	9/64

Wiggle Wiggle	Accents	12/58
Wiggle Wobble	Les Cooper	10/62
Wild	Dee Dee Sharp	10/63
Wild Cherry	Don Cherry	3/56
Wild in the Country	Elvis Presley	6/61
Wild is the Wind	Johnny Mathis	12/57
Wild One	Bobby Rydell	2/60
Wild One	Martha & the Vandellas	12/64
Wild Weekend	Rebels	12/62
Wildwood Days	Bobby Rydell	5/63
Will You Love Me Tomorrow	Shirelles	11/60
Willie and the Hand Jive	Johnny Otis	6/58
Win Your Love For Me	Sam Cooke	8/58
Wind, The	Diablos	4/54
Wings of a Dove	Ferlin Husky	12/60
Wipe Out	Surfaris	6/63
Wisdom of a Fool	Five Keys	12/56
Wish Someone Would Care	Irma Thomas	3/64
Wishing for Your Love	Voxpoppers	4/58
Witchcraft	Elvis Presley	10/63
Witch Doctor	David Seville	4/58
With All My Heart	Jodi Sands	5/57
With Open Arms	Jayne Morgan	8/59
With the Wind and the Rain in Your Hair	Pat Boone	1/59
With You on My Mind	Nat "King" Cole	9/57
With Your Love	Jack Scott	10/58
Without Love	Ray Charles	6/63
Without Love (There Is Nothing)	Clyde McPhatter	1/57
Without You	Johnny Tillotson	8/61
Wives and Lovers	Jack Jones	11/63
Wizard, The	Jimmie Rodgers	8/58
Wizard of Love	Ly-Dells	8/61
Wolverton Mountain	Claude King	5/62
Woman, A Lover, A Friend	Jackie Wilson	7/60
Woman Love	Gene Vincent	6/56
Wonder Like You	Ricky Nelson	10/61
Wonder of You	Ray Peterson	5/59
Wonderful Dream	Majors	8/62
Wonderful Summer	Robin Ward	11/63
Wonderful Time Up There	Pat Boone	2/58
Wonderful Wonderful	Johnny Mathis	1/57
Wonderful Wonderful	Tymes	8/63
Wonderful World	Sam Cooke	5/60
Wonderful You	Jimmie Rodgers	6/59
Wondering	Patti Page	5/57
Wonderland by Night	Anita Bryant	11/60
Wonderland By Night	Bert Kaempfert	11/60
Wonderland By Night	Louis Prima	11/60
Won't 'Cha Come Home	Lloyd Price	11/59

Won't You Come Home Bill Bailey	Bobby Darin	5/60
Woo-Hoo	Rock-A-Teens	10/59
Wooden Heart	Joe Dowell	7/61
Wooly Bully	Sam the Sham & the Pharohs	4/65
Work with Me Annie	Midnighters	4/54
Workin' For the Man	Roy Orbison	9/62
Workout Stevie, Workout	Little Stevie Wonder	10/63
World Outside	Four Coins	11/58
Worried Guy	Johnny Tillotson	2/64
Wringle Wrangle	Fess Parker	1/57
Wringle Wrangle	Bill Hayes	1/57
Writing on the Wall	Adam Wade	5/61
Written on the Wind	Four Aces	12/56
Wrong for Each Other	Andy Williams	4/64
Wun'erful, Wun'erful	Stan Freeberg	11/57

Y

Ya Ya	Lee Dorsey	9/61
Yakety Sax	Boots Randolph	2/63
Yakety Yak	Coasters	5/58
Years From Now	Jackie Wilson	8/61
Yellow Bird	Arthur Lyman	6/61
Yellow Dog Blues	Joe Darensbourg & the Dixie Flyers	1/58
Yellow Rose of Texas	Johnny Desmond	8/55
Yellow Rose of Texas	Mitch Miller	9/55
Yellow Rose of Texas	Stan Freberg	10/55
Yep	Duane Eddy	4/59
Yes I'm Ready	Barbara Mason	5/65
Yes Sir, That's My Baby	Ricky Nelson	9/60
Yes Tonight, Josephine	Johnny Ray	4/47
Yogi	Ivy Three	8/60
You	Aquatones	4/58
You Always Hurt the One You Love	Clarence "Frogman" Henry	5/61
You Are Beautiful	Johnny Mathis	1/59
You Are Mine	Frankie Avalon	3/62
You Are My Destiny	Paul Anka	1/58
You Are My Love	Joni James	10/55
You Are My Sunshine	Ray Charles	11/62
You Are the Only One	Ricky Nelson	1/61
You Beat Me to the Punch	Mary Wells	8/62
You Belong to Me	Duprees	8/62
You Better Know It	Jackie Wilson	9/59
You Better Move On	Arthur Alexander	2/62
You Bug Me Baby	Larry Williams	11/57
You Can Depend On Me	Brenda Lee	4/61
You Can Have Her	Roy Hamilton	2/61
You Can Make It If You Try	Gene Allison	12/57
You Can Never Stop Me Loving You	Johnny Tillotson	8/63

You Can't Sit Down	Dovells	4/63
You Can't Sit Down-Part II	Phil Upchurch Combo	6/61
You Cheated	Shields	8/58
You Cheated	Slades	8/58
You Don't Have To Be a Baby to Cry	Caravelles	11/63
You Don't Know Me	Jerry Vale	6/56
You Don't Know Me	Ray Charles	7/62
You Don't Know What You've Got	Ral Donner	7/61
You Don't Owe Me a Thing	Johnny Ray	1/57
You Don't Own Me	Lesley Gore	12/63
You Got What It Takes	Marv Johnson	11/59
You Lost the Sweetest Boy	Mary Wells	9/63
You Mean Everything to Me	Neil Sedaka	8/60
You Must Believe Me	Impressions	9/64
You Must Have Been a Beautiful Baby	Bobby Darin	9/61
You Need Hands	Eydie Gorme	5/58
You Never Can Tell	Chuck Berry	8/64
You Really Got a Hold on Me	Smokey Robinson & the Miracles	12/62
You Really Know How to Hurt a Guy	Jan & Dean	5/65
You Send Me	Sam Cooke	10/57
You Send Me	Teresa Brewer	11/57
You Should Have Seen the Way He Looked at Me	Dixie Cups	10/64
You Talk Too Much	Joe Jones	9/60
You Were Made for Me	Sam Cooke	3/58
You Were Mine	Fireflys	9/59
You Win Again	Fats Domino	2/62
You'll Lose a Good Thing	Barbara Lynn	6/62
You'll Never Never Know	Platters	9/56
You're a Wonderful One	Marvin Gaye	3/64
You're Gonna Miss Me	Connie Francis	9/59
You're Looking Good	Dee Clark	8/60
You're My Girl	Roy Orbison	7/65
You're My One and Only Love	Ricky Nelson	8/57
You're My World	Cilla Black	7/64
You're Sixteen	Johnny Burnette	11/60
You're So Fine	Falcons	4/59
You're the Apple of My Eye	Four Lovers	5/56
(You're the) Devil in Disguise	Elvis Presley	6/63
You're the Reason	Bobby Edwards	9/61
You're the Reason I'm Living	Bobby Darin	1/63
You've Been in Love Too Long	Martha & the Vandellas	8/65
You've Lost That Lovin' Feelin'	Righteous Brothers	12/64
Young and in Love	Dick & Dee Dee	3/63
Young Blood	Coasters	5/57

Z

""NON-OLDIE""
TITLE INDEX

Affair to Remember	Vic Damone	8/57
Amukirki	Les Paul & Mary Ford	11/55
Anyone Who Had a Heart	Dionne Warwicke	12/63
April in Paris	Count Basie	12/55
Ask Me	Nat "King" Cole	2/56
Baby's First Christmas	Connie Francis	12/61
Bad Man Blunder	Kingston Trio	6/60
Battle Hymn of the Republic	Mormon Tabernacle Choir	9/59
Bible Tells Me So	Don Cornell	8/55
Bible Tells Me So	Nick Noble	8/55
Blowin' in the Wind	Peter, Paul & Mary	6/63
Can I Steal a Little Love	Frank Sinatra	1/57
Can You Find It in Your Heart	Tony Bennett	4/56
C'Est La Vie	Sarah Vaughn	11/55
Cha-Hua-Hua	Pets	5/58
Chantez Chantez	Dinah Shore	1/57
Charade	Henry Mancini	12/63
Ciao-Ciao Bambino	Jacky Noguez	6/59
Comin' Home Baby	Mel Torme	11/62
Cry Me a River	Julie London	11/55
Delaware	Perry Como	2/60
Desafinado	Stan Getz & Charlie Byrd	9/62
Desert Pete	Kingston Trio	8/63
Dolly's Oh Susanna	Don Charles Singing Dogs	11/55
Don't Make Me Over	Dionne Warwicke	12/62
Don't Think Twice It's Alright	Peter, Paul & Mary	9/63
El Matador	Kingston Trio	2/60
Ev'ry Day of My Life	McGuire Sisters	9/56
Fascination	Jane Morgan	8/57
Flowers Mean Forgiveness	Frank Sinatra	12/56
Forgive My Heart	Nat "King" Cole	10/55
Frogg	Brothers Four	4/61
From the Candy Store on the Corner to the Chapel on the Hill	Tony Bennett	8/56
God Bless America	Connie Francis	11/59
Good Life, The	Tony Bennett	5/63
Greenback Dollar	Kingston Trio	1/63

Hey! Jealous Lover	Frank Sinatra	10/56
How Little We Know	Frank Sinatra	5/56
I Could Have Danced All Night	Sylvia Syms	5/56
I Left My Heart in San Francisco	Tony Bennett	8/62
I Loves You Porgy	Nina Simone	8/59
I Only Know I Love You	Four Aces	7/56
I Wanna Be Around	Tony Bennett	11/63
I'll Be With You in Apple Blossom Time	Tab Hunter	2/59
If I Had a Hammer	Peter, Paul & Mary	8/62
If I Had a Hammer	Trini Lopez	7/63
In a Shanty in Old Shanty Town	Somethin' Smith & the Redheads	5/56
Ivy Rose	Perry Como	10/57
Just Come Home	Hugo & Luigi	12/59
Kansas City	Trini Lopez	11/63
Lemon Tree	Peter, Paul & Mary	5/62
Liechtensteiner Polka	Will Glahe	11/57
Like, Long Hair	Paul Revere & the Raiders	4/61
Little Drummer Boy	Harry Simeone Chorale	12/58
Love & Marriage	Frank Sinatra	11/55
Love Theme from One Eyed Jacks	Ferrante & Teicher	3/61
M.T.A.	Kingston Trio	6/59
Mama Look a Bu Bu	Harry Belefonte	3/57
Mama, Teach Me to Dance	Eydie Gorme	7/56
Mary's Boy Child	Harry Belefonte	12/56
Ol' MacDonald	Frank Sinatra	11/60
On London Bridge	Jo Stafford	11/56
Pocketful of Miracles	Frank Sinatra	12/61
Pomp & Circumstance	Adrian Kimberley	7/61
Puff the Magic Dragon	Peter, Paul & Mary	9/63
Reverend Mr. Black	Kingston Trio	4/63
Saturday Night	New Christy Minstrels	10/63
Shelter of Your Arms	Sammy Davis, Jr.	11/63
Someone You Love	Nat "King" Cole	10/55
Stewball	Peter, Paul & Mary	11/63
Suddenly There's a Valley	Gogi Grant	9/55
Suddenly There's a Valley	Julius La Rosa	10/55
Suddenly There's a Valley	Jo Stafford	10/55
Take Five	Dave Brubeck	9/61
Talk to Me	Frank Sinatra	10/59
Tender Trap	Frank Sinatra	11/55

310

ARTIST INDEX

Artists having "non-oldie" songs are listed alphabetically at the end of this index.

314

315

316

Fox, Norman & the Rob Roys 35
Foxx, Inez 89, 172
Francis, Connie 36, 37, 39, 40, 43,
44, 47, 49, 50, 53, 54, 56, 57, 58, 59,
61, 63, 64, 68, 70, 72, 73, 76, 80, 82,
83, 87, 88, 92, 94, 98, 99, 110, 112,
121, 133, 134, 141, 147, 151, 181,
186, 190, 199, 222, 228, 244
Freberg, Stan 13, 14, 21, 28, 34, 203
Freeman, Bobby 39, 41, 61, 100, 212,
220
Freeman, Ernie 34, 160
Frogmen 68

Gabriel & the Angels 83
Gadabouts 22, 161
Gallahads 22
Gallop, Frank 40
Gardner, Dave 32, 163
Gardner, Don & Dee Dee Ford 79
Gari, Frank 64, 68, 70
Gaye, Marvin 86, 88, 94, 98, 102, 211
Gaye, Marvin & Mary Wells 99, 100,
167
Gaylords 5, 12, 157
G-Clefs 21, 72
Gene & Eunice 9, 12, 52, 158
Gentrys 105, 172
George, Barbara 73, 172
Gibbs, Georgia 8, 9, 19, 20, 22, 24,
43, 148, 157, 158, 162, 198, 222
Gibson, Don 38, 40, 43, 58, 69
Gilkyson, Terry & the Easy Riders
27, 159, 225
Gilmer, Jimmy & the Fireballs 93,
95, 112, 135, 142, 243
Gilreath, James 87
Gino & Gina 39
Gladiolas 28
Glazer, Tom & the Children's Cho-
rus 89
Glencoves 85, 89
Gone All-Stars 37, 233
Gordon, Barry 13, 160
Gore, Lesley 88, 92, 93, 95, 98, 99,
100, 105, 112, 135, 148, 224
Gorme, Eydie 39, 86, 148, 211
Gracie, Charlie 28, 29, 156
Grammer, Billy 43
Granahan, Gerry 26, 38, 39, 197, 238
Granata, Rocco 54, 225
Grant, Earl 42
Grant, Gogi 15, 20, 110, 117, 131,
140, 162

Grant, Janie 68
Graves, Billy 48, 212
Greene, Lorne 101, 135, 172, 227
Gregg, Bobby & His Friends 77, 211
Guaraldi Trio, Vince 83
Guitar, Bonnie 28, 157, 172

Haley, Bill & the Comets 3, 5, 6, 7, 8,
9, 12, 13, 14, 19, 22, 23, 39, 109,
117, 131, 139, 148, 160, 161, 186,
198, 226, 228
Hall, Larry 54, 228
Halos 70, 233
Hamilton, Bobby 41
Hamilton IV, George 23, 28, 34, 38,
89
Hamilton, Roy 9, 37, 66, 162
Hamilton, Russ 32, 172
Harnell, Joe 83, 127
Harper, Janice 33
Harpo, Slim 69
Harptones 4, 5
Harris, Betty 93
Harris, Eddie 68, 157
Harris, Rolf 89, 172
Harris, Thurston 34, 172
Harrison, Wilbert 47, 50, 109, 133,
141
Harvey & the Moonglows 7, 22, 42,
161
Hawkins, Dale 32, 41, 228
Hawkins, Ronnie 52, 226
Hawkins, Screamin' Jay 24, 39
Hawley, Dean 60, 159
Hayes, Bill 9, 27, 131, 156, 163, 221
Hayman, Richard 18, 162
Heartbeats 25, 68
Hearts 9
Helms, Bobby 32, 34, 35, 111, 243
Henderson, Joe 79
Hendricks, Bobby 41, 241
Henry, Clarence "Frogman" 25, 66,
69, 242
Heywood, Eddie 21, 126
Hibbler, Al 9, 13, 18, 22, 119, 157,
158, 162, 233, 242
Highlights 23, 243
Highwaymen 70, 73, 74, 134, 226
Hill, Bunker 81
Hill, Jessie 59
Hilltoppers 5, 13, 14, 23, 27, 35, 157,
158, 159, 160, 225
Hinton, Joe 100
Hirt, Al 97, 99, 126

Pastel Six 84, 211
Pastels 37
Pate Quintet, Johnny 37
Patience & Prudence 22, 24, 120, 162
Paul & Paula 84, 87, 89, 111, 134, 142, 198, 227
Paul, Les & Mary Ford 12, 19, 27, 41, 68, 156, 158
Penguins 7, 111, 157, 243
Pentagons 66
Pericoli, Emilio 79
Perkins, Carl 19, 110, 121, 156, 172, 197, 242
Perkins, Tony 34
Peterson, Paul 83
Peterson, Ray 50, 54, 60, 63, 71, 77, 155, 215, 221, 224
Phillips, Little Esther 82, 241
Phillips, Phil 51, 112, 172
Pickett, Bobby (Boris) 75, 82, 84, 134, 142, 173, 204, 242
Pierce, Webb 52
Pips 69
Pitney, Gene 66, 71, 73, 78, 82, 84, 87, 92, 94, 100, 102, 104, 105, 106, 147, 224
Pixie's Three 92
Platt, Eddie 38, 161
Platters 8, 12, 14, 15, 19, 21, 22, 23, 25, 28, 29, 36, 38, 43, 49, 51, 57, 62, 63, 66, 71, 109, 110, 118, 121, 131, 132, 139, 140, 148, 151, 160, 177, 183, 184, 186, 187
Playmates 37, 40, 43, 51, 63, 223
Poni-Tails 41, 173, 198
Pourcel, Frank 50, 127
Powell, Jane 22, 162
Powers, Joey 95, 173, 226
Prado, Prez 9, 40, 112, 119, 125, 131, 132, 139, 151, 227
Presley, Elvis 5, 6, 15, 19, 20, 21, 22, 23, 24, 25, 26, 27, 28, 29, 32, 34, 36, 37, 39, 40, 43, 49, 50, 51, 56, 59, 61, 63, 65, 66, 67, 68, 69, 70, 71, 72, 74, 77, 79, 81, 82, 86, 89, 94, 97, 98, 99, 100, 102, 103, 104, 105, 106, 109, 110, 111, 112, 113, 117, 118, 119, 120, 131, 132, 133, 134, 140, 141, 142, 147, 151, 156, 177, 178, 183, 184, 186, 187, 188, 197, 198, 211, 223, 225, 237, 239, 242
Preston, Johnny 53, 59, 60, 113, 118, 133, 141

Previn, Andre 51
Price, Lloyd 28, 44, 49, 50, 52, 54, 58, 60, 61, 94, 111, 119, 121, 132, 141
Prima, Louis 63, 163
Prima, Louis & Keely Smith 43
Pursell, Bill 86, 127

Quaker City Boys 44
Quin-Tones 42

Rainbows 9, 226
Raindrops 88, 92
Rainwater, Marvin 29
Ramrods 66
Ran-Dells 92, 204
Randolph, Boots 86
Randy & the Rainbows 89, 173, 221
Ray, Diane 92
Ray, Johnnie 22, 27, 29, 118, 224, 243
Ray, James 73, 78
Rays 34, 110, 121, 173
Rebels 84, 126
Reed, Jimmy 33, 58
Reese, Della 33, 53, 55
Reeves, Jim 29, 57, 60, 63, 119, 157, 207
Reflections 99, 173, 224, 227
Regents 69, 70, 219
Reisman, Joe 24, 219
Renay, Diane 97, 99
Rene, Henri 24
Revels 53
Reynolds, Debbie 32, 57, 111, 117, 132, 140, 161, 228, 241
Reynolds, Jody 39, 173, 215
Rhythm Orchids 27, 28
Rich, Charlie 56, 58, 105, 198, 228, 237
Richard, Cliff 53, 95
Riddle, Nelson 14, 20, 22, 80, 117, 125, 159
Righteous Brothers 88, 93, 102, 104, 105, 106, 111, 135, 142, 143
Rinky Dinks 41, 157, 239
Rios, Augie 44
Rip Chords 95, 99, 198, 242
Ritter, Tex 21, 70, 162
Rivers, Johnny 99, 101, 102, 155
Rivieras 48, 97
Rivingtons 81, 87
Robbins, Marty 24, 29, 35, 39, 42, 47, 48, 54, 58, 60, 63, 66, 80, 83, 110,

111, 118, 119, 133, 140, 161, 197, 215, 227
Robert & Johnny 38
Robertson, Don 20, 126
Robinson, Floyd 51
Robinson, Smokey & the Miracles 64, 76, 84, 87, 93, 95, 101, 104, 105, 106, 148, 207, 226
Robic, Ivo 52
Rochell & the Candles 66
Rock-A-Teens 53, 127
Rockin' R's 49
Rocky Fellers 87, 223
Rodgers, Eileen 22, 42
Rodgers, Jimmie 33, 35, 38, 39, 40, 42, 43, 49, 51, 53, 57, 83, 111, 117, 132, 140, 226
Roe, Tommy 80, 82, 94, 97, 113, 134, 228
Rogers, Julie 102
Rogers, Timmie 33, 197
Ronald & Ruby 38, 159
Rondo, Don 24, 32, 163
Ronettes 93, 95, 99, 100, 102, 104
Ronnie & the Hi-Lites 77
Ronny & the Daytonas 101, 106, 198, 228, 233, 242
Rooftop Singers 86, 135
Roommates 68
Rose, David 75, 79, 125, 134
Rosie & the Originals 64, 173, 243
Ross, Jack 77, 220
Ross, Spencer 57, 127
Routers 83
Rover Boys 21, 158, 197
Royal, Billy Joe 105, 106
Royal Teens 37, 43, 173, 197
Royaltones 43
Ruby & the Romantics 86, 88, 93, 113, 135
Ryan, Charlie 60, 158, 199, 242
Rydell, Bobby 51, 53, 58, 60, 61, 63, 66, 69, 70, 73, 77, 80, 83, 88, 102, 147, 211, 220
Rydell, Bobby & Chubby Checker 74, 86, 167

Safaris 60, 173
Sakamoto, Kyu 88, 135, 173
Sam the Sham & the Pharohs 104
Sands, Jodie 29
Sands, Tommy 28, 29, 38, 198
Santamaria, Mongo 87, 127

Santo & Johnny 52, 55, 58, 121, 125, 133
Sapphires 97
Scott, Bobby 14
Scott, Freddy 92, 95
Scott, Jack 40, 43, 44, 51, 57, 59, 60, 62, 224
Scott, Linda 67, 70, 73, 78
Secrets 95
Sedaka, Neil 44, 49, 53, 59, 62, 64, 67, 69, 73, 77, 80, 83, 86, 88, 92, 95, 111, 113, 134, 141, 147, 198, 219, 220, 228, 243
Sensations 76, 173
Seville, David 25, 39, 40, 111, 132, 203, 219, 244
Shangri-Las 101, 102, 104, 106, 135, 215, 240
Shannon, Del 65, 67, 70, 72, 74, 84, 100, 102, 104, 109, 134, 142, 224
Sharp, Dee Dee 78, 80, 83, 87, 94, 148, 211, 212
Sharpe, Ray 51, 225
Shaw, Georgie 13
Shells 64
Shep & the Limelites 25, 68, 70, 73, 173
Shepherd Sisters 33
Sherman, Allan 93, 204
Sherrys 83
Shields 42, 111, 155
Shirelles 39, 62, 63, 66, 68, 70, 73, 74, 75, 78, 80, 82, 84, 87, 89, 93, 111, 113, 121, 133, 134, 141, 142, 148, 151, 224
Shirley & Lee 12, 22, 25
Shirley Trio, Don 70
Shondell, Troy 72, 74, 173, 243
Silhouettes 37, 111, 132, 173, 241
Simmons, Jumpin' Gene 101, 204
Sims Twins 73
Sinatra, Frank 34, 47, 51
Singing Nun 85, 95, 113, 135, 142, 173, 221, 241
Sir Douglas Quintet 104
Six Teens 22
Skip & Flip 51, 59
Skyliners 48, 51, 53, 60, 111
Slades 42, 155
Slay, Frankie 74
Small, Millie 99, 101
Smith, Carl 51
Smith, Huey "Piano" 33, 44, 233
Smith, Jimmy 79

323

••NON-OLDIE••
ARTIST INDEX